PUNCTUATIONS

DUKE UNIVERSITY PRESS *Durham and London* 2019

PUNC.
TU.
A.
TION.S

how the arts think the political

michael j. shapiro

Printed in the United States of America
on acid-free paper ∞

Designed by Aimee C. Harrison

Typeset in Sabon and Avenir
by Copperline Books

Cataloging-in-Publication Data is available from the
Library of Congress.
ISBN 978-1-4780-0588-9 (hardcover : alk. paper)
ISBN 978-1-4780-0656-5 (pbk. : alk. paper)
ISBN 978-1-4780-0726-5 (ebook)

Cover art: Santu Mofokeng (b. 1956), *Chief More's Funeral, GaMogopa*, 1989. Gelatin silver print.
© Santu Mofokeng Foundation. Image courtesy
Lunetta Bartz, MAKER, Johannesburg.

Duke University Press gratefully acknowledges the
Department of Political Science at University of
Hawai'i at Mānoa, which provided funds toward
the publication of this book.

for Sam.

Connie.

+ Hawi.

CON.TENT.S

I am especially grateful to the students with whom I interacted as I assigned, presented, and discussed drafts of my chapters: political science graduate students in my department at the University of Hawai'i, Manoa, and in the International Relations Institute at PUC (the Pontifical Catholic University of Rio, where I teach in July). Thanks are also due to the manuscript's reviewers, including Brad Evans (who outed himself as one of the them), for their supportive and very useful criticism. I am also grateful to my many colleagues at my university and elsewhere who invited me for colloquia, panels, workshop sessions, and mini courses in which I presented parts of the project: Jonathan Luke Austin, Heriberto Cairo Carou, Francois Debrix, Luis Lobo-Guerrero, Jon Goldberg-Hiller, Kyle Grayson, Nickolas Robinson, Joseph Tanke, and Cyrus (Ernie) Zirakzadeh. Special thanks also to João Nogueira and Roberto Yamato at PUC-Rio for arranging my Rio teaching, to my Prague colleagues Petr Kouba and Martin Nitsche at the Institute of Philosophy in the Czech Academy of Sciences, and to Stanislav Synek in the Faculty of Humanities at Charles University for arranging and supporting my guest seminar where I presented and discussed chapters in fall 2018. Thanks go to my Prague students for their generous and engaged responses to the materials and to Bill Callahan, who helped me obtain an image from the London exhibition "Soul of a Nation." I also want to single out my friend, colleague, and frequent coauthor Sam Opondo, who read chapter drafts with discernment and made valuable suggestions.

Finally, I am grateful once again to the Duke University Press personnel who managed the project—my acquisitions editor Courtney Berger for her usual outstanding work at conducting the review process, Sandra Korn and Susan Albury for their generous assistance in conducting the production process, Aimee Harrison for her excellent work on the book design, and to the rest of the Duke team for their assistance with the images, permissions, copyediting, and cover design.

DEFERRALS, PUNCTUATIONS, MEDIA TEXTUALITIES

Deferrals and Breaks

Legacies of some of my earlier inquiries are among the conceptual perspectives framing the investigations in this book. In an analysis of the way Greek tragedies construct the politics of familial conflict, for example, I emphasized the way Aeschylus's tragedy *Seven Against Thebes* resists resolution. Rather than offering an unambiguous moral lesson, the play embraces a seemingly irreconcilable ontological divide. It cleaves to the tragic genre as it stages a struggle between two brothers, Eteocles, the King of Cadmus, and his rebelling brother, Polynices. As I put it, rather than issuing "a moral statement in behalf of particular, coherently developed Protagonists. . . . [*Seven*] dramatize[s] conflicting values and social practices, connected to different cosmologies, which yield different normative systems."[1]

At the end of the play, after it becomes apparent that the Greeks entertained "conflicting codes, those connected to the civic order and those connected to family and lineage," there is no attempt to reconcile them. In the final scene, the chorus, representing the *agon* in the midst of Greek life, divides "into two groups, one following Creon and the corpse of Eteocles (in support of civic justice), and the other following Antigone, who in defiance of civic law (but in accord with the law of lineage) is going to bury Polynices."[2] Rather than existing as *a* community of sense, the Greeks maintained a radically divided order. Reconciliation was perpetually *deferred*, an aspect of Greek civic life that many of the ancient tragedies thematize.

More recently, in a monograph concerned with the political significance of sublime experiences, I referred approvingly to another aspect of deferral, Jacques Rancière's concept of an "aesthetic break." I suggested that the political effects of such breaks or impositions on duration register themselves as encounters that disrupt usual sense-making practices. They "summon, shape, and render visible and voluble oppositional communities of sense" because the aesthetic breaks that intervene in durations "precipitate another duration, a negotiation process in which new interactions and alternative sense-making possibilities emerge."[3]

Still concerned with the critical political insights one can extract from such deferrals and breaks, my investigations in the chapters that follow treat them as immanent in the punctuation rhythms and structures of artistic texts. Analyzing diverse artistic practices, my focus is on the ways that systems and practices of intelligibility are contested in artistic media genres whose critical interventions inhere in the spatio-temporal (counter) rhythms that inhibit one's unreflective acceptance of the senses of experience that belong to consensual communities. Conventional narrative configurations, as they are composed in diverse artistic genres, facilitate what Paul Ricoeur refers to as a "grasping together" of disparate events, which fall into a consensual place through plots that create narrative wholes in which there is a progression with a beginning, middle, and end.[4]

Some writers, however, favor a destructive approach to such wholes, Marguerite Duras, for example, in whose works one finds "fragmented syntax" and an "inhibited flow of narration" in stories whose political effects result from semantic voids aimed not at "an encouragement of the reader's subjective agency . . . but exactly the opposite, . . . the inhibition of the process of reading." Duras referred to that way of writing as an aesthetic with a "potential for opening something entirely new."[5] Duras's approach to narrative accords with the view of the political potential of the arts that Rancière has repeatedly asserted, their ability to articulate arenas of nonclosural contention. They function as a "key locus where disagreement can be staged in order to produce new communities of sense."[6]

Punctuation

The investigations throughout this book favor the moments of inhibition to which Duras is committed, treated in my analyses as the grammatical concept/metaphor punctuation, which applied to artistic works involves "interruptions that disturb the tranquil integrity of a work,"[7] opening the work to alternative sensibilities. Punctuation-formed temporal structures in critical versions of the arts allow political initiatives to emerge by facilitating alternative or oppositional communities of sense. Although as Rancière suggests in a remark about visual representations, "There is no straightforward road from the fact of looking at a spectacle to the fact of understanding the state of the world; no direct road from intellectual awareness to political action," critical artistic practices nevertheless create a "dissociation: a break in a relationship between sense and sense," and therein lies the potential for the impact on thinking politically.[8]

Accordingly, when I refer to the compositional rhythms that deliver moments of dissociation as punctuation, I am emphasizing the intervening spaces, subjects, and objects that operate in artistic texts to shape the way the composition of the text delivers its challenge to political sensibility. In the register of language, punctuation is simply the part of grammar (notably the syntax) involved in constructing the way micro moments of deferral participate in linguistic and other forms of intelligibility. The punctuation marks that shape intelligibility, however, create more than mere clarity of meaning. For example, the diacritical marks in Jacques Derrida's *The Truth in Painting*—"foreign, discarded, archaic marks of punctuation,"[9]—which mark out spaces that intervene to fragment the text, serve to identify the work's hybridity as a mixture of the discursive and the figural. That punctuation practice delivers a painting pedagogy: "painting [is] not just surrounded but 'invaded' by discourse."[10] It's a pedagogy delivered by Derrida's text, which because it's punctuated with blanks, mimes the very hybridity it attributes to painting.

Thus, while didactic approaches to punctuation focus on "proper use" under the assumption that the writer or artist wants to communicate within the reigning structures of intelligibility, those interested in creative (counter-) expression value punctuation "for its expressive, artistic use."[11] That latter orientation implies a need to expand the meaning of punctuation, so rather than restricting my analysis to the usual approach, which limits the perspective to punctuation *marks*, I am construing punctuation in an extended metaphorical sense as part of the way diverse, critically oriented artistic genres—in architecture, cinema, literature, music, painting, photography, and poetry—alternatively participate in and challenge practices of intelligibility with rhythmic pacing that defers definitive closure, encourages critical reflection, and enables a rethinking of community coherence.

My methodological perspective is inspired by three approaches that explicitly invoke punctuation. The first belongs to Theodor Adorno, who famously addressed himself to the critical value that punctuation marks provide when extended beyond grammar. Beginning by suggesting that they work "hieroglyphically [as] an interplay that takes place in the interior of language," he proceeds to compare them to musical cadences, suggesting that "only a person who can perceive the different weights of strong and weak phrasings in musical form can really feel the distinction between the comma and the semicolon."[12] Adorno's turn to a musical rendering of punctuation is aimed at showing how punctuation brings the text close to the voice and thus to the will to intelligibility behind the punctuation choices. His insights help me structure chapter 1 on popular music

The second approach belongs to the writer/filmmaker Alain Robbe-Grillet, who referred to punctuation when asked how he translates literary forms into cinematic ones:

> [Question] As an innovator of both the New Novel and the New Cinema, do you perceive any similarity between these two art forms. [Answer] The New Novel and the new Cinema are rooted in phenomenology. . . . In my work I don't begin with a preconceived story line. Objects give rise to thoughts which become my novel or my film. A blue shoe, a broken bottle, and the sea inspired me, and became the point of departure and the evolutionary force for my film *Glissements progressifs du plaisir.* [Question] Objects then, are often your creative point of departure. How else do they function in our work? [Answer] As punctuation. Punctuation devices, which denote transition in novels, such as commas and periods, have its cinematic counterpart. For example, the objects around which I developed my *Glissements* scenario, recur throughout the film. They connect, by inference, and by their connotative power, one cinematic shot to the next.[13]

Thus, for example, in Robbe-Grillet's *Glissements* (a murder story), two built spaces that keep recurring serve as punctuations—the apartment shared by two young women, one of whom is found dead, and the prison cell of the one accused of the murder. A commentary on how the film's punctuation works points to Robbe-Grillet's innovative cinematic style: "The punctuation passages constitute a device rarely, if ever, used in narrative cinema, implying a double level in the film: on the one hand, the diegetic or fictional world of character and action . . . and on the other, elements of the literal dimension of the text,"[14] where the latter are the objects that punctuate that fictional world, shown in shots that slow the process of reception in order to direct attention to the nature of that world instead of animating the action sequence.

J.-F. Lyotard provides a similar insight, noting that the critical effect of images lies in their ability to "slow down the eye, and judgment, forcing the mind to take position in front of the sensory."[15] Robbe-Grillet exploits that critical effect. Rather than inserting a "fade" or a "dissolve" to punctuate the film (which are how transitions in the narrative of most commercial films are managed), "for the punctuation in this film, Robbe-Grillet uses singular images of objects that may or may not play into the narrative."[16] Robbe-Grillet's approach helps me shape the analyses in the chapters on images and literature (chapters 4 and 5, respectively).

The third belongs to Roland Barthes, who in his treatment of photography distinguishes a photograph's *punctum* from its *studium*. While the *studium* expresses the content that is recognizable for those familiar with the context of the photograph's referents, the *punctum*, a nonreferential aspect of the photograph (which Barthes calls "the second element"), "will break (or punctuate) the *studium*. . . . it is this element which arises from the scene, shoots out of it like an arrow, and pierces me. . . . [it] is also: sting, speck, cut, little hole."[17] Significantly, and in contrast with André Bazin's well-known insistence that the photograph *punctuates* time by arresting it (capturing the image, he says, in a "convulsive catalepsy"), for Barthes, it functions as a "symptom of time";[18] the *punctum* lends the photograph an implicit duration (e.g., the way a scene, an object, or a portrait connotes a life's temporal trajectory for the viewer of the photograph). I adapt Barthes's notion of attention-getting, temporal punctuations not only to images but also to literary texts (in chapters 4 and 5, respectively).

For my purposes, a primary aspect of what makes punctuation critical and thus politically relevant are *re*-punctuations that reveal the contestability of institutionalized interpretive practices. The arrests and contrapuntal rhythms that some forms of re-punctuation engender, provoking moments of reflection, arise in the work of professionals—writers, musicians, architects, and cinema directors—but are also produced at times from the actions of people whose movements violate expected narrative trajectories, for example, skateboarders who (as I note in chapters 2 and 3) are involved in countermovements to the purposive flows of the people who etch the movement trajectories that constitute the patterns authoritatively designed for the expected traffic of the people, goods, and services in life worlds. Each of these chapters treats artistic interventions that challenge those authoritative designs.

Before providing a chapter-by-chapter synopsis, however, I want to exercise various dimensions of my conceptual approach by first commenting on the way diverse artistic genres testify to the vagaries of intelligibility, then providing examples from poetry and commemorative architecture of the critical effects of punctuation for the political thinking advertised in my title, and finally offering an elaboration of the relationship between the arts and communities of sense with a reading of a science fiction novel that imagines a radically different basis for the creation of communal coherence.

The Perils of Intelligibility

In order to introduce the critical aspects of my investigations, I want to elaborate on my presupposition that intelligibility is an ambiguous achievement. Learning to participate in the reigning structures of intelligibility enables one to share information, that is, to communicate effectively. Those who can merely communicate, however, are (in the words of Gilles Deleuze and Félix Guattari) "functionaries" able only to manage "ready-made thought."[19] Dwelling in the realm of "opinions," they're locked within "the forces of recognition," unable to exercise an imagination of possibilities of "*terra incognita*."[20] Paradoxically, what has enabled some creative writers to avoid the "sluggishness of the brain" and the "facilitating paths . . . of dominant opinions"[21] have been circumstances that have made them linguistically ill-equipped. Thus, Jean-Paul Sartre attributes Gustave Flaubert's creativity to the deferral of his linguistic ability. Coming late into language, Flaubert (*The Family Idiot*) was not robbed early on of his "native poetry."[22]

Similarly, Samuel Beckett, alerted to the perils of falling back into "ready-made language," began writing in French in order to avoid English, which he knew "too well."[23] Like Kafka's "Great Swimmer" (and Kafka himself by implication), Beckett sought "to be a stranger *within* his own language."[24] In response to a request to say something about his approach to writing, Beckett makes evident the rationale for his choice of a less familiar language: "I will all the same give you one clue, *Le besoin d'être mal armé* ("the need to be ill-equipped"),[25] in other words, to be unfamiliar enough with the language of expression to be unable to use "ready-made" phrases. It is evident, however, that the remark is a *double entendre*; Beckett is also referring to the writing style of the French poet Stéphane Mallarmé, a poetic innovator who (as I note in chapter 1) reordered the syntax of the poetic line. Influenced by musical punctuation, Mallarmé interspersed blank spaces in his poems, making his poetic punctuation mime musical rests. Leo Bersani captures its implications well: There is a "current in Mallarmé's thought [to] . . . displace our attention from the sense of words to those 'cadences' through which wordless impressions simultaneously structure and erase language."[26] The blank spaces in Mallarmé's poems are interruptions that momentarily suspend reception and render the reader a reflective accomplice in the poem's sense-making. Mallarmé's innovative poetic punctuation arrests anticipatory understandings and turns his poems into "event spaces."[27] The poems are open structures whose various meanings emerge through active reading events, encouraged by the blanks or voids within the poetic lines. Like Duras's fragmented narratives, they perform a critical textuality that I want to illustrate here by resorting to another artistic genre, architecture, because such narrative styles are objects of investigation throughout my chapters.

Textualities

The critical effects of Mallarmé's textual practice are observable in a striking equivalence between his blanks and voids and the design of architect Daniel Libeskind's "Jewish Museum" in Berlin, which Libeskind explicitly likens to a text aimed at encouraging diverse readings. Invoking a venerable yet dynamic Jewish text dedicated to ongoing interpretation, Libeskind likens his museum to the Talmud: "The museum is open to many interpretations and many routes, just like the pages of the Talmud where the margins are often as important as what is being commented on in the center of the text. This experience is dependent on the engagement of the visitors with the implication of an ongoing history."[28] Invoking the textual concept of narrativity, Libeskind adds, "The spaces inside the museum are to be construed as 'open narratives.'" Resisting the concept of a museum as a "collection," Libeskind's design "seeks to estrange [the museum's contents and routes] from viewers' preconceptions. . . . to defamiliarize the all-too-familiar ritual objects and historical chronologies."[29]

With his emphasis on the way the museum is open to diverse readings by visitors, Libeskind has created an event space in which the historical experience of the Holocaust remains inert until activated by visitors attempting to manage a space that lacks a prescribed route. In Roland Barthes's terms, the museum-as-text is a "methodological field." It is a text that, through the interpretive trajectories to be inscribed by visitors/readers, harbors the "infinite deferment of the signified . . . [a text that] must not be conceived as 'the first stage of meaning' . . . [but] as its *deferred action.*"[30] That deferral for Libeskind is based on his decision not to materialize a particular meaning of the Holocaust but to provide a space for "unmeaning and a search for meaning."[31]

In his description of how his design—a "series of complex trajectories, irregular linear structures, fragments and displacements,"[32] the Jewish Museum's configuration—should be approached, Libeskind says that it has to be read "between the lines . . . one is a straight line, but broken into many fragments; the other is a tortuous line, but continuing indefinitely. . . . They fall apart . . . become disengaged, and are seen as separated . . . they expose a void that runs through the museum . . . a discontinuous void"[33] (see figure I.1). Representationally, the void constitutes the way Libeskind acknowledges and incorporates Berlin's "void of Jewish life" after the Holocaust. Functionally, however, the void defers attempts to consummate what the history of Jewish life and its "erasure" can and will have meant. Most significantly for how the design engages the visitor, in contrast with traditional museum design, the walls of the museum play no important role. They are there to "lend shape to [the] spaces and define their borders." It is "the void 'between the lines' that Libeskind seeks to capture, a void so real, so palpable, and so elemental to Jewish history . . . a negative center of gravity around which Jewish memory now assembles."[34]

A visitor attuned to the usual memorial museum is confronted with six voids and must struggle with disorientation. Rather than an orienting path that would supply a narrative of how to remember Berlin's Jewish life, the design burdens the visitor with a singular reading task. The effect of the museum's void punctuations is thus like the effect of the blank spaces punctuating Mallarmé's poems; Libeskind's museum, like Mallarmé's poems, is an event space that does not offer guidance toward a shared, common sense. Rather than allowing visitors to rely on a rigidly curated narrative and be induced to recognize what they expect to see, the museum forces them to think. Architecture is thus one among a variety of media technologies that negotiate the conditions of possibility for common versus oppositional sensibilities.

Technologies of Common Sense

My heading opens up a historical trajectory too vast to attempt to cover comprehensively. Instead of providing a genealogy of the technology-community coherence relationship, I want to jump into one critical historical moment, Martin Luther's invention of a reading "congregation," which was a revolutionary displacement of religious authority from the church hierarchy to the assemblage of believers. As is well known, the rapid expansion of Luther's rebellion was enabled by the coincidence between the event of his religious dissidence and the development of printing. At the same time, his German-language Bible became a vehicle for the spread of German literature, an effect that ultimately participated in the development of Germany's consciousness of itself as a nation. Subsequently taking advantage of print media, Johann Gottlieb Fichte published his *Addresses to the German Nation*, in which he exaggerates the national community of sense that such a shared language can produce.

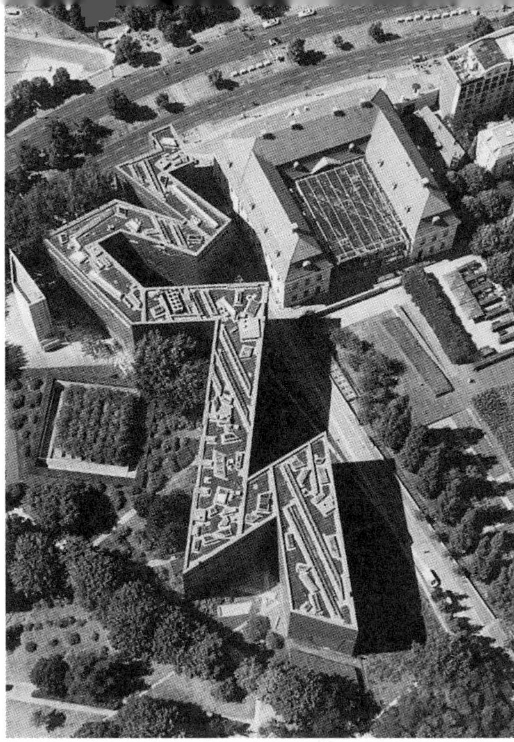

Figure I.1
Libeskind's Jewish Museum.

Its "supersensuous" aspect, he suggests, comprehends "the sum total of the sensuous mental life of the nation deposited in language . . . [which] proceeds from the whole previous life of the nation,"[35] and adds, "What an immeasurable influence on the whole human development of a people the character of its language may have—its language, which accompanies the individual into the most secret depths of his/[her] mind . . . united within its domain in the whole mass . . . who speak it into one common understanding."[36]

In a fictional commentary on another European venue, which emerged after the fallout associated with the disintegration of the Austro-Hungarian Empire, Joseph Roth provides an antidote to Fichte's optimism about the effects of language on national coherence. Roth's story, "Rare and Ever Rarer in This World of Empirical Facts," reflects on the arbitrariness of "attempts to lend historical weight to a newly emerging Czech national identity."[37] His protagonist, Heinrich, a writer, is recruited to invent national coherence by "script[ing] a popular and widespread emotional depth" 'for the new so-called autonomous Czech people.'"[38]

Although languages within developing national cultures have had centrifugal as well as centripetal effects, the latter spurred by state practices of cultural governance (sponsorships of diverse arts aimed at producing shared communal sensibilities, e.g., France's Grand Opera and Britain's

National Theater),[39] national allegiance began competing effectively with religious sensibilities in a Europe in which, thanks to Luther, Christendom had developed a significant fault line. Without going into the vicissitudes of the religious ferment that transpired after Luther—its more extreme manifestations bathed the European continent in blood and at the same time shaped much of the pattern of European sovereignties (compellingly and artistically rendered in Aldous Huxley's *The Grey Eminence*)—I want to reference a consequence that Fredric Jameson suggests: "After Luther, religion comes in competing brands [at least as far as Christendom is concerned]."[40] It should be noted, however, that Luther's intervention into the church's orthodoxies was not a singular event. In relatively close historical proximity to Luther's assault on the "brand" were other challenges in cities all over Europe: Jan Hus in Prague, Huldrych Zwingli in Zurich, John Calvin in Geneva, and Erasmus in Rotterdam and Deventer, all preceded (and influenced to a degree) by John Wyclif in Oxford.[41]

Carrying on with his thumbnail historical sketch, Jameson delegates Christendom to the past, suggesting that as religion's hegemonic dominance has been attenuated by secular forces, "It is . . . plausible to assume that the end of religion is on us with secularization, and probably with Luther's revolution, which transformed a culture organized by religion into a space in which what is still called religion has become an essentially private matter and a form of subjectivity (among many others)."[42] Certainly, Jameson's restriction of religious subjectivity to the domain of privacy is belied by the many ways that the practices of religious rites and rituals find their way into public spaces and events.

As Émile Durkheim famously points out, "Religious phenomena are naturally arranged in two fundamental categories: beliefs and rites,"[43] making clear that together they generate the coherence of religious groups, as rites "translate common ideas ["beliefs"] into common practices."[44] Moreover, I hasten to add, "the "religious phenomena" to which Durkheim refers provide the interpretive frames through which adherents of diverse religious "brands" address themselves to public issues. Durkheim's analysis of the ideational and practical aspects of religious life occurred in a period that precedes the subsequent proliferation of the contemporary competing "forms"—for example, the contemporary films and television series that Jameson analyzes to address complex social and cultural enigmas. To take one instance: the importance of television as a competing form is evident in a *New York Times* editorial vignette by a Haitian comic who describes a mentoring relationship with an elderly Haitian woman he tutored in a program for high school volunteers teaching illiterate elders from the community to read and write English. To describe the ultimate success of the endeavor, he draws on two characters from the popular television series *Game of Thrones*, assuming that his readers are sufficiently attuned to that media genre to get the reference: "She was my Davos Seaworth and I was her Shireen Baratheon."[45] Crucially, media history, like economic history, is (to use Fernand Braudel's term) *conjunctural*.[46]

Rather than being displaced, older forms remain to compete with newer ones. Although the enigmas treated in popular culture to which Jameson refers may not insinuate themselves into the perspectives of many of those absorbed in the beliefs and rituals of traditional religious life, the contemporary contention between an adherence to an ancient religious textuality (however various religious authorities may inflect it) and contemporary media genres (e.g., visual media and social media and artistic creations now disseminated in a proliferation of media platforms) constitutes an exemplary struggle over how individual and collective subjectivity is to be understood and practiced by the competing communities of sense that the alternative media help to create and assemble.

As is well known, Jameson's suggestion about the political triumph of secularism over religious commitment has considerable support among theorists of nationalism who have suggested that nationalism as the religion of modernity has largely displaced theological religion as a political force. The displacement model, however, neglects the way religion in some of its most intensely practiced modes (those that harbor commitments that color all aspects of one's life world, e.g., evangelical Christianity) is the basis for connecting believers to the extra-religious forces of capital formation and governance. As William Connolly points out, "In politics diverse elements *infiltrate* into the others, metabolizing into a moving complex," which he conceives as an "evangelical-capitalist resonance machine," consisting in a complex of affective and ideational attachments.[47] In the case of evangelical Christianity, Connolly detects a form of abjection of those with differing commitments, an antidemocratic, antipluralist political sensibility: "Given the intensity of the ethos binding the parties [a capitalist-friendly governance and evangelical Christianity] together amidst variations in religious doctrine, economic creed, and life conditions; any constituency or social movement that crosses them is subject to sharp castigation and accusations."[48]

That political sensibility articulates itself as a partitioning of worthy versus unworthy artistic initiatives. For example, evangelicals find affirmation in a series of novels: "The cutting edge of the evangelical Right is organized around a vision of the Second Coming, dramatized in the best-selling series of novels, *Left Behind*" (50 million copies sold as of 2005). Moreover, "To embrace this vision is to place a series of defiled doctrines, institutions, and constituencies under daily suspicion: it is to foment a collective will to revenge against nonbelievers held to be responsible for the time of tribulation and obstacles to future bliss awaiting believers."[49] Castigating support for versions of the arts that are embraced by "unbelievers," a right-wing think tank that oils the gears of the "evangelical-capitalist resonance machine," the Heritage Foundation, continually attacks the NEA (National Endowment for the Arts), claiming that it funds art projects that are "offensive to most Americans."[50] In contrast to the Heritage Foundation's commitment to an "ethical regime"[51] of the arts (strictures on what can appropriately be represented), a critically oriented approach to the arts, which permits thinking as opposed to moralizing, is what Rancière refers to as the "aesthetic regime of the arts," which "frees it from any specific rule, from any hierarchy of the arts, subject matter, and genres."[52]

Heeding Rancière's position on the contemporary aesthetic regime of the arts and endeavoring to illustrate the political significance of struggles in which various forms of belief orthodoxy are at stake, I turn to Philip Dick's prescient, fearlessly nonconformist (and likely offensive to believers) exploration of contention between that venerable textual community, Christianity, whose adherents find themselves in Dick's futuristic epoch as "Neo-Christians," supported by a venerable media platform (sacred texts), and a new community created by biosemiotic media that penetrate bodies rather than merely displaying signs aimed at inducing belief. The new media in Dick's novel *The Three Stigmata of Palmer Eldritch* are shared mentalities induced by pharmaceuticals that generate an affective symbiosis among users, a shared sensuality that displaces a shared spirituality. Without requiring reinforcing rites and rituals to maintain adherents, the pharmaceutically induced communities of sense are maintained by the way the drugs grip mentality and impose affect. The novel articulates the way Dick sees the objects in his stories, "as clues to other universes, other societies."[53]

In this novel, the critical effect of Dick's textual intervention into contentious conditions of possibility for community—a text that doubtless belongs to the "aesthetic regime of the arts"—is owed in part to the temporal structure of the media genre in which his story is situated. As Steven Shaviro points out, science fiction derives its critical effects by operating "(conceptually if not grammatically) in the future tense." As a genre, it is a form of "discognition," which he describes as "a kind of thought experiment, a way of entertaining odd ideas . . . of asking *what if* questions. . . .

Science fiction . . . proposes counterintuitive scenarios. . . . its effort is . . . to work through the weirdest and most extreme ramifications of these scenarios and to imagine *what it would be like* if they were true."[54]

I want to add that the conceptual attachment to the future that characterizes science fiction has critical implications for other temporalities. Its speculations render the entire historical trajectory of shared temporal experience radically contingent. As Bernard Stiegler's corpus of work on technics and time shows, the bases of communities of sense are fragile. Over time, they form and reform as a result of the continual "adoption" of a new technology, which "constructs communities" as it connects people in new ways.[55] To cite one of his examples: "cinema is a temporal object,"[56] and its emergence as "cinematic time" reveals the radical contingency of past and present versions of the life world, each shaped by a different temporally situated technology whose adoption "constructs and reformulates communities."[57]

A relevant instance that speaks to Stiegler's example is the small and rather "static . . . college educated, well-traveled group" that was introduced to "European filmmaking" in the art theaters developed by Dan Talbot in Manhattan. That "group" also developed a shared sensibility about postwar Germany's life world after watching the films of Werner Rainer Fassbender in his theaters.[58] Similarly, the temporal structure of science fiction attracts another relatively small community of sense among those who want to escape the conceptual strictures of the present in order to speculate on what might be. Like traditional religion, which, as Durkheim notes, introduces "speculation upon all that which evades science or distinct thought in general,"[59] science fiction introduces speculation rather than scientifically based investigation, not to create communities of believers (the quest of religious speculation) but rather to suggest "new lines of inquiry that analytic reasoning and inductive generalization would never stumble upon by themselves."[60] Challenging all the technology-assisted communities of believers, Dick's science fiction novel is a critical intervention that I want to engage and amplify because it encourages thinking about the possibilities of alternative, nondogmatic communities of sense.

Philip Dick's Drug-Induced Community of Sense

Drawing on the sociability clichés of the social contexts evoked in the Mattel toy company's Barbie and Ken doll variations and articulating those avatars with a drug-induced communal bonding, Dick's novel invents a drug-imposed fusion/translation experience that forges a community among a group of colonists on Mars. They achieve their communal connection by taking the drug Can-D, which projects them into the Barbie and Ken–type dolls Perky Pat and her boyfriend, Walt. As a result, the Mars community they inhabit becomes a surrogate of Earth's most banal version of U.S. West Coast culture. A main protagonist, an aspirational tyrant, the eponymous Palmer Eldritch, intervenes in that community with a competing pharmaceutical, Chew-Z, which produces a psychosis-like reaction that intensifies the Can-D fantasy. In contrast with the "consensual hallucinations" that Can-D induces, Eldritch's product enslaves the minds of the colonists, placing their shared hallucinations under his domination.

Mimicking religious communities, the drug-taking colonists (whether on either Can-D or Chew-Z) identify themselves in pseudo-religious terms as believers and evoke a Pauline commitment to the spirit over the flesh.[61] As they put it, "We lose our fleshly bodies, our corporeality. . . . And put on imperishable bodies instead, for a time. . . . Or forever, if you believe as some do that it's outside of time and space, that it's eternal."[62]

Introduced into that narco-created community is Anne Hawthorne, a "Neo-Christian" and thus a carrier of an older media platform, Christianity's religious texts that technologies of writing have made available. Her appearance stages an encounter between two belief-creating technologies, Christianity's sacred texts and a drug that induces mind fusion in the settler community. In reaction to her attempts at proselytizing among the mind-fused community members, an adherent of the latter, Fran Schein, says to Barney Mayerson (an executive in the Can-D pharmaceutical enterprise who arrived on Mars with Anne), "You don't want that Neo-Christian nut to live with you. We've had experience with that; we ejected a couple of them last year. They can cause terrible trouble here on Mars. Remember, *we shared her mind*. . . . she's a dedicated member of some high church or other, all the sacraments and the rituals, all that old outdated junk; she actually believes in it."[63]

In contrast with Christianity's promises about inhabiting eternal time, the eponymous protagonist Palmer Eldritch claims to have delivered what Christianity's purveyor of the "good news" only promised: "Well you got what St. Paul promises, as Anne Hawthorne was blabbing about; you're no longer clothed in a perishable, fleshly body—you've put on an ethereal body in its place. . . . You can't die; you don't eat or drink or breathe air . . . you'll learn in time. Evidently on the road to Damascus, Paul experienced a vision related to this phenomenon."[64]

Dick's text sides with neither of the communities of shared beliefs/hallucinations. It operates at the level of meta belief, inquiring into the way alternative technologies activate belief structures and pointing to their political consequences, the power and authority effects acquired by belief or hallucination wizards. It reveals the functioning of two kinds of enterprise that control or manage the technologies that engender consensual communities: religious authorities who disseminate textual interpretation and pharmaceutical entrepreneurs who control pharmaceutical distributions and the interpretation of the drugs collective ontological consequences. To pursue those political consequences, I want to shift the conversation back from Dick's Mars to earthly geopolitics and contrast the historical role of social science's approach to beliefs with a politics of aesthetics that sets up the inquiries in my various chapters.

The Historical Contingency of Beliefs

Philip Dick's artistic intervention suggests that the belief systems consolidating communities enfranchise various versions of political authority. In order to appreciate that political pedagogy, we need to recognize the historical contingency of beliefs and the political resources deployed by those who operate as the knowledge agents on behalf of their validity. For that purpose, I evoke a historical moment I have analyzed elsewhere, inspired by a conversation that took place in the Arctic region in 1924 between a Danish anthropologist and an Inuit shaman. Describing that conversation in his ethnography of the arctic region, Barry Lopez writes, "A central Eskimo shaman Aua, queried by Knud Rasmussen, a Danish anthropologist, about Eskimo beliefs, answered, 'We do not have beliefs, we fear.'"[65] In response to that encounter, I suggested: "Instead of attributing the shaman's answer to a misunderstanding, Lopez's discussion encourages inquiry into the genealogy of our concern with such cognitive concepts as beliefs. Rather than being concerned with the validity and reliability of statements about beliefs, the question that would direct such an inquiry would pursue the forces that have made the concept of belief so central to a social science such as anthropology."[66]

Continuing in that pursuit, I distinguished the contexts of Inuit security practices from those in contemporary nation states: "Aua's response reflects the Inuit way of [managing] security. In their everyday lives they practice an epistemology of fear in order to protect themselves [because] . . . to feel fear is to be constantly alert to imminent danger. By contrast 'we,' [in advanced industrial societies] . . . practice an epistemology of belief because for us security is mediated by various agencies—insurance companies, the Defense Department, the police, the army, and so on."[67] To put the implications of where politically relevant beliefs are usually situated: they are part of a legitimation apparatus (a *dispositif*) in which the social sciences have participated. Whereas Inuits, as they must, use their personal experiences to assess immediate danger (practicing their epistemology of fear), modernity's belief systems are commodities for agencies involved in indirect influence. They traffic in an epistemology of belief and market their security products to those who must rely on their reports on what constitutes danger.

For example, during the Vietnam War, social scientists working at Oak Ridge National Laboratories carried out investigations of "defense beliefs," funded by the U.S. security agencies concerned with how to sell their approach to the war to the U.S. public. As I put it, "the sponsoring agencies were interested in the reception of security policy."[68] The researchers therefore functioned as part of a legitimation structure. Oakridge Laboratory's "social science staff, focused on 'public opinion on national security matters' . . . reported on the American public's support for various kinds of military hardware."[69]

From Beliefs to Witnessing: Alternative Media Genres

Social scientists employing the technologies of survey instruments or the protocols of ethnographic investigations to assess beliefs are involved in a practice of what Rancière calls "unavowed fiction," for as he puts it, "Fiction is a structure of rationality which is required whenever a sense of reality must be produced. It is . . . a form of presentation of things that cuts out a frame and places elements within it to compose a situation and make it perceptible."[70] Rancière adds, "Politicians, journalists or social scientists must use fictions as well as novelists, whenever they have to say: this is the situation, these are the elements that compose it."[71] Heeding Rancière's blurring of the boundary between fiction and nonfiction, I want to suggest that rather than wondering about the extent to which an artistic text or a social science study is fiction, the critical questions to ask are about the political resources deployed by the text. As Michel Foucault insists, "to analyze a discursive formation," one must ask for whom it is an "asset."[72] My claim here is that there are more politically astute fictions than those that summon the beliefs that buttress structures of power and authority. They are those that challenge entrenched knowledge agents and thereby redistribute assets. Accordingly, the artistic texts that attract my attention throughout this investigation are those that intervene in the structures of recognition from which beliefs emerge. They access realities that official approaches reinforcing institutionalized forms of intelligibility obscure.

Briefly, for purposes of illustration, among such approaches that open access to an alternative, politically relevant sense of reality is Claude Lanzmann's documentary film *Shoah* (1985), which he describes as "fictions of the real." Composing his *Shoah* with scenes of witnessing based on personal memory, Lanzmann's text effects an "aesthetic transformation"[73] as it blends cinematic time with historical time, creating scenes of how the past exists in the present for the film's characters. As both a work of art and a documentary, Lanzmann's witnesses—those who survived the concentration camps—are best thought of as "actors," "playing out what they lived through."[74] Rather than merely presenting memories, they are reexperiencing what they went through as Lanzmann stages the past (for those he asked to reexperience it—for example, using a borrowed railway car to have them and the viewer experience a train ride with the old Polish locomotive engineer, Henrik Gawkowski, who drove the train more than forty years earlier, when its passengers were headed for extermination in the Treblinka camp).

By filming the testimonies of those still alive that experienced the Holocaust, Lanzmann's film creates a realist temporality articulated with camera movements that affect both his protagonists and viewers. The grammar of his *Shoah* displaces static memory governed by the past tense, with the future anterior, how it will have been after the past is repeated. As his witnesses reexperience what was past, they participate in Lanzmann's aesthetic transformation, which makes the event endure rather than recede.[75]

In contrast with the competing belief systems within which the event of the Holocaust is alternatively understood as something now surpassed—for example, the current revisionism of "state-builders" in Poland who promote a version of the event that preserves "the nation's honor"[76]—Lanzmann's text delivers what André Bazin famously calls "image facts," "fragment[s] extracted from the world which resist our attempts [at explication] . . . or to deplete [their] force through an act of naming or making sense,"[77] while at the same time submitting that facticity to a repetition that activates imagination.

He brings back an event that is "temporally removed," reinserting it into the spaces in which it occurred. Noting the temporal structure of the film, Gertrud Koch points to the film's "complex montage . . . [which]

plays on multiple levels with real and filmic time [for example, bringing the viewer on] a walk through the forested terrain of a death camp [to provide] a realistic sense of the spatiotemporal certainty: the presence of an absence in the imagination of the past. . . . Past and present intertwine; the past is made present and the present is drawn into the spell of the past."[78]

Similarly, if we heed the increasingly available sets of image facts that bear on the military's use of "military hardware" (about which the Oakridge social scientists solicited "beliefs" to help legitimate war strategy), we are positioned to rethink such security issues by examining visually oriented texts that testify to the enduring effects of that hardware, which static belief protocols cannot capture. For example, it was the cinematic event known as Italian neorealism that made such effects palpable to large audiences in the immediate post–World War II period. Bazin describes the effect of the new film genre, neorealism, while referring to Roberto Rossellini's *Paisa* (1946) as "An Aesthetic of Reality" that provides "a fragment of concrete reality in itself multiple and full of ambiguity."[79] Describing that reality effect, a commentator elaborates: "This ambiguity is lessened to a degree when one image-fact is placed alongside another but they regain a certain autonomy and ambiguity regardless of this arrangement. They retain a materiality and weight beyond the use they are supposed to serve in regards [to] the narrative and the meaning the filmmaker wishes to elicit from the image. In neorealism, there is a density to objects that allows them to retain an independence or integrity beyond their manipulation or use by the filmmakers."[80]

In his *Paisa*, Rossellini shifts the focus of warring violence from weapons and strategies, the war genre most familiar to film viewers, to the social realities affected by the war. Sandro Bernardi captures the innovative aspect of Rossellini's films: "Rossellini's work . . . consisted above all of a 'cleansing of the eyes,' an attempt to free cinema, vision, and therefore knowledge from the stereotypes accumulated over time . . . over centuries . . . [he] used cinema to think."[81]

A more recent technological event that also provides "an aesthetic of reality" (applied to contemporary militarized violence) is the democratizing event of video, a technology that makes everyone a potential filmmaker capable of producing citizen documentaries. The effect of that technology is similar to the effect of the earlier technology print (treated above), which, as Condorcet famously remarked, had the capacity to "unmask and dethrone" hierarchal authority, as "men found themselves possessed of a means of communication with people all over the world [yielding] . . .

a new tribunal . . . which no longer allowed the same tyrannical empire to be exercised over men's passions."[82] As Rune Saugmann Andersen points out, in the case of the new visual medium, "the authority granted video as a faithful witness means that the spread of video entails a transformation of the authority with which politics is spoken—and, crucially, who can speak effectively."[83]

A recent intervention by "civilian investigators" testifies dramatically to Saugmann Andersen's remark. On February 20, 2014, after a "paramilitary police force loyal to President Viktor Yanukovych killed forty-eight protestors demonstrating against the government's Russia-favoring policy," the young civilian investigators "used cellphone videos, autopsy reports and surveillance footage" to renarrativize the event with evidence that proved Yanukovych's denials false.[84] They mounted a forensic intervention that accords with Eyal Weizman's observations about the forensic opportunities afforded by civilian access to now privatized satellite imagery (once exclusively a resource of governments).[85]

Human rights groups have now been able to make use of citizen-produced images to provide video testimony that contests governmental accounts of events.[86] Importantly, the aesthetic transformation of authority that video technology makes possible is also spatial. It is a technology that has migrated from private space, where its main function was as a "registrar of the private sphere," to public space, where its users could bear witness to events and make them continually repeatable.[87]

The transformation effected by video technology therefore turns citizen-subjects from passive viewers of violent events (whose beliefs and opinions, based only on official and mainstream media sources, can be solicited) into political actors who bear witness in ways that challenge official accounts. The development of that citizen-controlled technology testifies to the way media genres can intervene in the politics of subjectivity. They can create and activate oppositional communities of sense by disturbing the matrix of subject positions that is otherwise anchored by institutionalized structures of power and authority, served by knowledge agents attuned to authoritative and static information frames.

Accordingly, the diverse investigations in the chapters of this book provide a politics of aesthetics that is articulated by artistic texts. The critically oriented media genres on which I focus in each chapter provoke thinking outside of the conventional modes of recognition that serve entrenched modes of authority. Specifically, the chapters that I summarize in this introduction treat critical, subjectivity-making punctuation effects in popular music, urban soundscapes, architecture, images (photography, painting, cinema), and Holocaust literature, respectively.

Chapter 1: How Popular Music Thinks the Political

I begin with this chapter because it's the place where I elaborate what I have termed challenges to reigning structures of intelligibility and because it is where I develop the concept of alternative communities of sense. After beginning the chapter with a review of Adorno's extension of punctuation from language to music, I figure challenges to musical intelligibility by turning to David Michael Hertz's analysis of the expressive freedom exacted in the French symbolist movement in musical and literary composition, in which he elaborates the parallel challenges to traditional forms of intelligibility of Richard Wagner and Stéphane Mallarmé (who (re)punctuated music and poetry, respectively). Noting Hertz's emphasis on the ways that symbolist language and music create startling, arresting effects, I illustrate that mode of critical innovation and note its political implications by analyzing the compositional style of the jazz composer/musician Thelonious Monk, whose musical innovations exemplify the ways in which the African American oppositional community is articulated in modes of distinctive aural intelligibility.

After distinguishing the way Monk's music articulates the counterintelligibility involved in African American *sociolects* (M. M. Bakhtin's term), I turn to films within which the musical scores feature engagements between alternative intelligibilities, belonging to alternative communities of sense. The bookends of that part of the analysis are Spike Lee's *He Got Game* (1998), in which the musical score is a virtual duel between the symphonic music of Aaron Copland and the rap music of Pubic Enemy, and Gillo Pontecorvo's *The Battle of Algiers* (1966), in which sound as well as image articulates the colonial division during the Battle of Algiers. Pontecorvo and his cowriter, Franco Solinas, solicited a soundtrack (from composer Ennio Morricone) that features a clash of the incommensurate musical cultures of Algiers's French and Arab populations.

The chapter ends on a note of musical reconciliation, an example of what Gregory Clark calls "civic jazz." It's a moment involving the fashioning of an intercultural acoustical community of sense at "the Moab music Festival," where the Marcus Roberts Trio was joined by a bluegrass musician, the banjoist Béla Fleck (at the Utah stop of the of the trio's tour). I conclude by noting that the musical hybridity achieved in the encounter succeeds in uniting elements of African American and Euro American communities of sense (where, for example, the labor coalition and the possibility of "interracial sympathy" during "the Reconstruction" that W. E. B. Du Bois had famously hoped for had failed).[88] While my emphasis throughout most of the chapter is on how popular music *thinks* the political, this is an instance in which the music *does* the political by reaching across a divide to initiate a thinking together that becomes a moment of being together.

Chapter 2: Urban Punctuations: Symphonic and Dialectic

The focus in this chapter is on urban interventions that reveal (and at times disrupt) the rhythms of the urban life world and on their micropolitical implications. Emphasizing a musical metaphor for those rhythms, the symphonic, the textual bookends of the chapter's investigation are two films: Walther Ruttmann's 1927 documentary, *Berlin: Symphony of a Great City*, which films the daily movements of bodies in the various parts of Berlin's life world during one day, and Ola Simonsson and Johannes Stjärne Nilsson's 2007 feature film, *Sound of Noise*, in which an anarchic group of musicians perform a musical score that is represented dialectically against the city's professional symphony. They play the city of Stockholm, using medical equipment (and the body of a hospital patient), a bank's shredding machine, the city's electrical wires, and heavy construction equipment (whose clanging and banging disrupts an event at a symphony hall) to realize that score. The Ruttmann documentary is viewed with attention to Beethoven's tonality (as articulated by Adorno), and the Simonsson-Nilsson feature film is read with reference to John Cage's theory of music and the interarticulation of aesthetic and ludic practices.

In between those readings, the chapter treats not only soundscape interventions but a variety of others—for example, by the artist Krzysztof Wodiczko, who invented "critical vehicles," technological prostheses worn by immigrants to re-punctuate the network of interactions in public space (between 1993 and 1997), and by circuses, for example, "Circus Amok," an assemblage that usually operates in the street, making an "'inappropriate' use of preordained urban zones. . . ." [Like other interventionist artistic performances], they "eat away at the rigid urban grid."[89] It's a circus that introduces a "ludic city"[90] in which urban space is reoriented in a conjunction of laughter and serious reflection.

With such ludic practices in mind, I end the chapter by asking how the ludic articulates with the aesthetic and suggest that like the intervention of the aesthetic, play introduces moments of indeterminacy in situations and domains that are taken as fixed. Clowning and other playful moments of urban intervention reorient the "'psychogeographic' potential of the urban grid."[91] Such disruptions derail people's usual utilitarian, goal-oriented fulfillment-seeking and encourage new ways of thinking about identities and space and thereby new ways of moving/acting together. I argue that an aesthetic of play operates "against the normative, the rational, and the ideal [while signifying] . . . the absence of essence [and] . . . excess beyond binary opposition."[92]

Chapter 3: Architectural Punctuation: The Politics of "Event Spaces"

This chapter's primary conceptualizations are based on Bernard Tschumi's understanding of architecture as dynamic such that buildings are not to be understood merely structurally but rather as "event spaces" that result from human intrusion and Eyal Weizman's perspective on "forensic architecture . . . a critical field of practice [whose aim is] to disseminate evidence of war crimes in [an] urban context." The chapter begins with a discussion of an exhibition that contained a facsimile of the bullet-punctuated door to Fred Hampton's Chicago apartment, testifying to his assassination (along with Mark Clark's) by the FBI and Chicago police in a predawn raid on December 4, 1969,[93] and ends with an analysis, based on two texts, of the architectural barriers separating Israel and Palestine (the "separation wall" and series of check points that punctuate the landscape).

The first text is by Palestinian architect Yara Sharif, whose construal of the design problem is considered from the Palestinians' perspective, which involves the creation of a more "elastic space born from the will to connect—a space of resistance that keeps on changing with the . . . interventions [that] respond to [an imposed] instability through the tactics of an emergent architecture, which in its nature might seem ephemeral, yet is quick in its effects."[94]

The second text is Hany Abu-Assad's film *Omar* (2013), in which the Separation Wall is one of the film's primary protagonists. I argue that through the way the film interarticulates action and setting—as it mobilizes an aesthetic subject involved in the microevents to which Sharif refers—we can better appreciate Sharif's descriptions of the dynamics of architectural resistance (which are enacted by Abu-Assad's eponymous protagonist, Omar).

In between the analyses of these "event spaces"—Fred Hampton's apartment and the Israel-Palestine border region—I review a variety of architectural projects and provide illustrations of architecture as a protagonist in artistic texts in five films: John Ford's *The Searchers* (1956), Paul Mazursky's *Scenes from a Mall* (1991), the Wachowski Brothers' *Bound* (1996), Stephen Frears's *Dirty Pretty Things* (2002), and Tomas Alfredson's *Tinker, Tailor, Soldier, Spy* (2011), and in three novels: Colin Harrison's *Bodies Electric*, Joe Gores's *32 Cadillacs*, and Qui Xiaolong's *When Red Is Black*.

I end the chapter with a return to a discussion of what Eyal Weizman's practice of forensic architecture is about, noting that in response to the technologies of the occupation, which sequester and immobilize people and impede the sharing of information and access, are the techniques of forensics. In accord with how Weizman construes forensics, the chapter's aim throughout is to interrogate the built environment in order to (in Weizman's words) "make objects reveal information by subjecting them to additional force."

Chapter 4: Image Punctuations: From the Photographic to the Cinematic

The initiating focus of this chapter is an analysis of the photographs of the South African Santu Mofokeng, whose compositional work abounds in "deep shadow and blur" (as Teju Cole puts it). That style, which renders the details difficult to comprehend articulates an intimacy with a historical experience—South Africa's history of apartheid—the details of which are elusive to uninitiated outsiders. The political resonances of the apartheid world that his art conveys, as he intervenes in the history of South Africa's historiography to shed light on an unjust political reality, have methodological implications for other image-oriented texts that seek to intervene critically into historical events. Theorizing such interventions with resort to Roland Barthes's concept of the "punctum" noted earlier—points and aspects of disruption in images that have the effect of arresting one's ability to impose traditional modes of intelligibility—I discuss the way such arrests open the image to innovative political reception. After pursuing a variety of photographic, art historical, and cinematic examples to illustrate the critical method, I return in my conclusion to

Mofokeng's photographic practice to move the analysis from the singular case of South Africa's apartheid to a more general concern with how images can engage and activate what Deleuze and Guattari famously refer to as "assemblages," collectives with shared experiences that have hitherto failed to rise above the level of public recognition.

In the body of the chapter, I turn to art history, with a main focus on Paul Cézanne's color punctuation and the way his canvasses decenter the viewer. As I put it, the absence of a stable center in Cézanne's paintings displaces the viewing subject from a single viewing focal point and thus accords with one of Gilles Deleuze's insights about the way cinema resists the stability of perceptual centering: "cinema does *not* have subjective perception as its model because [in accord with the "continuous movement through space and time" in a Cézanne canvas] the mobility of its centers and the variability of its framings always lead it to restore vast acentered and deframed zones."[95] Cézanne therefore provides a threshold to analyze cinematic punctuation, which I do with readings of two of Michelangelo Antonioni's films, *Red Desert* (1964) and *The Passenger* (1975).

In the conclusion, in which I return to the politically pregnant photographs of Santu Mofokeng, whose details are glossed in the Teju Cole commentary from which I quoted, I focus on one of Cole's words that stands out, intimacy: "The spaciousness and blur of Mofokeng's pictures come ultimately with this intimacy with this 'gossamer' world'"[96] (where *gossamer* is Mofokeng's word for the spirituality imminent in the black South African life world, manifested in church services).

To ascend to a more theoretical level, the "intimacy" to which Cole refers—and elaborates by noting that it's a world "that is elusive to the uninitiated or outsiders"—can be captured with the concept of assemblage, which Deleuze and Guattari use to conceive the way bodies form collective attachments through their shared capacity to affect each other. Mofokeng references that capacity and its effect on black South African self-recognition when he remarks that his intended viewers are black South Africans who can recognize the violence of apartheid in the photographs. To end the analysis, I reflect on the implications for a micropolitics of subjectivity of the textual hopscotch of image practices I have treated throughout this chapter (with a special emphasis on chromatic shifts).

Chapter 5: Holocaust Punctuations

Beginning with the observation that the Holocaust stands as an alarming punctuation mark in modern history, in this chapter, inspired by the survivor/Nobel Prize–winning writer Imre Kertész's insistence that fiction's "creation is a path to remembrance," I analyze the fiction of the Austrian Peter Handke, struggling with his national patrimony of "death-cult masters" (in his novella, *The Long Way Around*), the Hungarian Kertész, who wrote to "become the name-giver instead of the named" (in *Fatelessness* and other novels), and the German W. G. Sebald, who wrote a journey of detection through a fictional character (in *Austerlitz*), all of whom have distinctive styles that continually defer closural interpretations of events.

I point out that Handke's, Kertész's, and Sebald's compositional styles, deployed with durational (i.e., becoming) subjects, punctuate their texts in ways that impose on their readers the need to reflect on their own temporal trajectories, to "live through" what is in the pages. Moreover, because their readers, like Bakhtin's authors, are "axiological yet to be," their approaches to the Holocaust articulate, in each of the texts, an influential ethics of the event. As a result, the experiences of their protagonists impose on readers a task of sense making that encourages not only a rethinking of the Holocaust—seen through lenses that articulate biography with history—but also parallel phenomenological reflections in which they confront the comportment toward events of their own durational selves.

I go on to suggest that what is fundamentally shared in their texts are the observations and acts through which Holocaust-affected individuals seek to reclaim what Cathy Caruth calls "unclaimed experience." Apart from the cleansing that the writing of all three accomplished for them, what I also stress is what their texts can do for readers and for the event, beyond the suggestion that readers are encouraged to reflect on their own durational trajectories (the entanglement between biographical time with historical time). Their texts encourage an ethico-political attunement derived through an incessant temporalization of encounters with persons and things in one's every day experience.

Throughout the chapter, I focus on how the writers accomplish such effects, suggesting that what should draw our analytic attention are their aesthetic strategies, especially the textual vehicles to which they turn to formulate what must be thought anew. Emphasizing *how* the texts think the political, I conclude by picking up key encounters that testify to the ways the three writers enact *time*, which [to quote Rancière] "means the form of coexistence of facts that defines a situation and the mode of connection between events that defines a story,"[97] because the ways they tell the stories serve to counteractualize the Holocaust by amplifying it from a passing and now abstract historical moment to a series of concrete, experiential, and enduring effects that must be continually engaged. Finally, and important, are *my* engagements, in which (borrowing from Foucault's remarks on his approach to his lectures on *The Will to Know*) I "alternate concrete investigations and theoretical punctuations, but in an irregular way according to requirements"[98] that each chapter shapes.

HOW "POPULAR" MUSIC THINKS THE POLITICAL

Music as Oppositional Language

Theodor Adorno's remarks about how to conceive the critical aspects of punctuation (quoted in the Introduction) is the initial inspiration for my application of the concept of punctuation to music:

> There is no element in which language resembles music more than the punctuation marks. The comma and the period correspond to the half-cadence and the authentic cadence. Exclamation points are like silent cymbal clashes, question marks like musical upbeats, colons dominant seventh chords; and only a person who can perceive the different weights of strong and weak phrasings in musical form can really feel the distinction between the comma and the semicolon.[1]

The main implication I draw from Adorno's comparison is that musical intelligibility (like language intelligibility) is structured through punctuation. As is the case with literary forms, there are many aspects of musical punctuation: rhythm, phrase length, the dynamics of statement and response, the pacing that derives from the music's pattern of rests, and the interaction between the music's diegesis and anti- or extranarrative moments. Crucially for my purposes, in addition to being a grammatical operator, punctuation can serve as a concept/metaphor that helps us appreciate the individual and interpersonal rhythms of interactions in the life world and the dynamics of aggregation that eventuate in official and institutionalized versus oppositional communities of sense, which operate in the field of musical genres as they do in other artistic fields. Because my analysis focuses mainly on the critical political effects of challenges to traditional or institutionalized forms of intelligibility, I am drawn to compositional styles that depart from institutionalized and thus expected forms. Such departures provide conditions of possibility for enfranchising (intentionally or unintentionally) those who seek to distinguish themselves collectively as a distinctive, alternative, or oppositional community of sense (where, as Jacques Rancière puts it, the "phrase 'community of sense' [references] a collectivity shaped by some common feeling . . . a frame of visibility and intelligibility . . . which shapes . . . a certain sense of community").[2]

Focusing on musical punctuation and on music as punctuation, the primary materials of my analysis are musically expressed contentions among alternative acoustic communities of sense manifested in two films: Spike Lee's *He Got Game* (1998) and Gillo Pontecorvo's *The Battle of Algiers* (1966). The contrapuntal soundtracks that punctuate both films are structural realizations of M. M. Bakhtin's characterization of Dostoevsky's writing style, an interaction of voices that constitute a "polyphonic reactive activity," a "method of integral dialogic juxtapositions,"[3] which is realized in the form of clashing voices in Dostoevsky's novels and through engagements of reactive voices and music in the case of the two films. Before turning to my first illustration, Lee's film, however, I want to elaborate the language-music homology by treating the parallels between literary and musical challenges to traditional modes of intelligibility. Among the places where those parallels have been cogently thought through is David Michael Hertz's analysis of the expressive freedom exacted in the French symbolist movement in musical and literary composition (which has been subsequently featured in the developing field of "Word Music Studies").[4]

Hertz's analysis begins with the parallel challenges to traditional forms of intelligibility of Richard Wagner and Stéphane Mallarmé, who re-punctuated music and poetry, respectively. Wagner's challenge is issued through a "fracturing of the musical period."[5] By departing from symphonic music's traditional quadratic form, "Wagner sews a new motif into the heart of cadence [so that]. . . . Musical punctuation is defunct at the expense of organic continuity."[6] Mallarmé's challenge operates through obfuscation of "the syntactic hierarchy of the poetic line."[7] Influenced by musical punctuation, Mallarmé interspersed silence (effectively like musical rests) with "blank space[s]."[8] His use of that mode of punctuation was influenced by Charles Baudelaire, a writer whose style challenges traditional literary punctuation. Pointing out that in Baudelaire, "Language is used to create startling, arresting effects," Hertz proceeds to show its parallel in music in the way Wagner's and Franz Liszt's compositions generate similar effects ("through changed patterns of both syntax and semantics").[9]

Stylistic re-punctuations derived from musical forms are also featured in the writings of Raymond Roussel, whose musically influenced writing style constituted an influential challenge to traditional literary practice. Originally aiming to be a musician and composer (he studied piano and started composing songs at age sixteen), Roussel decided that he would rather work with words; "he found that 'the words came easier than the music.'"[10] Nevertheless, what Michel Foucault refers to as "the muffled phonetic explosion of arbitrary sentences"[11] that characterizes Roussel's writing indicates the imbrication between sound and word that shaped his compositions. As Roussel himself points out (in an essay on his method of writing),[12] he improvises with phonic combinations. That practice bears comparison with the improvisations of the jazz musician John Coltrane, who played along the same paradigmatic axis of meaning (in his case the verticality of music; changing its chordal harmonies).[13] Just as Coltrane tried to find sounds that went beyond what had heretofore been heard but at the same time referred to what had already been heard, Roussel, as Foucault puts it, was involved with "encountering the 'already said,' and with his 'found language' [worked] to construct, according to his rules, a certain number of things, but on the condition that they always refer back to the 'already said.'"[14]

Roussel's sound-influenced narratives also bear comparison with Debussy's challenges to traditional musical intelligibility. As Leon Botstein describes the effects, "Emancipat[ing] pitch and rhythm as well as harmonies from relationships defined by tradition and rules, Debussy's sequence of sounds is suggested by their gradual unfolding, one from the next, permitting new and unexpected sounds and colors to emerge from the actual (if non-natural) and non-artificial character of sound."[15] Debussy's anti-narratives are interruptions of his work's temporal continuities. His "abrupt juxtaposition[s] of contrasting and often unrelated ideas exhibit [those] anti-narrative tendencies in [the] occasional discontinuit[ies] of his music's moment-to-moment motion[s]."[16]

Thus, like Mallarmé, whose poesis is influenced by musical structures, Roussel's experiments with language are music-influenced. However, while Mallarmé's texts play with topology or spacing—his writing form is a "graphicality"[17] that interrupts continuity with blank spaces; in contrast, Roussel works with a "verbal doubling,"[18] with an effect that is more temporal than spatial, one in which he "reverses the triangle of time. . . . By a complete revolution, the near become distant, as if only in the outer windings of the labyrinth Roussel can play guide. He leaves off just as the path approaches the center where he himself stands."[19] Going continually from a sentence to a countersentence, Roussel shows ultimately how fragile are the word combinations with which intelligibility is achieved and thus how one can create counterintelligibilities. The "arresting effects" and counterintelligibilities to which Hertz refers and which Foucault discovers in the compositions of Roussel—as well as the syntactic (i.e., spatial) punctuation of Mallarmé—are also characteristic of the compositional style of the jazz composer/musician Thelonious Monk, to whom I turn to illustrate the ways in which the African American oppositional community is articulated in oppositional modes of aural intelligibility.

Monk's Challenge to Musical Intelligibility

Given that (among other things) "'[a] nation's emergence is predicated on the construction of meaningful sounds,'" much of the contribution of African American jazz musicians to 'sounding *reality*' has resisted the "Euro-American state's desire for a unitary nationalizing enterprise."[20] As Houston A. Baker Jr. has pointed out, the challenge of some African American artists to white dominance has proceeded through a "deformation of mastery." A more radical challenge than an earlier practice of coding and concealing, the deformation of mastery is a form of "distinguishing," achieved by enacting, in Baker's terms, "a go(ue)rilla action in the face of acknowledged adversaries"[21]—for example, the way Duke Ellington's music foregrounds the "black spokesperson" (in his *Jump for Joy*) and makes "audible extant forms in ways that move clearly up, masterfully and re-soundingly away from slavery."[22] One can discern a similar (if less strident) distinguishing in the counterintelligibility performed in Thelonious Monk's compositional style, which abounds in "startling, arresting effects." It is a "new parataxis," a "syntactically-oriented replacement of the old periodic manner of building forms," which Hertz ascribed to symbolist music and poetry.[23] Adopting a similar set of syntactic changes, Monk's jazz compositions have been compared by the social critic Nelson George to the basketball moves of Earl ("the pearl") Monroe: "Earl Monroe, a stylish guard who played for the New York Knicks in the 1970s, employed tempo changes only Thelonious Monk would understand."[24] To locate that strategy within the language metaphor with which I began: Monk's melodic revisions operate along the syntagmatic axis of language, which the linguists Roman Jakobson and Morris Halle designate as the horizontal axis, the language axis of temporal sequencing (realized through spatio-temporal punctuation).[25] "[M]usic in its most banal sense of the term. . . consists . . . entirely of notes (the particles of music) and rests . . . ,"[26] and Monk's riffs on familiar popular pieces, primarily from Tin Pan Alley musicals, are distinguished by their original phrasing lengths and their "rests" or pauses. Monk "makes hesitation eloquent,"[27] as Nathaniel Mackey puts it; his "rhythmic phrasing complicates the sense of time . . . [a] time feeling he wanted."[28] That "phrasing" also involves innovative spacing, rendering Monk's musical style as "grammatico-figural" as well.[29]

How does one move from innovations in musical intelligibility to political statement? Although at times jazz compositions have fused form and content to deliver explicit political meaning—for example, John Coltrane's "Alabama," a piece with musical resonances that capture the rhythms of Martin Luther King's eulogy at the funeral of the two young African American girls who died when "dynamite Bob" blew up a black church in Alabama[30]—Monk's music makes no direct political statements that can be discerned in (for example) his riffs on such popular songs as George Gershwin's "Nice Work If You Can Get It" and Al Dubin and Harry Warren's "Lulu's Back in Town." Rather than radical departures, "playing popular songs, or 'standards,' was the basic procedure for a jazz musician of Monk's generation."[31]

Nevertheless, if we heed the fundamental oppositionality of the approach to intelligibility in general of much of the African American assemblage as it developed in the twentieth century, we can recognize the political sensibility inherent in their musical forms. "Black talk" is "a form of counter-intelligibility (or what George Lipsitz calls a 'strategic anti-essentialism')[32] . . . owed in part to its African discursive heritage and in part to the necessarily coded form of discourse developed among people who have not, in varying degrees and at different historical moments, been free to express themselves directly [or to participate] . . . in mainstream American civic expression."[33]

Given the linguistic predicates of African American musical forms, we have to reflect critically on the appropriate grammar required to appreciate what Monk and his musical generation have contributed politically to their listeners. According to a Monk biographer, Gabriel Solis, the "approach [requires] not so much an analysis of what Monk and his music *are* or even were, but of what they *have* been to the community loosely defined as the collection of people with Monk as a common interest."[34] To put it more incisively, the bebop style of Monk and others has been received as "a music of revolt." "It is especially the intransigent opponent of Tin Pan Alley. Indeed the war against the horrible products of the tunesmiths . . . has been brought to successful conclusion only by the beboppers, who take standard melodies at will, stand them on their heads, and create new compositions retaining only a harmonic relationship with the original."[35] Much of jazz's fundamental oppositionality is captured in a review of a New Orleans novel in which jazz is a major protagonist. Referring to a moment in the novel when a street preacher, who hangs moralistic signs on the back of his church wagon, hangs one that reads, "JAZZ KILLS," the reviewer writes, "The novel makes clear that jazz does indeed kill—not by its decadence, as the proselytist suggests, but by its novelty, its ingenuity. Jazz kills the old art forms, rag and swing. Jazz enacts violence on a song—one band is shown 'teasing apart the 'Tiger Rag' like an old sweater until it unraveled into something unrecognizable."[36] And Christopher Small summarizes the way jazz functions as an oppositional practice, taking it beyond its destructive impact on older art forms: as jazz performers compose as they play, they are involved, he writes, in a "struggle between freedom and order."[37] Their performances constitute "a movement back and forth between the spaces of black vernacular orality and the values and assumptions of the white social order."[38]

Accordingly, as "Monk reshaped popular songs"[39] by restructuring the intervals in the original versions, he engaged in acts of defamiliarization that effectively changed the receptive effects of the music. Articulating a distinctive "metapoesis" to engage a "very specific addressee or set of addressees. . . ,"[40] his compositions resonate with "black vernacular orality." They are attentive to such a "very specific addressee." Focused on that addressee, Nathaniel Mackey has concerned himself extensively with the order-freedom struggle imminent in African American jazz compositions. He takes up the grammatical metaphor initiated by Amiri Baraka in his *Blues People*, where Baraka points out that the special meaning of *swing*, practiced in the big-band jazz of Fletcher Henderson, Duke Ellington, and Jimmy Lunceford in the twenties and thirties, which functioned as a verb (expressed as the improvisational character of Afro-American music), became in the versions of many (white) imitators "a less dynamic, less improvisatory, less blues-inflected music, and, in the political level, a containment of black mobility."[41]

The improvisatory privileging of the verb in Afro-American compositions/performances, according to Mackey, is comparable to the linguistic practice (to which Small refers), an oblique coding style developed "among a people whose ability to act is curtailed by racist constraints."[42] Mackey singles out Monk's style in his tune "Jackie-ing," in which "even a so-called proper noun is a verb in disguise—present-participial, provisional subject to change."[43] Accordingly, to appreciate the musical othering of African American jazz composers/musicians, he adds, "we need more than content analyses based on assumptions of representationality. The dislocating tilt of artistic othering, especially as practiced by African American artists, deserves a great deal more attention than it's been given."[44]

Popular Music and Disjunctive Soundscapes

Mackey's grammatical framing of the oppositionality of African American jazz styling places pressure on the concept of "popular music." That styling evokes a fault line within the U.S. population, a fracturing within what can be designated as the "popular." For example, what had been a "popular" tune in Euro-American–dominated media (e.g., what had been repeatedly played as part of America's "top 40" tunes on radio broadcasts) was revised by African American jazz artists, who "deterritorialize . . . many of the punctual structures of pop."[45] The force of that deterritorialization became dramatically apparent when the epoch of rock and roll descended on *Your Hit Parade*, the popular music program, which began on radio (1935–55) and ended on television (1950–59), when the program's singers, Snooky Lanson, Russell Arms, Gisele McKenzie, and Dorothy Collins, proved to be unsuited for performing rock music. I recall watching how out of his element Lanson was as he attempted to do Elvis Presley's appropriation of black sound—noted years later in a commentary on the show's demise: "Snooky Lanson's whitebread rendition of '*Hound Dog*' sealed the show's fate."[46]

At a minimum, the deterritorialization that occurred as a result of the new musical genre rendered "the term pop . . . problematic."[47] It shifted the focus from commercial success to forms of nonconformist cultural reception, making clear that, "what is termed pop [music]," that is, its "musicality . . . has nothing to do with the level of commercial success . . . If . . . a popular artist chooses to create an expression which does not conform faithfully to pre-existing forms, which does not adhere to a model known in advance but rather transforms existing models and forms so as to produce an expression both singular and new, then that expression will indeed be musical"[48] in a way that resonates for a particular assemblage within the social formation. It is thus evident that to appreciate the fault lines that divide alternative musical expression in what constitutes the dispersion of popular music, we have to heed the "cultural economy" rather than the commercial economy. As one analyst puts it, "creativity and innovation in the modern cultural economy can be understood as rooted in the production system and its geographic milieu, i.e., in the creative field [in which one can observe] . . . the formation of cultural communities."[49] To recognize the existence of alternative cultural communities, we therefore have to heed the fault lines in "the geography of the creative field,"[50] which early television failed to encompass.

The specific fault line with which I am concerned divides the "popular" and thereby divides politically inflected alternative modes of musical intelligibility. It is what Jennifer Lynn Stoever calls "the sonic color line," which has a venerable history: "sounds, heard and unheard, have histories. If we listen we can hear resonances with other times and places . . . segregation's hostile soundscapes."[51] Early in the twentieth century, black musical forms—for example, bebop—operated "beyond the grasp of the market place."[52] It and other forms of African American musical creativity entered what finally emerged as a racially shared public sphere only after it became apparent to the record companies that African Americans spend money on recordings. For example, after Perry Bradford, a "black show-business entrepreneur [rebuffed by the large labels] . . . convinced a smaller label to let him make 'Crazy Blues' with Mamie [Smith], within a month of its release on Okeh Records 75,000 copies were sold."[53]

The sonic color line nevertheless persisted. Stoever points out that the African American singer Lena Horne's voice helped to signal the tensions in the American soundscape (well before the fiasco of *Your Hit Parade*) because she "shifted strategically across the sonic color line and back again," as she "wielded one of the most distinctive voices in American culture (in the mid-1940s)."[54] An African American singer whose vocals were "vexing white definitions of 'black sound' [even] . . . while signaling her social and political commitments to black people through vocal phrasing and sonic detail,"[55] she evoked different reactions from African American and Euro-American communities of sense: "While the black press contextualized Horne's voice in terms of race consciousness, white press reviews of Horne revealed how the listening ear had shifted with color blindness to listen for the 'right kind of black,' 'Chocolate Cream Chanteuse,' the tile of *TIME*'s 1943 feature."[56] Lena Horne's ambiguous and contentious position in the American soundscape points to the sonic oppositionality I explore in the next section.

Sounding America: The Clash of Sociolects

As I've noted, M. M. Bakhtin privileges the novel as a site for contending voices, which he at times refers to as clashing sociolects, alternative speech styles among subcultural groupings within the social domain that are centrifugal, that pull away from a "verbal ideological center."[57] Similarly, Roland Barthes refers to the "intimidating character" of sociolects, which exclude those outside and constrain those within.[58] An exemplary clash of sociolects, in which Lena Horne's contentious subject position shows up, occurred in a Hollywood-situated James Ellroy crime story, "High Darktown." It's the mid-1940s, and Ellroy's protagonist, a police detective named Lee Blanchard, is holding a young black woman (identified only as "Cora"), threatening to arrest her unless she informs on a local black burglary ring. In typical off-the-record police talk, he says, "Questions and answers. Tell me what I want to know and you walk, fuck with me and I find dope in your purse and tell the DA you've been selling it to white nursery school kids."[59] As the conversation progresses, Cora takes over as interrogator with the remark, "Why do you do this shitty kind of work," and when invited to answer her own question, she "started ticking off points on her fingers" (while speaking black talk):

> One, you yourself figured your boxin' days would be over when you was thirty, so you got yourself a nice civil service pension job; two, the bigwig cops loves to have ball players and fighters around to suck up to them—so you gets the first crack at the cushy 'signments. Three, you likes to hit people, and *po*-lice work be full of that; four, your ID card said Warrants Division, and I knows that warrant cops all serves process and does repos on the side, so I knows you pickin' up lots of extra change.[60]

At that point Blanchard, having heard enough, throws his hands up in surrender. Later, it's his turn to ask a question, after Cora clues him in about the details of High Darktown (an upper-middle-class black suburb): "'How do you know all this?' he asks. Cora: 'I am from *High Darktown*, sweet.' Blanchard: 'Then why do you hold on to that Aunt Jemima accent?' Cora laughed. 'And I thought I sounded like Lena Horn,'" she replies before pointing out that it's a survival choice, "you dig"? Thus, her black talk, in her case a way of speaking "through a mask darkly"[61] is a venerable survival strategy *within* as well as across the sonic color line, which from some points of view Lena Horn famously rendered ambiguous. The literary sociolects that punctuate Ellroy's crime story "give visibility to [the text's] plurilingualism. . . . they perturb the supposed unity of narrative discourse, introducing discursive ruptures and discontinuities that 'imitate' or transform real-world linguistic and social phenomena."[62]

Cinematic soundtracks can also enact a perturbation that evokes the "ruptures and discontinuities" in the social order. Exemplary in that respect is the clash of musical idioms that punctuate Spike Lee's film *He Got Game* (1998). His soundtrack, in which there are alternations between the symphonic music of Aaron Copland and the rap music of Public Enemy, punctuates the film with ruptures and discontinuities that challenge any attempt to ascribe a cultural unity to American society. Focusing on that challenge, I turn to a consideration of how Lee's soundtrack contributes to the way his film thinks the political.

He Got Game

The contrapuntal soundtrack of Lee's film punctuates a film narrative that is on its surface an American basketball story, framed by a fraught relationship between an African American father, Jake Shuttlesworth (Denzel Washington), in prison on a murder conviction for killing his wife (accidently, as a flashback shows), and his son Jesus Shuttlesworth (Ray Allen), a high school basketball star who is attracting intense recruitment efforts by major college basketball programs. Jake is temporarily paroled (but remains under carceral control, wearing an ankle bracelet to monitor his movements) to try and convince his son to sign a letter of intent to play for the New York governor's *alma mater.* Summoned by the warden, he's informed that the governor is offering him a commuted sentence if he succeeds.

Jake Shuttleworth's (ultimately failed) attempt to get his son to sign the letter of intent constitutes the drama of the film narrative, and a religious metaphor, conveyed with the name Jesus (inspired by Earl Monroe, nicknamed "Black Jesus" during his playing days) for the protagonist and a coach named Billy Sunday (John Turturro), named after a baseball player/evangelist whose recruitment speech is evangelical in tone, frames the drama, with attention to the interarticulation of moral economy and the political economy of college sports. Nevertheless, the land- and cityscape scenes constitute much of the way the film thinks politically. The political theme *within* the film narrative is about the exploitation of black bodies by the sports system that profits from their performances (e.g., a sports agent conspires with Jesus's girlfriend and her lover to control Jesus's career) and by the prison-industrial complex that lives off the disproportionate incarceration of African Americans. However, if we heed Martin Lefebvre's analysis of the tensions in cinema between landscape and setting, we can observe a national-level metapolitical frame, which constitutes what the film's moving images and soundtrack say about the American land- and cityscapes.[63]

Lefebvre points out that "the gaze by which landscape emerges in painting [is also] manifest in the work of filmmakers." While in some films the landscape as setting contributes to the film's narrative, "some filmmakers have freed the film's setting from its service to the story."[64]

In such cases, "landscape . . . is *space freed from* eventhood" (which in the case of Lee's film is freed from the drama of the recruitment of Jesus Shuttlesworth).[65] So while setting as Lefebvre notes is the space where the story or event takes place, landscape can have different connections with setting, at times in a "supporting role as background or setting to events and characters," and at times as "a completely distinct aesthetic object."[66]

In the film, the land- and cityscapes often function as "a completely distinct aesthetic object" and is musically marked throughout the film. There is thus an answer to one reviewer's critical response, "Why does Jake become involved with the prostitute, [Dakota Burns] (Milla Jovovich), next door in his cheap hotel? . . . Why does the movie have so many damned holes in it?"[67] It is precisely because the relationship with Dakota, which operates outside of the main narrative, is part of the way the "cheap hotel" and the urban milieu in which it is located constitutes a "completely distinct aesthetic object." Dakota and her (African American) pimp are part of the life world that is marked by Public Enemy and juxtaposed to the (largely nonurban) world of major college sports that stretches westward. Moreover, consonant with the tendency of the contemporary "aesthetic regime of the arts . . . a fragmented or proximate mode of focalization which imposes raw presence to the detriment of the rational sequences of the story,"[68] the encounter with Dakota is a result of "the greatest achievement in the history of Western literary fiction . . . the dismantlement of the continuity of narrative action . . . the isolation of the random occurrence . . . the any-moment-whatever."[69]—in this case, cinematic punctuations that tell us about the contingencies of encounter and the discontinuities in a life-world that defy traditional regulative ideals (figure 1.1).

Within the film is an exploration of a range of corrupt college recruitment practices, with an emphasis on the avarice of those who would live off the athletic skills of a young black athlete: politicians, colleges, family members, friends, and lovers. While the film story is focused on two major venues for the capture of the African American body, the penal system and the sports system—depicted in parallel montage at both the outset and final sequence of the film as the father is shown shooting baskets in a prison exercise yard while the son shoots baskets on a practice court—the soundtrack enacts a different contrast. It punctuates the film narrative with the vernacular-inspired symphonic music of Aaron Copland and the rap sounds and lyrics of Public Enemy. Lee states that he selected Copland's music because, "When I listen to [Copland's] music, I hear America, and basketball is America."[70] Copland drew from vernac-

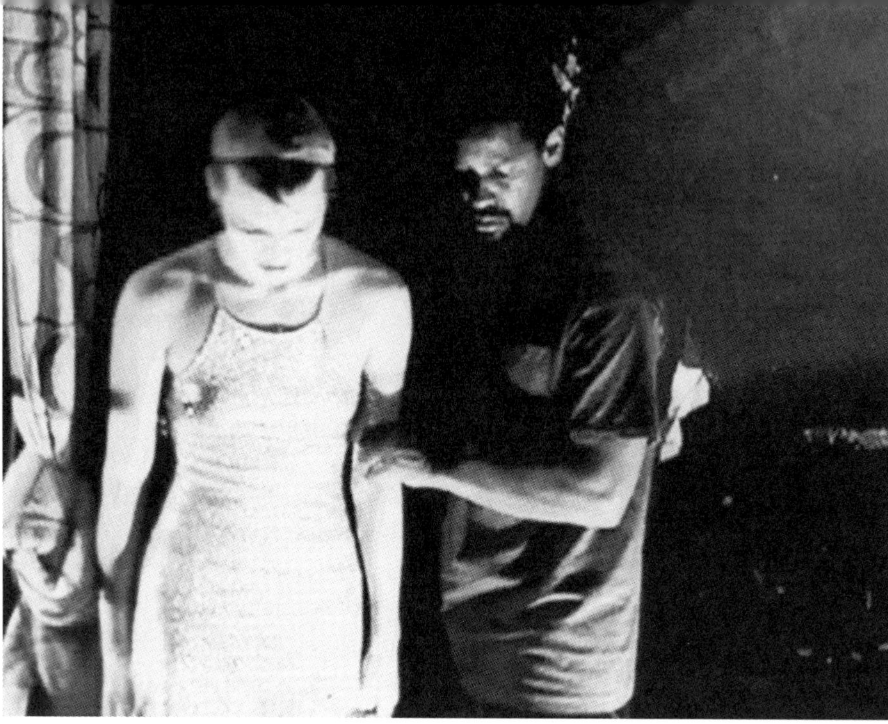

Figure 1.1 Jake and Dakota.

ular sources, from what he called "the music of the common man." His aim was to transcend specific idioms to create a uniquely American music: "Our concern," he wrote, "was not with the quotable hymn or spiritual; we wanted to find a music that would speak of universal things in a vernacular of American speech and rhythms."[71]

There is a philosophical as well as a political impetus sustaining Copland's orientation. In effect, Copland had adopted the philosophical basis and ultimate goal of Immanuel Kant's analysis of the aesthetic object (most notably in his "Analytic of the Beautiful"), the desire to demonstrate the existence of universal *sensus communis*. Accordingly, Copland's aim was to have the reception of his compositions contribute to a shared national community of sense. That aesthetic aim bears comparison with another Kant-inspired universalizing aesthetic impulse, that of Thomas Mann, whose novelistic tetralogy, *Joseph and His Brothers* (written between 1925 and 1942), is punctuated by diverse musical idioms but aimed ultimately at providing what he conceived as a unifying blending.

In a published speech, *The Theme of the Joseph Novels*, Mann notes that although "some people were inclined to regard *Joseph and His Brothers* as a Jewish novel . . . yet, all that is Jewish, throughout the work, is merely foreground, only one style element among others, only *one* stratum of its language which strangely fuses the archaic and the epical and analytical. In the last book is a poem, the song of annunciation which the musical child sings for the aged Jacob, and which is a composition of psalter recollections and little verses of the German romantic type." He goes on to insist that the character of the work is not meant to simply lay different idioms side-by-side. Rather, "the whole work, which seeks to blend a great many things . . . conceives and imagines everything human as a unity."[72]

Just as Mann sought to unify humanity (in his case to respond to a looming totalitarianism in Europe as he sat in exile in the United States), Copland sought to unify the American political experience. But which America does Copland's music seek to unify? While his earlier music (prior to what is adopted in Lee's soundtrack) was "reflective of his Jewish, New York, and Paris experiences," his post-1935 music (his most familiar music) is inflected toward a general American nationalism. His "*Billy the Kid, Rodeo, Lincoln Portrait, Fanfare for the Common Man*, and *Appalachian Spring* [upon which Lee drew] speak to a wide breadth of American sensibilities."[73] We cannot assume that those "sensibilities" within this "wide breadth" are solely Euro-American ones, associated only with the spatial history of the Euro-American "ethnogenesis" (the moving frontier involved in the whitening of the continent),[74] for that is one among other emphases in Copland's music, his "western works": "Copland's western works are fundamental to his pre-eminence in American music because the West looms so large in the national consciousness. . . . It is well known that Copland's use of open intervals and wide spacing, clear orchestration, and plain folk-like materials has given Americans a powerful musical image of their frontier."[75]

However, having traveled in Mexico and contemplated the freshness of Mexico's "'Indian background'" . . . [Copland's] ideal of America became [a reprieve from] the oppressive influence of European culture [and] an alternative to the fragmented reality of industrial modernism."[76] Having developed an interest in music's social and political relevance, he sought to develop a musical language that would exemplify an American aesthetic with a stylistic simplification that would render it open to widespread reception all over the American continent. Inspired by the music of Virgil Thomson, whose film soundscapes influenced Copland's score for the first film version of *Of Mice and Men* (1939), he sought "to evoke an American Landscape."[77]

Nevertheless, much of Copland's music had a city focus—for example, his first film score for *The City* (1939), a Ralph Steiner documentary.[78]

And he was at times focused on the same territory that has been much of the space referenced in the compositions of Public Enemy, the street (e.g., his "proletarian song, "Into the Streets May First [1934]").[79] The music from which Lee drew for his soundtrack was Copland's rural western music, however, which had already become "the Hollywood musical code for the American pastoral."[80] The melodic landscapes of Copland's music, their "rising and falling pitches,"[81] articulate well with the western landscapes they accompany in the film, and the rhythms of Lee's filming often match Copland's musical rhythms. Ultimately, plurivocal though his musical works as a whole may be, Copland's drive was to universalize and blend the American ethnoscape. Accordingly, the Copland music that accompanies the film's early scenes is what Michel Chion famously calls empathetic; it is selected to "express its participation in the feeling of the scene[s]."[82]

In contrast with Copland's universalizing impulse, which seeks to engage reception at an ideational level specifically to evoke allegiance to a shared humanity, Public Enemy's compositions—also with empathetic effects—consist in staccato rhythms and politically inflected lyrics as they engage a somatic as well as ideational experience of a history of racial oppression. They gesture toward a communal sensibility not only "by cognitive symbols" but also "through the interaction of individual rhythms and the people who embody them,"[83] for example, "the politics of chains and whips." The music urges resistance, for example, "Be a dissident. Who ain't kissin it,"[84] which brings together the memory of physical abuse and an ethos of resistance.

As a result, their music aligns (in Carter Mathes' *a propos* terms) with "sound as an evasion of sedimented or regulated meaning,"[85] and with "the sonic as a realm of resistance to and critique of an American narrative of black life."[86] For purposes of this analysis, "Rappers," as Tricia Rose suggests, "have redefined the concept of communal authorship,"[87] specifically black life as it exists in "the traditional black urban landscape."[88] Moreover, rap has followed jazz as another improvisational mode of sonic resistance; it "parallels jazz in many ways" (as Reginald Thomas points out).[89] Like jazz, rap features syncopated rhythms and as a result has been viewed as compatible with the form and spirit of jazz—even to the point where the pianist "Dr. Billy Taylor recorded a 'jazz rap' . . . [in which he] used lyrics to try to paint a picture of urban life, as rap music often does."[90] Rap, like jazz, emerges from the African American "discursive forest."[91] In Tricia Rose's terms, it's a "secondary orality,"[92] and like jazz, it operates on one side of the "sonic color line."

Although much of the implicit pedagogy of Lee's *He Got Game* is the exposure of a racial fault line (as has been the case in many of his other films), Lee, like Copland and Mann, also manifests a concern with blending and interarticulating as well as distinguishing. Thus, in the opening sequence, as the credits are running and Copland's music is punctuating the cinematic montage, the scenes cut back and forth between pastoral landscapes and concrete basketball courts in urban settings, with young white teenagers shooting baskets in the former (e.g., one shooting at a basket fixed to a barn) and black teenagers shooting baskets in the latter, initially to the clanging sounds of Copland's *John Henry*, followed by his "Hoe-Down" from his 1942 ballet *Rodeo* as the scene cuts to a urban playground game.

Krin Gabbard's remark, "Spike Lee has made a powerful statement by combining images of young black men playing basketball with music written by the one composer in the classical tradition considered by many to be 'the most American,'"[93] implies that Lee is saying something about the inclusion of African Americans in what it means to be "American," even in an America whose resonances are articulated by a white composer. It also seems to be the case that the opening sequence, punctuated by Copland's music, is meant to bridge the racial divide. There are cuts back and forth between white and black youth (both men and women) shooting baskets in different venues as well as involved in pickup games. And ultimately, speaking to the aim of bridging divides, are two telling scenes near the end of the credit sequence. In the first, a young African American has dribbled a basketball across one of the borough bridges (figure 1.2), followed closely in the second by an African American holding a basketball under a pole holding perpendicular street signs, one of which is for a street named "Division" (figure 1.3). The two images thus speak to basketball's potential for bridging divides.

Nevertheless, the film maintains some stark divisions. While Copland's music, with its interarticulated vernaculars, references a shared America, Public Enemy's staccato rhythms and inner city–directed lyrics speak to and mimic other sensibilities, providing a more strident political edge with (among other things) a commentary on a biased juridical system (e.g., from "He Got Game": "Even Murders excused. White men in suits don't have to jump") and on the exploitation of those marketing sports logo wear and drugs (e.g., from "Politics of the Sneaker Pimps": "I see corporate hands up in foreign lands. With the man behind the man gettin' paid behind the man"). As Lee's soundtrack punctuates his images with the musical scores of alternative American thought-worlds, the viewer

Figure 1.2 Borough Bridge Scene.

Figure 1.3 Division.

sees alternative, musically marked American experiences. The effect is a politics of aesthetics that distinguishes alternative ways of referencing political community.

In contrast with an aesthetic that aims toward fashioning the "in common" (Aaron Copland's) is Public Enemy's more radical political aesthetic, which, when arrayed against Copland's musical America, creates different political subjects by "reconfigur[ing] what are given to be facts."[94] Public Enemy's contribution to Lee's soundtrack is thus a counter aesthetic that discloses dissensus and "establishes a grid that makes it possible to think through the forms of political dissensuality . . . by undoing the relations between the visible, the sayable, and the thinkable."[95]

In short, they help reframe a sports story, making it one that addresses America's racial politics, the spaces of its realizations, and the encounters through which what constitutes Lee's version of "America" is continually renegotiated.

Like the rest of Lee's film corpus, *He Got Game* is part of the cinematic event that he fashioned throughout his film career. Attentive to the dispersion of the sociolects constituting city talk—"that symphony of speech . . . the city's greatest source of vitality"[96]—Lee developed a cinema of critical urban encounter. While "black talk" abounds, his films include other ethnic sociolects that participate in the action to create a view of the urban that emphasizes discursive encounter (note, e.g., the ethnic talk interludes, alternating between Brooklyn's African Americans and Italian Americans in his *Summer of Sam* (1977), which sorts alternative interpretations of the "Son of Sam" serial killer's motives. There, as in all his films, the city emerges as among other things an interethnic cacophony, which reveals the multiple perspectives through which events are interpreted. Taken as a whole, Lee's film corpus adds up to his version of "America." Summing up the Spike Lee event, David Sterritt writes, "One of the secrets of [Lee's] success is his intuitive awareness that African-Americans, Italian-Americans and *Anything*-Americans are socially and psychologically grounded in both parts of their hyphenated racial-ethnic designations; they are African or Italian or Anything by ancestry and they are Americans by birth."[97]

I turn now to another important cinematic event that explores a different fault line, Gillo Pontecorvo's *The Battle of Algiers*, which many credit as the inauguration of "Third Cinema."[98] For example, "*The Battle of Algiers* marked a paradigm shift in film art, deeply influencing what came to be known as Third Cinema,"[99] and "The True heirs of *Algiers* have been the numberless filmmakers from Brazil, Argentina, Bolivia, Cuba, Senegal, Mali, Tunisia, Morocco, Palestine and Algeria itself—inspired by Pontecorvo's supreme empathy to tell their own stories of nationalist striving."[100] It was also an event in the context of the prior role of film during the colonial period: "In colonial Algeria, motion pictures played a small yet essential role in supporting the empire by exporting a particular image of the country as an exotic haven whose benign, colorful subjects could prosper only under French control. The local population was treated as raw material that could be molded to fit the needs of the motherland."[101]

For purposes of comparison, Pontecorvo's *Algiers* counteractualizes the support for colonial domination that had been the cinema's prior orientation. Just as two incommensurate forms of music create a soundtrack that punctuates a film that thinks about a racial fault line (Lee's), in *Algiers,* two incommensurate musical forms punctuate a film that thinks about a colonial fault line. As I have noted elsewhere, in *The Battle of Algiers,* Pontecorvo "was aiming at creating a counter-point between the sound images and visual images. And crucially [as Pontecorvo notes] . . . often the sound image trumps the visual image."[102]

The Battle of Algiers

Edward Kamau Braithwaite, a Barbadian poet, provides an instructive threshold for appreciating the contrapuntal soundtrack of Pontecorvo's film. Seeking a way to model the rhythms of the Caribbean life world, which he says he could not retrieve by listening to Beethoven, Braithwaite refers to a parallel between the rhythm of a pebble skipping on the surface of the water and Calypso music.[103] Similarly, the rhythms of the Algerian life world shape the images and sounds in Pontecorvo's film as "[t]he city of Algiers . . . articulates and supplies the rhythmic orchestration of the film," a "colonial city that is a physical, social and architectural embodiment of French-Algerian colonialism."[104]

To show how sound as well as image articulates the colonial division during the Battle of Algiers, Pontecorvo and his cowriter, Franco Solinas, solicited a soundtrack (from composer Ennio Morricone) that features a clash of the incommensurate musical cultures of Algiers' French and Arab populations. While the images of the former are accompanied by (among other music) classic European marches that sound like fight songs, the latter are framed with the percussion rhythms of chants and choruses that have somatic resonances, intensifying during dramatic moments (e.g., when Arab women are donning European clothes in order to infiltrate French venues and place bombs). Moreover, while the French settlers are represented as enjoying a leisurely life with expansive vistas, the Algerian population, crowded into the confining spaces of the Casbah, are often seen in surging crowds as they respond to French policing tactics (as well as a freelance bombing of an Algerian neighborhood). As I have put it elsewhere:

> Given the cuts and juxtapositions that mark the film's statements-through-editing, what is shown is a people seeking to control their political destiny in the midst of a self-indulgent and privileged settler community. The crowded and segregated Casbah, surrounded by the wide boulevards characteristic of French urbanism, supply the physical side of the colonial *mise en scene*, while a bio-political *mise en scene* is created with a montage of shots that juxtapose the surveilled and im-

Figure 1.4 Casbah.

poverished Algerian inhabitants, compressed in a crowded quarters, with the leisurely life of bourgeois French settlers, relaxing in bars and cafes and entertaining in large, well-appointed estates.[105]

The physical aspect of the colonial *mise en scène* is articulated as a claustrophobic, virtually quarantined Casbah, juxtaposed to the wide boulevards characteristic of French cities (figures 1.4 and 1.5). And the biopolitical *mise en scène* is articulated with a montage of shots that reveal the surveilled and poor Algerians, moving in and out of narrow passageways.

While much of the structure of colonial separation is observed spatially, it is the soundtrack that provides much of the film's political sense. Pontecorvo notes that he sought to create a counterpoint between the sound images and visual images, with the former bearing more significance than the latter.[106] And tellingly, he figures his main protagonist, the Algerian people of the city, musically. He characterizes them as a "chorus" (realized in Morricone's soundtrack, which contrasts French martial music with a percussive representation of the emotions of the Algerian people, conveyed in a musical idiom close to an Algerian *baba saleem*). As one commentator points out, Pontecorvo's problem was "how to outflank normal viewing habits and solicit identification with a group hero."[107] That perspective is articulated musically as well as visually in the form of a chorus rather than as a collection of individual soloists. Although the group effect is also expressed through visuality, scenes of surging crowds, it is the soundtrack which more than any other aspect of the film delivers the affective register of the political struggle. For example, at one point the Algerian women produce a collective chant, "an eerie wall of sound that creates a strangely menacing form of passive resistance."[108]

Before the film explores the city's "colonial spacing"[109] in the 1950s, it opens with a look at a critical moment in the independence struggle, the moment in which France sends a large detachment of troops to quell the Algerian resistance. The film's initial scene shows the French soldiers leaping from trucks and fanning out over the city to the tune of martial music. Then what effectively begins as a rousing symphonic first movement shifts to a typical second movement, a slow meandering scene in which the soundtrack slows as the viewer gets a glimpse of the film's climax, the point where the revolutionary operative Ali La Pointe, the fictional protagonist, a street hustler played by Brahim Hadjadj, and his cohorts have been discovered hiding behind a wall.[110]

The film then cuts to an earlier scene in which the soundtrack carries Bach's "St. Matthew Passion" during scenes of French brutality, followed by a flashback to Algerian public space, accompanied by a soft melodic background, as the viewer is introduced to a younger version of Ali La Pointe, at that time hustling in the street (running a Three Card Monte table) before ultimately becoming a key player in the resistance. Subsequently, as the resistance and counter-resistance intensify, the soundtrack becomes more prominent; it features alternations between French martial music and the above-noted percussive Algerian musical genres.

Figure 1.5 French Quarter.

The contention among the sounds that punctuate the film, however, are not only in musical genres. They include radio voices as well. Throughout the film, the Revolutionary Algerian Party's (FLN) clandestine broadcasts are heard exhorting the Algerians to resist French colonialism (and urging the French to heed the UN's attempt to resolve the dispute), and in counterpoint there are French broadcasts to the French community, disparaging the Algerian resistance and urging solidarity among the European population.

Ultimately, the uprising was crushed. After showing the process by which Colonel Mathieu had defeated the FLN, however, the film ends with the liberation of Algeria with a scene of a woman dancing in the street in celebration of the achievement of independence. That image is simply the last of many moments in which the film narrative is punctuated by active women. In addition to playing a major role in the action—for example, women are shown cutting their hair and changing their clothing style so they can pass as Europeans to gain access to the French public areas where they plant bombs—women also play a major role in the soundtrack. As the screenwriter Solinas points out, during the end of the film, when a "spontaneous . . . resurgence of Algerian resistance to colonial occupation" is shown, there is a moment in which 'calm has returned, although from the Casbah continue to be heard those cries . . . incoherent rhythmic, nightmarish cries . . . the trilling calls (*ju-ju*) of Algerian women that have a tenacious presence throughout the film.'"[111]

Gender Punctuations and an Encounter of Communities of Sense

Heeding the contribution of Algerian women to the soundtrack of the resistance in the film, I want to note a contribution to the linguistic/sonic legacy of the colonial experience since the revolution by drawing from the writing of the contemporary Algerian novelist Assia Djebar. Both her fiction and nonfiction, influenced by the history of the French-Algerian encounter, draws from Arabic and French vernaculars and effectively picks up the tune sung by women during the resistance. Assessing that postcolonial Algerian multilingualism (which Djebar's novels feature), Réda Bensmaia refers to the vernacular as a "play of multiple languages such as dialectal Arabic, Berber and French, and more recently English."[112] Such multilingual, multiethnic vernacular interarticulations are geographically pervasive, albeit with different affective results. As Russell Potter puts it, "All (sub)cultures, in a sense, are part of the vernacular continuum, which in some cases bridges cultural identities and in others intensifies old antagonisms; that one or another subcultural moment is stocked with bits and pieces from other subcultures (past or present, allied or opposed) should hardly be a scandal."[113]

Mildred Mortimer captures the musical structure of Djebar's approach to "bridging," the polyphonic vernacular in her nonfiction:

> Alternating oral history and autobiographical fragments with historical accounts of the French conquest of Algeria, Djebar creates a complex structure that resembles a five-part symphony . . . and at the same time imitates a North African *fantasia*, the spectacle of charging Arab cavalry. . . Djebar reminds us that the *fantasia* is always accompanied by "tzarlrit," the *youyous* of shrill cries of women's voices, *le cri dans la fantasia*. She uses [a] symphonic and fantasialike structure to blend her voice with those of traditional Maghrebian women.[114]

And as I've noted elsewhere, in her novels, Djebar "'Arabizes' her written French to supply voices to those who have not been a part of the 'Algeria' historically constructed by France. Writing a 'multilingual French,'" Djebar, as she summarizes it, employs "French for secret missives; Arabic for our stifled aspirations toward God; Lyico-Berber which takes us back to the most ancient of our mother idols. The fourth language, for all females, young or old, cloistered or half-emancipated, remains that of the body."[115]

Djebar's efforts to recover and enfranchise colonial subjects and at the same time create musico-literary space for international/intercultural blending are exemplary. They provide an inspiration for me to turn from my emphasis on oppositional communities of sense to those events of communal fusing—moments of coming-to-be-in-common—that are staged in diverse genres of the arts—music and literature especially.

Conclusion: Forging Intercultural Communities of Sense

With some exceptions, notable theorists and enthusiasts of democratic community have found inspiration from the sociopolitical perspicacity of Alexis de Tocqueville, especially as expressed in his observations during his travels on the American continent in the mid-nineteenth century, where he became convinced that there was something in the "American character" (what he famously referred to as "habits of the heart") that predisposed them to a democratic polity. Less often noted are limitations of Tocqueville's ethnographic gaze, the notable blindness in his insights, which are evident in both his brief exposure to the city of Algiers and his extended encounters in nineteenth-century America, where he associated with (was often hosted by) Euro-American (i.e., white) families.

With respect to his interpretive encounter with Algiers: Tocqueville visited the city in connection with his duties in the French Chamber of Deputies and viewed it through the lens of one favorably predisposed to French colonial domination. As I have put it, "[Tocqueville's] report on the Algerian colony constitutes a firm justification for repressive colonial rule in the name of the glory of France: 'For France works to create civilized societies, not hordes of savages.'"[116] As for his observations about Algiers: Gazing at the city from his ship in the harbor, Tocqueville asserted that "the architecture of the city constituted an unambiguous representation of its modes of organization and enactment . . . 'the architecture portrays their necessities and customs . . . it portrays extremely well the social and political state of the Muslim and Oriental populations . . . [including among other things] the complete absence of political life.'"[117]

Attuned to the political architecture of European capitals, Tocqueville assumed (as Timothy Mitchell points out) that a "'building stands for an institution' whereas a more locally attuned reading would recognize that Algiers, like other middle eastern cities in the nineteenth century, did not 'offer an architecture or external framework pretending to portray its interior life.' Rather, 'social and political life in Algiers were constituted out of mobile boundaries, for example gates that at times enclosed various areas and at times were opened to permit transactions. One could not *see* the various aspects of an urban life organized on the basis of various functions deployed at different times. In Algiers, 'the life of the city was understood in terms of the occurrence and reoccurrence of practices, rather than in terms of an architecture—material or institutional—that stands apart from life itself, containing and representing the meaning of what was done.'"[118]

Tocqueville's widely celebrated ethnographic gaze on the American scene was no less obtuse. To identify its limitations, I return to a contrast I have offered elsewhere between Tocqueville and another nineteenth-century visitor, Antonin Dvorak, not only because it speaks to the limits of the Tocquevillean ethnographic gaze but also because it bears on the creative encounters among vernacular music with which I am concerned. Without going into the details of Tocqueville's observations about "The Three Races in America" (having associated intimately with only one of them), suffice it to say that for Tocqueville, America's future would be in "white" hands because he regarded the "Negro" as hopelessly incapacitated (unaware that African Americans role-played incapacity as a survival strategy), and he regarded Native Americans as unqualified for life in a democratic polity by dint of their temperament and cultural practices (observations based on rumors rather than investigation).

Although Tocqueville at one point mentions possible benefits of "racial mixing," having lamented the evils of slavery and the destruction of Native American cultures, nowhere does he show ethnographic interest in either (he traveled as far as Minnesota to peer at immiserated remnants of nearly destroyed Indian nations, and while traveling in the South, he observed slaves from an even greater conceptual as well as physical distance than his plantation-owning hosts). His gaze was a legacy of his class: "Habitually assum[ing] an aristocratic attitude toward American ideas and customs," the way he viewed America was conditioned by "the social position [that Aristocrats] had lost after the French revolution." Rather than immersing himself deeply in the various dimensions of vernacular culture, what Tocqueville observed was screened through his preoccupation with his "unworked through attachments to the aristocratic tradition."[119]

Antonin Dvorak arrived on the American scene with a different perspective nearly 60 years after Tocqueville. Dvorak, a descendant of farmers and tradesmen, welcomed and incorporated America's ethnic diversity into his musical compositions with the aim of creating an interethnic musical America that contained African American and Native American, as well as Euro-American musical idioms. He noted, for example, that "in the Negro melodies of America I discover all that is needed for a great and noble school of music. . . . There is nothing in the whole range of composition that cannot be supplied with themes from this source." Heeding that source, he "saturated himself with the spirit of the old tunes (e.g., 'Swing Low, Sweet Chariot' in the second theme of his first movement) and then invented his own themes." And mimicking what came to be characteristic of the blues, he occasionally used a flatted seventh "blue note."[120] He also "tried to combine Negro and Indian themes," for example, composing a largo movement for his *New World Symphony* after reading the famine scene in Longfellow's *Hiawatha*.[121]

The spirit of Dvorak's compositional hospitality to diverse ethnic musical traditions has been evident in many subsequent musical events. For purposes of geographic continuity, however, I refer to those that touch on Algeria and the United States. The contemporary ethnic hybridity that has emerged from the Algerian musical scene is evoked by Salman Rushdie in his novelistic homage to world music in *The Ground Beneath Her Feet*

(1999). The impetus for Rushdie's blending of diverse musical cultures is his cosmopolitan identity. As he has written, "We are now partly of the West. Our identity is at once plural and partial. Sometimes we feel that we straddle two cultures; at other times, that we fall between two stools. But however ambiguous and shifting this ground may be, it is not an infertile territory for a writer to occupy."[122]

Like Thomas Mann's approach to the form of his Joseph novels (*supra*), Rushdie mimics the musical diversity to which his novel refers. Specifically, as his prose mimics the polyphony that is the novel's thematic, it is expressed in sentences that contain American and British idioms, and Bombay argot as well as various idioms from diverse language vernaculars. The writing is stylistically homologous with the music of Rushdie's music-composing protagonist, Ormus Cama, who states at one point that his lyrics, "cockeyed words" and "vowel sounds," are simultaneously his and someone else's.[123]

As for the Algerian scene, Rushdie's character (effectively his alter ego in the novel), Rai, has a name that stands in for a genre of Algerian popular music. Rushdie's novel valorizes "world music," a genre that emerged in the late 1980s. The name (a marketing expression) refers to popular music produced by other than Anglo-American sources, for example, "Rai music" from Algeria (the likely basis for the name of Rushdie's character). It is also likely that the Algerian Berber singer Djur Djura provides the model for Rushdie's other main protagonist, the novel's world music singer, Vina Apsara. Djura's music, like Assia Djebar's prose, expresses a cultural hybridity. Having grown up in France, Djura's bicultural identity has encouraged her multigenre version of world music while seeking a universality of reception.

As for the U.S. (or "American") scene, among the most notable creative blending has been that initiated by jazz ensembles, because as Gregory Clark puts it, "a performance of jazz enacts a community," which results because "musicians must adapt to each other, making judgments about what is and what is not good for the music they are making."[124] Moreover, as Clark adds (as he pursues the dynamic of "getting along"), jazz ensembles exemplify "getting along [which] requires people to find out and even feel a connection with each other. It is a felt sense of being bound together by some sort of commonality that opens us to the influence of others and to change."[125]

The jazz composer Wayne Shorter puts "that getting along" this way: "When we get together we don't fight. We don't argue over who's going to do what when someone's playing. Say someone's playing a line and then someone else cuts across the line and takes over. We don't think of it as an interruption. Matter of fact, we don't think. We just use it as an opportunity."[126] The novelist Russell Banks amplifies Clark's and Shorter's insights with the suggestion that people already possess aspects of the kinds of otherness required for empathic modes of recognition. In his *Continental Drift,* Banks stages an affair between "Bob," a "white" New Englander for whom people of color are exotic and unfamiliar, and his paramour Marguerite, an African American woman he meets after he moves his family to Florida. Bob finds himself involved with a woman about whose habitus he knows very little. To convey the challenge that Marguerite's world presents to Bob, Banks intervenes in the drama with this meditation: "To understand your children, you attend to the child in you . . . to imagine Elaine [his wife] and Doris [a former paramour] and now Marguerite, the three women who in recent years have mattered most to him, all Bob has to do is pay attention to the woman in himself. It's harder in the case of Marguerite, but all the more interesting to him for that, because with her he has to pay attention to the black man in himself as well."[127]

Finally, I want to suggest that the empathetic attention-paying that Clark ascribes to the musical communities of sense, which result from the interactions in jazz ensembles, occurs in two ways, which I will designate discursive and excursive. The discursive mode took place when Miles Davis joined the Cannonball Adderley quintet in a jazz version of the 1950s standard, "Autumn Leaves" (available on the Cannonball Adderley's quintet album, *Somethin' Else*).[128] In a passage that recalls for me Bakhtin's above-noted characterization of Dostoevsky's novelistic form ("an interaction of voices that constitute a 'polyphonic reactive activity,' a 'method of integral dialogic juxtapositions'"), Clark captures the "polyphonic reactive activity" and "dialogic juxtapositions" among the musicians:

> The tune begins with piano, bass, and drum marking out in distinct rhythm a dark harmony that is augmented after a few bars by a sequence of slightly syncopated chords, played brightly by horns repeatedly, to answer in counterpoint. On that introduction, Miles Davis's muted trumpet pushes out the first phrase of this ballad's familiar melody, made of four phrases of four ascending notes, each phrase starting a step below the last. . . . Then it's Adderley's turn. His arpeggios on the tune's chord changes pour over what Davis has just played, as if his alto is letting loose what the trumpet pent up. . . . Adderley pays some choruses and then Davis returns. They play their separate ways together through a few more, bound together in the rhythmic and har-

> monic momentum of Hank Jones's piano, Sam Jones's bass, and Art Blakey's drums.[129]

In that collective versioning of "Autumn Leaves," the ensemble's discursive interactions constitute an episode of thinking together. Perhaps we can construe the playing-as-discursive interaction in this way (as I imagine the conversations): Adderley et al., "Here's how we imagine an introduction to the tune." Davis, "OK, here's how I imagine its melodic mood." Adderley: "Thanks for that, here's how I am inspired to continue." Davis: "OK, after that I want to come back this way." Jones, Jones, and Blakely: "We're with it; does this bring us all together?" Clark construes the result with a different figuration:

> Playing together, they all five begin to sound something like the way people sharing the same car on a train might look: each one deep in his own thoughts and feelings as the pulse of the wheels on the rails and the landscape rushing past the windows encompasses them more than they know at the moment in the intimacy of the same journey. In this "Autumn Leaves," as each musician engages the others in the differences that divide them, they are bound inexorably together by the time, place, and purpose they share.[130]

The encounter between the Adderley quintet and Miles Davis, in which a communal moment is forged, functions *within* the musical discourse of jazz. To conclude, I want to invoke an excursive musical moment (to which I refer in the Introduction), a reaching across genres in a moment that exemplifies what Clark calls "civic jazz." It's a moment involving the fashioning of an intercultural acoustical community of sense at the Moab Music Festival, where the Marcus Roberts Trio was joined by a bluegrass musician, the banjoist Béla Fleck (at the Utah stop of the trio's tour). Clark describes the moment: "Here jazz would meet bluegrass, bringing together two American musics that had much to divide them. When the concert began, the four musicians—three black and one white—let their musics roll across each other, calling out in one idiom and responding in the other, exchanging idioms and gradually developing a hybrid sound in a new voice of both jazz and bluegrass."[131]

As the collaboration progresses through the different sets, one can hear Roberts' piano style sound increasingly string band–like, while at the same time one can hear Fleck's banjo riffs sound increasingly less percussive and more jazz-like.[132] The musical hybridity that is achieved in the encounter succeeds in uniting elements of black and white communities of sense (where, for example, the labor coalition and the possibility of "interracial sympathy"[133] during "The Reconstruction" that W. E. B. Du Bois had famously hoped for had failed).[134] While my emphasis has been on how popular music thinks the political, this is an instance in which the music *does* the political by reaching across a divide to initiate a thinking together that eventuates in a being together.

URBAN PUNCTUATIONS: SYMPHONIC AND DIALECTIC

Urban Temporalities

Cities are traditionally viewed as geographic entities, a perspective based on their spatial extension and on the physical and juridical boundaries that both distinguish them from adjacent jurisdictions and shape the internal grid that designates the public and private spheres of control. The network of boundaries that distinguish residences, public parks, and commercial and governmental zones punctuate the city with "barriers" that direct and contain the flow of moving bodies and vehicles.[1] As Lewis Mumford has famously pointed out, however, the city is also a temporal entity that "through its concentration of physical and cultural power . . . heightened the tempo of human intercourse and. . . . through its monuments and written records, and orderly habits of association . . . enlarged the scope of all human activities, extending them backwards in time."[2]

The architectural theorist Sanford Kwinter provides a similar account, viewing the city as a "historical process rather than a stable object."[3] While their dual focus is on the historical sweep of urban development, one can discern shorter-term urban temporalities, daily and seasonal rhythms that speak to the specifics of the "cultural power" toward which Mumford gestured.

Although it's well known that modern capitalism has tended to have an increasingly greater influence on shaping society than have cultural practices, the city of Oslo stands as a space in which its seasonal temporal rhythms place culture in contention with the shaping forces of commerce, public administration, and the strictures of privacy. Specifically, Oslo has two official maps, one for winter and part of spring, during which time there is snow on the ground, and one for the rest of the year. The former is a ski map, available in the publication, *Skikart over Stor Oslo* ("Ski map of Greater Oslo"), which covers an area from the center of the city to *Nordmarka* (the north fields), where there are thousands of miles of ski tracks.

During the months in which the map shows the ski tracks crisscrossing the entire city, it authorizes the legal right one has while on skis to disregard all jurisdictional boundaries. Just as an amphibious vehicle dissolves the boundary between land and water, the skier is legally enabled; when one is on skis in Oslo, boundaries dissolve. Once the snow melts, the old boundaries reappear as depicted in Oslo's other map, configured primarily by commerce—with its boundaries between commercial and private spaces, and between all those spaces and public sectors. In terms of the forces that move bodies, skiing punctuates part of Oslo's calendar year, and the other dynamics of the city's life world take over the rest of the year. The city's winter ski choreography is an essential part of Norway's culturally sanctioned temporal rhythms in a society in which a culturally pervasive leisure practice is able periodically to suspend the usual aspects of the space-shaping forces of contemporary administrative, commercial, and proprietary practices.

In what follows, I take special note of urban spatio-temporalities and focus mainly on the way that a different set of cultural practices—the arts rather than a leisure sport—intervene to reveal (and at times disrupt) the rhythms of the urban life world and inflect the city's micropolitical relationships. My analysis focuses on moments when the "strategically structured monumental city with fixed assigned places . . . has to make way for other relations."[4]

To frame the rhythmic interplay between the city's continuities and disruptions, I employ a musical metaphor for those rhythms, the symphonic, and turn to films as the textual bookends of this chapter: Walther Ruttmann's 1927 documentary *Berlin: Symphony of a Great City*, which renders cinematically the daily flow of bodies in various parts of Berlin's life world in the early twentieth century, and Ola Simonsson and Johannes Stjarne Nilsson's contemporary feature film *Sound of Noise* (2010), in which an anarchic group of musicians perform a musical score that is represented dialectically against the city's professional symphony. They play the city of Stockholm, using medical equipment (and the body of a hospital patient), a bank's shredding machine, the city's electrical wires, and heavy construction equipment (whose clanging and banging disrupts an event at a symphony hall) to realize that score.

Walther Ruttmann's Symphonic Berlin 1927

What are the political resonances of the symphonic metaphor that Walther Ruttmann adapts to model the rhythms of Berlin's daily life world in his 1927 documentary, *Berlin, Symphony of a Great City*? Ruttmann's film was widely panned by critics at the time of its release by, among others, Siegfried Kracauer, who saw it as depthless, fragmentary, and lacking in a critical point of view, and by many others who have since lamented an absence of "social comment" in the film.[5] Such obtuse reception of a documentary, which Derek Hillard shows convincingly to be intensely ambivalent and critical of Berlin's urban modernity, is no doubt owed in part to how the symphonic as metaphor is ordinarily understood. Although symphony (*symphone* from the Greek) translates simply as "sounding together," and its realization as a played score (to orchestrate) is similarly understood as the achievement of harmonious coordination, symphonic form can model more contentious effects.

Accordingly, to highlight the tensions in Ruttmann's symphonically figured and accompanied film, I turn first to Richard Will's critical reading of Beethoven's *Pastoral* symphony, which shows that despite how the notion of a pastoral life world implies one that is untroubled and idyllic, the symphonic form of this so-named work disturbs that expectation. Specifically, in Beethoven's *Pastoral*, a storm with "unexpected form" and unprecedentedly irregular rhythms disturbs the idyll that the music creates in the symphony's first two movements.[6]

Such disruptive musical punctuation—dramatic shifts in "tonality"[7]—also appears elsewhere in Beethoven's musical oeuvre, for example, "the interruptive trumpet call" in act 2, scene 1, in his opera *Fidelio*.[8] There, as in his *Pastoral*, Beethoven articulates musical form with the plot (or "program"). In terms of the plot, "The atmosphere darkens as the work proceeds," and in terms of musical form, the trumpet call carries an "expressive force . . . in a sphere beyond the ordinary."[9]

Beethoven's disruption of musical form in his *Pastoral* has often been missed. At the outset of his demonstration of the idyll-disrupting discontinuities in that symphony, Will reviews the commentaries that fail to heed Beethoven's departures from traditional symphonic form—for example, Donald Francis Tovey's appraisal, which incorporates the third movement's storm within traditional symphonic form. Contesting that appraisal, Will insists that contrary to Tovey's claims, the storm does not fit comfortably within the formal traditions of the symphony: "Together with the program [the symphony's dramatic narrative] . . . the *pastoral* inhabits two generic worlds . . . that of the symphony and that of the programmatic symphony as it was practiced . . . by Beethoven's contemporaries and predecessors" [belonging] wholly to neither genre [because although] these latter works abound in passages like the storm and in continuous movements like those concluding the *Pastoral*. . . . The *Pastoral* mixes traditions freely . . ."[10] so that "the storm . . . poses a structural ambiguity."[11]

Structurally, there are tonal shifts that render the work as divided into a "'symphonic' first half consisting of the first and second movements, in which run-ons and other programmatic devices play no role, and a 'programmatic' half consisting of the scherzo and storm, and finale [so that] in each half, time seems to run differently."[12] Disjuncture is also created between "idyllic time" and "historical time,"[13] leading ultimately to the way the third movement's storm "disrupts the idyll [as] the music representing it disrupts the genre."[14] "Beethoven's storm . . . has not only an unexpected form but also unprecedentedly irregular rhythms and phrases as well as previously unheard or rarely heard harmonies."[15] Endorsing Will's insights, I want to suggest that the kind of symphonic metaphor that Ruttmann applies to the rhythms of Berlin's daily life world is in accord with the tensions in Beethoven's *Pastoral.* Rather than seeking to render Berlin life as harmonious and idyllic, Ruttmann's documentary discloses a Berlin modernity whose historical context "connects the experience of urban modernity to the experience of migration and dislocation."[16]

How then does Ruttmann's cinematic tonality aimed at capturing the structural and psychic dislocations of urban life as it impacts migrants and exiles work? Just as Beethoven's *Pastoral* delivers unexpected tonal punctuation that challenges musical reception by violating those symphonic forms that cleave to normalizing modes of musical expression, Ruttmann's editing abounds in disruptive cinematic punctuation, for example "in [the] final shot of a blinking light that punctuates darkness [and] brings the film almost full circle to its dawn beginning."[17] From the very outset (when the train headed from the countryside to Berlin is shot from many points of view: close ups, shots from in front, and shots from above), he provides disparate angles of vision: "a frenzied juxtaposition of shots . . . intended to produce in the viewer a shock-like reaction that confounds perception and destabilizes identity."[18]

Characterizing Ruttmann's continually unexpected cinematic punctuation, Derek Hillard refers to "conflicts of shots [that] reflect the dynamics of technology and the unpredictability of modern society . . . montages [that] allow the stimulaic clashes and perceptual uncertainties, . . . an "onslaught,"[19] which effectively reproduces Georg Simmel's famous representation of the perceptual vertigo he ascribes to the mental life of the metropolis.[20] Helping to achieve that effect, Edmund Meisel's soundtrack delivers an "expressive tonality," a series of "set-progressions to convey an increase or decrease in tension,"[21] which reflect the differential levels of activity and motion at different times of Berlin's daily cycle.

There are thus strong thematic resonances between sound and image in the film. The opening scene in which a train heads toward Berlin is ac-

Figure 2.1 The train's buffer parts.

companied by a march that resounds throughout a cinematic montage of images of the moving wheels of the train, its steel buffer parts (see figure 2.1), and its driving cylinders, with cuts to the steel tracks along which it's traveling, all suggesting a valorization of the industrial accomplishment embodied in a speeding train. The music then merges into the symphonic first movement with brass instruments sounding major chords, a dramatic tonality heralding the dawning of an event, the arrival of the train into the great city.

At that juncture, the soundtrack has resonances with Beethoven's third symphony, the *Eroica*, which constitutes a fanfare for a dramatic historical moment (connected with Napoleon Bonaparte's ascension to the rank of First Consul). As I have suggested, however, Beethoven's *Pastoral* is ultimately a better fit for the sense that Ruttmann's film ultimately provides about Berlin's modernity. After the train's arrival in the city, the musical score slows down and backs away from its tonal intensity, as the camera backs up and provides a panorama of the city's architectural density. Then silence reigns as the camera surveys the street in a series of fades in which each scene emphasizes the sparse activity of the early morning hours. That moment is followed by a quickening tempo as the third movement generates liveliness to the rhythms of men and women (but mostly men) alighting from trains and trams and heading to and entering their work places in large numbers.

Figure 2.2 Berlin's crowd.

Act II opens with a slow (typically second) symphonic movement as the theme turns to the slow awakening of the city's domestic rhythms: women airing bedclothes out of their apartment windows, children heading to school, people washing their cars, and people both on foot and in vehicles.

Then, as is also typical of symphonic form, Act III has the quickened musical tempo (already noted) that accompanies the quickening pace of city life, with people rushing to public transportation as the city's industrial and commercial activities intensify (figure 2.2). Without going into the rest of the sound-supported symphonic rendering of Berlin, I want to suggest that a focus on the coordination between music and image has misled critics by seeming to render the film as merely a benign celebration of the rhythms of a "great city." In contrast, a focus on the film's cinematic montage reveals ambivalence, for it constructs a more fraught Berlin modernity than what emerges in the soundscape-image coordination.

Although the film's soundtrack effectively matches the rhythms of the cinematic montage (actualizing Abel Gance's observation, "Cinema is the

Figure 2.3 Suicide scene.

music of light"),[22] Ruttmann's *Berlin* emerges primarily with images. Ruttmann translates symphonic tonality into a cinematic tonality to structure the film with a montage of imagistic scenes, where the most shocking punctuating event is a wholly unexpected shot of a suicide, when a woman jumps from a bridge (figure 2.3).

Anton Kaes's account of that moment is compelling. Following the film narrative at the moment of the suicide, Kaes first points to a storm-like moment and then to a juxtaposition between consumer goods for well-off women and a destitute woman, followed by the suicide:

> [There is] a quick shot of an expensive necklace in a store and a destitute old woman standing in front of it, begging. Suddenly a storm stirs up leaves, pedestrians are swept along and a woman runs across the street to reach a bridge over a river. As she stares at the choppy water, swirling like a vortex, we catch a glimpse of her wide-open eyes and frightened face. . . . Cut to the frenetic roller coaster descending downward. Suddenly a splash in the water. A long shot shows pedestrians pointing to the river, which has swallowed her body. The woman's suicidal jump from the bridge is not explained psychologically (we do not know who the woman is) but follows structurally. . . . The scene is remarkable because it is the only segment in the documentary that is ostensibly staged. . . . The shock of this private revolt against life itself

is further emphasized by harsh editing: a fashion show follows the suicide as if nothing had happened.[23]

That event (storm imagery included) bears comparison with Beethoven's storm in *Pastoral* inasmuch as it is a intensely disturbing moment, achieved with a montage of images that violently punctuate the urban flows and motions dominated by commercial and industrial practices (the forces that have both summoned migration and created turmoil for the psyches of much of the urban population). The disruptive force of industrial modernity is also figured at another (dramatic, albeit not deadly) moment when a train running on an overhead railway is seen "cutting through a domestic building at Dennewitzplatz."[24] Apart from those dramatic punctuating events, Ruttmann's cutting from the more pacific imagery of shimmering pools of water, with which the film opens, to the moving steel parts of locomotives and then to factory equipment at work constitutes the continual, if less dramatic, disruptions conveyed by his cinematic tonality.[25]

As is the case with Ruttmann's early twentieth-century Berlin, contemporary urban systems retain the flows and counterflows that challenge those versions of modernity that ascribe harmony and smooth coordination to urban life. In order to illustrate some contemporary urban counterflows, I turn to another "great city," Helsinki, which has a contrapuntal soundscape, and, importantly for this analysis, also has been historically punctuated by migratory events. Like Berlin of over a century ago, Helsinki, like other major urban centers, is (to borrow the apposite words of Ash Amin and Nigel Thrift) a "force field of passions that associate and pulse bodies in particular ways."[26]

Urban Impressions, Helsinki's Flows, and Countermovements

In the summer of 2013, from mid-May to mid-June, I was a guest scholar at the Helsinki Collegium for Advanced Studies at the University of Helsinki. To get to my office every day, I walked from my apartment on the edge of town to downtown Helsinki. As I approached the downtown area on my first day and neared Mannerheimkatu, a major traffic thoroughfare, I heard a clacking sound, whose origin I couldn't at first place, registering itself above the traffic noise (in Helsinki, as in any "typical city, the most dominating sounds are those of vehicles whizzing by or of cars honking at one another").[27] When I got closer and saw a public building with a wide expense of sidewalk where I crossed Mannerheimkatu, I could see the source of the sounds, skateboarders performing on the sidewalk and steps in front of the building and in the adjacent park. What are the implications of Helsinki's ubiquitous skateboarders, whose repetitive movements and sounds (as they rehearsed their moves) punctuated the city's sensorium, as their "play" constituted what Henri Lefebvre famously called "an escape from the localization and 'punctualization' of activities?"[28]

Their movements are an example of "non-instrumental, playful behavior [involved dialectically in] a continual negotiation with various forms of discipline."[29] How then can one effectively conceptualize the transversality that the skateboarders enact against the city's more purposive (and audible) rhythms, goal-oriented movements and sounds as people head to work in the mornings on foot and in motor vehicles, shop in stores by midmorning, break for lunch in determined flows, head home, and in some cases head back downtown in the evening to frequent bars and restaurants and consume diverse forms of entertainment (more or less the same temporal trajectory covered in Ruttmann's documentary)?

The late cultural/dance theorist Randy Martin had addressed those questions on March 13, two months before I became intrigued with how to think about the counterarticulations of the urban skateboarders. Contrasting risk behavior in finance (especially investment in derivatives) with that in the arts, which are involved with "a different kind of currency," Martin notes that he is reminded of "skateboarding and other kinds of movement practices moving through and etching out certain kinds of openings and closures in the city. We might say [he adds] that this is, indeed, a kind of mapping of a different way of valuing risk that acts on what could be and begins to announce what I would term a 'social kinesthetic,' a sensibility for how it is that we move together, that we're oriented towards movement that we could say is a way of reclaiming and reinvesting in a different principle, a lateral, distributed, but also difficult-to-concretize principle of people moving together but not as one."[30]

Martin here is referring both to oppositional communities of sense, which are articulated as co-motion (as the forms of "moving together") and to an antifinancial perspective on urban life. As he puts it elsewhere:

> Valuing the ways in which we are linked together without being one, that we share certain sensibilities of moving together without needing to model or imitate someone, opens conceptions of sovereignty as self-production that just might serve as a momentary realization of the future in the present. The much vaunted and readily dismissed ephem-

erality of dance (and finance) would thereby assume a generative durability, an elaboration of times and spaces in which collectivity itself would gain and circulate its own currency. This self-conferred tenancy would claim a different ground from which the uncertain movement of precarity might circulate its politics.[31]

Urban Sounds: Listening Together or Apart

Having taken up Martin's reference to being and moving together, I turn to an analysis of the historical soundscapes of cities, which I initiate by noting (along with David Garrioch), "Cities have always been noisy places"[32]—for example, the sounds of the past that have "disappeared almost completely . . . the rattle of swords and musketry or the cries of the hawker."[33] Historically, urban noise has been politically inflected, as evidenced by the way the urban soundscape has reflected power relations: "whoever controlled sound commanded a vital medium of communication and power. . . . The usurpation of church bells by secular rulers, to mark dynastic celebrations and their passing, illustrates the importance of bells both for disseminating information and as a political tool, conferring legitimacy."[34] Eventually, however, auditory uniformity and control were attenuated as urban society experienced "the gradual decline of auditory signals as a means of regulating behavior in large cities."[35] What emerged and still characterizes the modern city is a decentralized soundscape, a variety of (sometimes overlapping) acoustic sub-communities in which alternative sounds mark the city's "multiple identities."[36]

That multiplicity of sound is well illustrated in a musically inflected documentary, which when contrasted with Walther Ruttmann's symphonic *Berlin*, render's the Havana 1953 soundscape as a "suite." "Unlike Ruttmann's city symphony [with its] emphasis on heavy machinery and lack of attention to human relationships,"[37] Fernando Pérez's *Habana Suite* (2003) explores the ambient soundscape (for example, the hissing of steam from a factory chimney and the rustle of hospital bedding), sounds that result from the diverse activities of individual Cubans shown in close-ups working (e.g., cooks, nurses, gardeners, road construction workers, or simply those engaged in different parts of their day: eating, walking, cycling, driving, dressing, and so on). Unlike Ruttmann's *Berlin*, which moves through sequential parts of the day, focusing on emerging assemblages, Pérez's *Habana* shows parallel activities as it cuts back and forth among the stories of five characters, all of whom are involved in trades during the day and artistry in the evening. Recognizing that Ruttmann's sound is imposed while Pérez's is collected from the city, Amanda Holmes captures the documentary's sound and image effects and thereby provides a contrast between Berlin's turn-of-the-twentieth-century industrial modernity (focused very much on class contrasts) and Cuba's postrevolutionary, late-twentieth-century (more classless) modernity: "A close analysis of the interplay between image and sound reveals how *Suite Habana* constructs an organic relationship among Havana's inhabitants and the objects that make up the city environment. One sequence introduced by the voice from an ambient radio presenting [a] guitar piece 'Suite Habana' (by Cuban composer Eduardo Martin) demonstrates the attention to sound in the film and its parallel with the creation of musical composition."[38]

Whereas in societies with notable class differences, sound production and reception were clearly partitioned—for example, between upper bourgeois citizens entering a concert hall to hear classical music and proletarian classes listening to marching bands in the street—Havana offers a striking contrast in which shared musical idioms punctuate the entire city. Even in societies with notable class divisions, however, contemporary technology has rendered much of musical reception invisible. Who knows what a person using ear buds has selected from the playlist on her or his individual listening device? That technology adds an epoch to Jacques Attali's genealogy of music space, from the street to the concert hall to the airwaves.[39]

Reflecting on an earlier development of such a singular listening device, the "Walkman," Jean-Paul Thibaud describes the Walkman listener as one who "transforms the public scene [providing] a new tonality to the city street."[40] The Walkman listener is effectively muting "intense urban noises that punctuate the flow of [their] musical audition,"[41] the public intersubjectivity that results from the sharing of the ambient noise of the city's soundscape (evident in Pérez's documentary): "[D]ecomposing the territorial structure of the city and recomposing it through spatio-phonic behaviors,"[42] the prior Walkman listeners and those who are now plugged into current individual listening devices use a technology that has attenuated the effects of the former spatial practices that organized ways of listening together.

Nevertheless, there remain multiple acoustical communities of sense that at times operate in separate venues and at times come together in musically shared spaces to effect intersubjective episodes of musical blending. I offer two examples, one actual and one contrived. The former is treated in Gregory Clark's account (described in chapter 1) of an exemplary musical event, an intercultural acoustical community of sense evinced at the Moab music Festival, when the Marcus Roberts Trio is joined by the banjoist Béla Fleck at the Utah stop of the tour. As Clark describes the moment: "Here jazz would meet bluegrass, bringing together two American musics that had much to divide them. When the concert began, the four musicians—three black and one white—let their musics roll across each other, calling out in one idiom and responding in the other, exchanging idioms and gradually developing a hybrid sound in a new voice of both jazz and bluegrass."[43] The latter is developed in one of the multiple narratives in David Simon's HBO series *Treme* (2010–2013), a music-punctuated fictional version of the way New Orleans's population managed the aftermath of Hurricane Katrina, where the focus is on a disjunctive aspect of New Orleans's musical culture, a continuing story of the relationship between Albert "Big Chief" Lambeaux (Clark Peters) and his son Delmond (Rob Brown). While Albert positions himself as the guardian of the traditional moral economy of New Orleans music, Delmond is associated with modern, commercially oriented jazz. For Albert, the percussive, Indian version of jazz is a cultural treasure with ontological depth and a ritual function (primarily to be performed in the street during Mardi Gras by elaborately costumed "Indians"), while Delmond, at least at the outset of the series, is a performer (trumpeter) of a commoditized modern jazz in concert venues (primarily Lincoln Hall in New York).

As *Treme*'s seasons progress, the division between Albert Lambreaux and his son Delmond attenuates. In his role as a cultural icon steadfastly resistant to commoditized forms and venues of music, Albert initially refuses to perform in a musical style and music venue that renders the music as an exchangeable good. *His* preferred music venue is the street (which Jacques Attali famously identifies as the space of festival and ritual that preceded music's migration into the confined spaces of clubs and concert halls).[44]

Late in the series, however, Albert changes his attitude about his son's musical vocation and the venues in which he performs. At the same time, Delmond has developed a passion for New Orleans's musical heritage and begins working on a temporally hybrid music that incorporates his father's traditional/ethnic, percussive musical rhythms within versions of modern jazz to preserve the embodied resonances of the former and emphasize the swing, dance-provoking aspects of the latter. As *Treme*'s last season begins, Albert has agreed to perform in nonstreet venues with Delmond's ensemble.[45]

While the increasingly infirm Albert is no longer able to move with his music (in New Orleans's musical parades), the hybrid music in which he participates encourages movement in the audience, thereby recovering an aspect of the jazz tradition whose attenuation Ralph Ellison had earlier lamented. Ellison referred to the "thinness of much so called modern jazz" (which Albert had lamented), its loss of wholeness, which can be attributed to its distance from the public events that gave it its connection with movement, "the small Negro public dance," which he regarded as its most authentic cultural venue.[46] As I have suggested, while the city's soundscape reflects the multiple practices of identity/difference which at times unites and at times divides the city's subcommunities, the vagaries of the gaze also contribute to that dynamic. I address that in the next section.

Enabling Presence/Challenging Invisibility/Reanimating Lost Sounds

Helsinki has been a site of another notable mode of urban punctuation. To appreciate Helsinki's participation in contemporary urban modernity, I want to insert a paradigmatic image of urban life, where bodies are congregated densely while their gazes remain oblique—Ernst Ludwig Kirchner's rendering of a Berlin street scene at Potsdamer Platz in 1913 (figure 2.4).

Kirchner's painting "captures two aspects of modern life . . . the kinetic energy of urban life—which he referred to as 'lines of force'—and the [requirement of maintaining] interpersonal indifference in situations of close interpersonal proximity."[47] The steadfast obliqueness and indifference of the urbanite gaze is especially visited on immigrants and refugees whose presence is virtually invisible to long-term residents, adding to the alienation that newly arriving people experience as they seek to accommodate to their new environment.

In order to intervene in that dynamic (in Helsinki as well as in other urban centers: Barcelona, Paris, Marseille, New York, Houston, Stockholm, Warsaw, Rotterdam, and Boston), the artist Krzysztof Wodiczko invented "critical vehicles," technological prostheses worn by immigrants to re-punctuate the network of interactions in public space (between 1993 and 1997). His interventions are driven by his vocational commitment: "Artists are in a special position to . . . engage public issues . . . by creating work that is challenging and disrupting."[48] Especially notable with respect to how his art disrupts the usual flows in urban space is Wodiczko's *bâton d'étranger* (alien staff), "a piece of storytelling equipment and a legal and

Figure 2.4 Berlin street scene.

Figure 2.5 Wodiczko's baton.

ethical communication instrument and network for immigrants."[49] "Resembling the rod of a biblical shepherd, it is equipped with a mini-video running a short biographical sketch of the wearer, and a loudspeaker powered by batteries the wearer carries in a shoulder bag. The small image on the screen induces observers to move closer for a better look, diminishing the 'usual distance between the operator . . . and the passersby.'"[50]

The result, as Wodiczko puts it, is the provocation of "an incitement to infringe on the barrier between stranger and non-stranger."[51] The interruptions that Wodiczko's technological prosthesis-wearing immigrants effect re-punctuate the pattern of daily interpersonal encounters, familiarizing wary residents with strangers thought to be too exotic to engage. Politically speaking, his interventions address "inequalities and stratification [necessary because, as he puts it] . . . public space is often barricaded and monopolized by the voices of those who are born to speak and prepared to do so."[52] His prosthetic devices "equip unheard individuals . . . so that they can more effectively break the silence"[53] (see figure 2.5).

While Wodiczko's interventions are aimed at calling attention to those whose presence tends to be ignored within diverse urban settings, there is

Figure 2.6 Hitler in Heldenplatz.

an intervention that calls attention to those who, once present, have tended to have their disappearance ignored. In a sonic intervention with historical depth, the Scottish artist Susan Philipsz created voice-like sounds deployed twice daily in Vienna's Heldenplatz (Hero's Square), where three days after German troops annexed Austria on March 12, 1938, Hitler addressed tens of thousands from the palace balcony. Two weeks later, the transports to the Dachau death camp began[54] (figure 2.6). What is broadcast is "the eerie sound of fingers rubbed on water-filled glasses," selected both because the sounds are voice-like and designed, according to Philipsz, to "remember all those who had disappeared," and because the sounds of glass evoke much about the era: "the lead crystal motif [relates to] . . . some imposing chandeliers in the palace. . . . Radio sets had crystal elements in the 1930s, the radio was a vital propaganda tool for Hitler. And of course, there was Kristallnacht, . . . when synagogues and Jewish businesses in Germany and Austria were ransacked."[55] Given the venue of Philipsz's artistic intervention into Vienna's urban soundscape, her sound installation constitutes an episodic archive which, over its duration (planned for an eight-month period), resonates with Mumford's previously noted observation that cities are temporal as well as territorial entities, while at the same time making an ethico-political statement about the importance of remembering a historical moment that many want to ignore.

Other Artistic Urban Disruptions

Social theorists have long recognized that cities epitomize diversity, not only ethnically but also in terms of political subcultures, for they contain not one but a variety of (overlapping) public spheres (organized on the basis of gender, ethnicity, national origins, etc.), each embodying alternative communities of sense. Rather than merely describing the patterns in particular urban formations, however, my concern is with how the arts disrupt the dynamic through which such patterns are shaped, or, in the perspective of Sander Bax et al., how the arts constitute interruptions of the dynamics through which the public sphere (in all its pluralities) is constituted.[56] Noting that "the public sphere is constituted by a combination of social, political and media forces [which are] continuously being interrupted," they refer to those interruptions as "temporary halts."[57] Similarly put (in Krzysztof Ziarek's terms), the interruptions are moments when "art frees forces into a becoming which is apart from the habitual relations of representation, action, and knowledge that form and regulate social praxis."[58]

Here I want to distinguish those moments of continuity versus interruption that are internal to the historical culture of certain urban formations from those occasioned by outside interventions. Among the former are scheduled carnivals, for example, the yearly Mardi Gras in New Orleans, the yearly carnivals in Brazilian cities, and the carnivalesque processions through Avignon on Bastille Day. Because those interruptions are scheduled and contained by long-established protocols, their effects are politically innocuous. They introduce a very temporary level of anarchy into the city, articulated mostly in the form of relaxed rules about personal display and interpersonal intimacies. In contrast with carnivals, which are internally generated reprieves from the normal daily operations and flows in urban space, circuses intervene from outside, traveling from place to place to stage a series of acts by characters whose antics alternatively amuse, terrify, and astound. Those traditional and expected interruptions, however—to the extent that they are scheduled by enterprises or political agencies—constitute a "ritual interruption," which "may disrupt the everyday social order, but only to actually confirm it."[59]

Nevertheless there are nontraditional (nonstate- or city-sponsored) circuses that bring to the dynamics of urban normality a degree of chaos, created especially by clowns, whose antics challenge "expected forms of normalcy" and thereby open lines of flight from "social constraints" while at the same time "inviting reconsideration of the order of things."[60] As M. M. Bakhtin puts it, clowns are among the figures that provide a "distinctive feature that is as well a privilege—the right to be 'other' in this world, the right not to make common cause with any single one of the existing categories that life makes available."[61]

The filmmaker Federico Fellini was for that reason "fascinated by circuses, clowns and itinerate performers,"[62] expressing his fascination as an "attachment to the chaos, the music, the monstrous hallucinations, and the death risk that this type of spectacle, based on wonder, fantasy, mockery" offered. He animated that fascination in his documentary *I Clown* (1970), in which he emphasizes the dialectical relationship between two kinds of clowns, "the White Clown and the Augusto, two characters [who] embody a myth that's inside all of us: the reconciliation of opposites," for example, "the mother and the bratty child," "the teacher and the kid," which he sees as a "teacher and [an unruly] kid."[63] Referring to that opposition, Fellini characterizes it as "the famous antithesis *yin* and *yang*" and "Hegel and the dialectics."[64]

Although Fellini lamented the disappearance of the joyous and oppositional spirit of the circuses of his childhood, which mobilized grotesque characters to parody the social order, there remain subversive versions with clowns and other characters that stage such parodies. Exemplary in this respect is an Australian assemblage, Circus Oz, which stages productions that parody patriotism and traditional protocols of masculinity by clowning in ways that reverse gender roles and "deliver an aura of unruly uncooperativeness."[65] The productions are "politically purposeful," characterized especially of late by an anarchic physicality that satirizes masculinity, while representing the female as a "gender outlaw."[66]

To appreciate the parodic praxis conducted by Circus Oz, we can heed M. M. Bakhtin's analysis of the carnivalesque applied to "the varied popular-festive life of the Middle Ages and Renaissance." That life form reached its summit, he points out, in the sixteenth century, a period in which laughter punctuated public space, provoked by the popular festivals that took place periodically in the streets of cities and towns. Subsequently, "in the new official culture there prevails a tendency toward the stability and completion of being toward one single meaning, one single tone of seriousness."[67]

I should note as well that insofar as carnivalesque-induced laughter intervenes in contemporary social life, it tends to have left the streets for built entertainment venues and the "airways" (e.g., comedians performing live in concert halls or on television), thereby imitating Attali's genealogy of music, which chronicles the movement from street performance to the enclosed concert hall and other such architectural venues, and thence to the airways. Nevertheless, the Rabelaisian spirit of parody (uncrowning and other forms of identity deconstruction), which Bakhtin treats in his history of laughter, continues to punctuate urban life, introducing moments of anarchy into structures of institutionalized seriousness and chaos into practices of identity recognition.

In the case of Circus Oz, the identity targets are not kings (the targets of medieval clowns, e.g., the "red-snouted Catchpole" that Bakhtin describes);[68] they are practices of gender recognition. At a minimum, Circus Oz bids to encourage reflection on the politics of gender roles by lampooning tradition and playfully producing alternatives. Radical circus acts and parodic clowning are more than merely irreverent; they oppose state- and civic-sponsored cultural governance and "challenge . . . biopolitical processes [that seek to install] . . . normalizing behaviours and regulated conduct amongst people."[69]

The chaos engendered when parodic play and other subversive acts (in circuses or in more freelance practices) intervene in social formations, however, can have differential effects. They can provoke and legitimate reactive violence or liberate political reflection. Here I want to juxtapose the former, a fictional circus visit to a Hungarian town in Bela Tarr's film *The Werckmeister Harmonies* (2000)—arguably an allegory of Hungarian politics—which provokes a fear-driven chaos that leads to the installation of a violent totalitarian form of governance, with the traveling assemblage Circus Amok, whose aim is anarchistic, seeking to challenge the normalcies associated with politics as usual.

In *The Werckmeister Harmonies*, an adaption of Laszlo Krasznahorkai's novel (with the same title), a Hungarian town is disrupted by the arrival of a circus, which features a leviathan (an enormous stuffed whale), an enigmatic prince who is sequestered within the enormous container housing the whale, and a circus staff, consisting of a director and factotum. What is most instructive (from philosophic and political points of view) about the circus's arrival is the way its impact is mediated by the radically different political perspectives of the film's three main protagonists: Janos Valuska (Lars Rudolph), György Eszter (Peter Fitz), and Tünde Eszter (Hanna Schygulla), who represent alternative images of harmony and disharmony.

Janos Valuska (the local village eccentric), who first appears while orchestrating a model of the planetary system with the bodies of drunken patrons in a local bar, is an advocate of a cosmological version of harmony. He marvels at the order of the cosmos and is especially fascinated by its rhythms, particularly the occasional appearances of eclipses, which he mimes with the celestial choreography he has created with the bar's clientele during the opening scene. Tarr's filming elaborates the eclipse image by making the film a virtual shadow play (a play of light and dark constitutes the film's rhythmic narrative). For example, the viewer sees the circus's arrival through the witnessing of Valuska, who watches what is in effect another eclipse, as the tractor-pulled circus wagon enters the frame, its headlights illuminate and then darken the sides of a building. As rumors abound about the dark intentions of the circus's Prince, leading ultimately to the creation of an angry and dangerous mob, Valuska remains resistant to the town's growing fear and chaos. Allegiant to a perceived cosmological reason—seeing the celestial order as an expression of a divine plan—he is distracted from his immediate surroundings. Preoccupied with eternal rather than contingent events, he seeks attunement to a changeless order rather than power.

In stark contrast, Tünde Eszter, the estranged wife of György Eszter, is after power. Along with her associate, the town's chief of police, she plans to exploit the fear and resulting chaos to displace the town's former communal order with a martial, authoritarian regime. While Valuska is perplexed by the words of "the One" (the Prince) and by the resulting chaos, and Tünde is exploiting it to seize control, the protagonist, György, having given up on natural harmonies (he is an accomplished composer working on tuning protocols to implement a musical harmony but cannot get the Werckmeister tuning system to work), sides with the novel and the film's sensibility by appreciating interpretive chaos. The chaos precipitated by the circus's whale and the perplexing, incomprehensible words of the characters who accompany it merely confirm his newfound anarchistic outlook. He had ultimately realized that (as the novel puts it), "the present state of the area never had the slightest shred of meaning in the first place . . . as if the only order inherent in it was that it fitted it for chaos . . . desiring to take action against something that simply doesn't exist nor ever will exist . . . is not only exhausting . . . but quite pointless. . . . Henceforth. he says, 'I will abjure all independent and lucid thought as if it were the crassest stupidity.'"[70]

By the end of the film, Tünde and her coconspirators have taken control of the town, a situation that references a period of Hungarian political history (the authoritarian eras of Mátyás Rákosi and János Kádár from 1948 to 1989, in which their leadership imposed totalitarian orders). The film ends with shots in which Tarr redeploys the trope of light versus dark, along with an architectural metaphor to represent the policing of politically unacceptable ontologies. The last look at Valuska shows him seated in a brightly lighted psychiatric hospital room, clad in a white hospital gown. Beside him is his contrapuntal friend, the contrasting, darkly dressed György Eszter, who during his visit to the hospital recounts how he too has been quarantined. He tells Valuska that he has been allocated a very small part of his former residence (a closed-in summer porch), while his ex-wife and her police chief collaborator are occupying its main rooms. Both Valuska's cosmological ontology of a celestial order and György's anarchistic ontology of disorder have been displaced (symbolically and spatially) by the enforced harmony of totalitarian politics, justified by a vision of a Hobbesian war of all against all that has been precipitated by the intervention of the traveling circus.

Running versus Being Amok

An important aspect of sensorial and ideational effects in Tarr's film is in scenes of the crowd that forms in the town's central square and ultimately runs amok as hundreds of them (effectively miming Elias Canetti's famous account of out-of-control crowds) march to a local hospital and take their madness out on helpless hospital patients, the town's most vulnerable population. The film's soundtrack reverberates with the loud sounds of the mob's boots in a long take of their march to the hospital, contrasting with the earlier softer sounds of the footfalls of Valuska and György marching through town together. The mob's footsteps replicate Canetti's description of the rhythms of a rioting mob's feet: "a long stretch of time in which they continue to sound loud and alive."[71]

In contrast with the effect of a circus's intervention in Tarr's film is Circus Amok, an assemblage that (like skateboarders) usually operates in the street; making an "'inappropriate' use of preordained urban zones. . . . [like other interventionist artistic performances] they "eat away at the rigid urban grid."[72] They are circus anarchists who themselves run amok rather than inducing that reaction in their audience. Their anarchic enactments provoke critical reflection and provide the conditions of possibility for new intimacies; their effect, as their founder and main player Jennifer Miller puts it, is "laughter [which] opens up the spirit, to think, to be concerned, to see, to have energy moving from one to the other."[73]

Circus Amok's performances have been mainly concerned with major social and political issues: "Circus," as Miller puts it, "works incredible well with issues of social justice. . . . [It's a] celebratory form" that is at once "enticing" and serious, encouraging a "sense of concern" that engages both "activists and people who are toiling away out there."[74] In terms of political content, the targets of Circus Amok's parodic vignettes have included the 2008 financial crisis (in a skit entitled "Sub Prime Sublime"), and a 2012 rendering of New York's stop-and-frisk policing practice (entitled "Moo"). In this latter engagement: "The audience encounters a circus under siege! Creditors are knocking down the doors, performers disappearing left and right, and there's a cow on the loose! How will the show go on? Astounding acrobats, bodacious bovines, and catastrophic clowns all forge ahead while a wire-walker teeters on the edge of sanity. Cops and Carol Channing mix it up."[75]

In terms of form, Circus Amok's performances revive an early tradition of "clowning" [which they see as a] "historically political act," drawn from diverse street performances throughout history—"Commedia dell'Arte performers at Renaissance fairs, . . . the San Francisco Mine Troup, [and] Bread and Puppet theater [associated with the Bread and Puppet Circus]."[76]

Ultimately, as Miller suggests, Circus Amok aims to challenge the contemporary tendency toward non-face-to-face engagement (in which people are separately absorbed in various virtual spaces) by encouraging "a movement of real bodies meeting in real spaces to counter or be in discussion with all this virtual time we are spending."[77] Moreover, because laughter and playful parody are the signatures of their acts, Circus Amok introduces a "ludic city"[78] in which urban space is reoriented in a conjunction of laughter and serious reflection. Challenging governmental authorities and bureaucracies that order city space, Circus Amok displaces the imposed order with moments of contrived anarchy. In what follows, I pick up on that playful anarchy with a turn to the promised bookend of the analysis, the antisymphonic antics of a group of anarchic musician/composers in Ola Simonsson and Johannes Stjarne Nilsson's film *Sound of Noise* (2010).

Sound of Noise

To appreciate the musical orientation of the film's protagonists, who turn the city of Stockholm into a setting for an extended musical guerilla theater, we need to heed the musical thinking and compositional strategies of John Cage, a major inspiration for the film. Like Jennifer Miller's Circus Amok, Cage wanted to project a circus atmosphere into the midst of urban life—in his case in the form of an anarchic community piece, *Musicircus*. Anarchy gets a surcharge in Cage's "composition" (if that word can be applied to his piece). Without a score, it is organized as "an invitation to bring together a number of groups of any kind [and have] them perform simultaneously anything they wish."[79] As Cage describes the piece, "You won't hear anything; you'll hear everything." Constructing himself as a "benign anarchist," he claims to prefer anarchy to governance (uttered in his Charles Eliot Norton lectures, 1998–1999).[80] Cage's Norton lectures constitute a manifesto in behalf of musical anarchism, which he saw as organized around the concepts of experimentalism, chance, and silence, all motifs that lend themselves to a communitarian musical habitus that eschews "hierarchical arrangements and interferences of legislative society . . . [an] anarchistic way of composing and living [articulated as a commitment] to listen affirmatively, anarchistically to the nonintentional, silent world that surrounds us."[81]

Although symphonies have performed some of Cage's compositions, his musical approach is fundamentally antisymphonic. For example, the experimental, nonintentionality that he pursued brought him into contention with the conductors Pierre Boulez, who claimed that Cage's type of writing was "no longer music," and with members of the New York Philharmonic (and their conductor, Leonard Bernstein), who resisted Cage's instructions about the placement of his *Atlas Eclipticalis* among other pieces in a program devoted to "The Music of Chance."[82]

To listen to a Cage composition is not to hear a traditional orchestra; it is to hear reoriented sounds that don't belong to ordinary orchestral scores. What are conjoined, for example, are "silence dissonance noise altered instruments words radios piano tin cans orchestra sounds magnetic tape amplifications voices electronic clatter scratches sound fragments songs reading thumps common clamor."[83] Rather than a music that takes its place in an orchestral history of composition, it is one that "opens the mind to the world around us."[84]

Framing the issue of his challenge to ordinary musical intelligibility with the issue of coercive controls over language intelligibility—"Cage has said that syntax in language is like the army in society; to rid ourselves of it we must demilitarize language"[85]—Cage sought to distance himself from the forces that have shaped musical taste and instead to listen to the world. To allow the world to find its way into a musical composition according to Cage is to heed its resonances, "which can be released by setting it into vibration."[86] For Cage, demilitarizing music also involves eschewing the "hierarchical relationship between audience and performers [which implied breaking down the walls of the concert hall], no fees for performers, no ticket charges, and especially [quoting Cage] . . . 'maNy / Things going on / just a space of time / aNd / as many pEople as are willing / performing in The same place.'"[87]

Cage's resistance to the commercialization and enclosure of musical performance sets up a dialectic between music as organized intentional performance within closed fee-demanding venues and the contingencies of publicly available, music-enabling noise. That he reassigns the noise-music relationship is exemplified in a fragment of his poetic meditation on structure: ". . . a canvas of Time is provided hospitable to both noise and mUsical tones upon which music may be dRawn."[88] That dialectical shift is effectively enacted by the group of anarchist percussionists in *Sound of Noise*, who are assembled after some of them quit conventional musical venues to join an ensemble of six drummers who use the city of Stockholm to realize the score: "Music for One City and Six Drummers," created and arranged by two former music students who go rogue.

The two are featured in the film's second scene; Sanna (Sanna Persson Halapi) is driving a van at excessive speed, and Magnus (Magnus Börjeson—a composer as well as an actor) is playing a set of drums in the back, increasingly frenetically to match the speed of the van. His performance is thus summoned by the rhythms of his momentary situation; it ends when the van escapes from a pursuing motorcycle policeman, who is foiled when Magnus throws the drums out of the back of the van, causing him to tumble from his motorcycle while swerving to avoid the debris.

The film's opening scene introduces (with an array of family photos shown on screen) the Warnebring family, whose two sons constitute one of the film's two dialectics; one son, Oscar, is a musician and symphony conductor, and the other, Amadeus, a tone-deaf police detective, is his antithesis. While Oscar is insulated in his role as symphony conductor, Amadeus becomes mobilized as a main protagonist from the moment that Sanna and Magnus abandon their wrecked van. He pursues them throughout the rest of their musical adventure, as the anarchist ensemble performs a musical score that uses diverse parts of the city to realize the composition. Amadeus chases but never arrests the group (whose performances effectively overcome the arresting effects of standard musical venues), but his trajectory of movement serves to help map the film's second dialectic, that between enclosed-venue symphonic music versus its antithesis, the scoring of the city, whose sounds the rogue musicians bring to life.

Shortly after their adventure on the road, Magnus shows Sanna his musical score, which she pronounces to be a "masterpiece" (figures 2.7–2.9). Thereafter, their task is to assemble the drummers to rehearse in their rented warehouse. During the recruitment, the viewer is shown a variety of stultifying musical venues, which each musician abandons after breaking out of the musical scores within each. Two examples: in the first, Johannes (Johannes Bjork) appears playing his drum and cymbal set with a dance band that plays slow foxtrots in a night club catering to middle-aged couples. Looking bored with his role (quarantined within an anachronistic musical routine), Johannes spots a butterfly that he sees flying past and breaks his routine to strike his cymbals, making them resonate with the vibrations of the butterfly wings (effectively a John Cage moment). Asked to resume his place in the musical piece, he instead goes crazy on his drums, disrupting the club's traditional order as he unleashes his creative impulses before leaving.

The second example takes place in Stockholm's symphony hall, where Oscar Warnebring is rehearsing the orchestra in a rendition of Haydn's *Surprise Symphony* (the epitome of a piece requiring creative restraint). It is a piece that especially frustrates the drummer, Anders (Anders Vestergard), whose role at one point in the symphony is to play a single beat on his kettle drum (while the conductor keeps complaining about his timing). Like Johannes, Anders finally cracks and goes rogue on his drums, after saying that he "hates Haydn."

Once the rogue drummers are assembled and rehearsed, they hit the city to perform Magnus's four movements, designed for four venues: 1) "Doctor Doctor Gimme Gas in My Ass" (performed with rhythmic beats in a hospital operation room on a patient, admitted for a hemorrhoid operation, and on the surrounding equipment); 2) "Money 4 U Honey" (performed in a bank, using the rhythm of a shredder, first flicking the paper kronor notes to a musical beat and then shredding them); 3) "Fuck

Figures 2.7–2.9 The score.

the Music, Kill! Kill!" (performed in front of Stockholm's symphony hall using the destructive rhythmic pummeling of "4 heavy machines [e.g., a bulldozer], one drill, one sledgehammer," with which they break up a fountain, a set of steps, and part of a road, and 4) "Electric Love" (performed at a central power station, where they rappel up the electric towers and rhythmically strike the wires, making the city lights blink off and on).

Movement #3, "Fuck the Music, Kill! Kill!" is especially notable because it brings the film's two dialectics together. Inside the hall is Oscar Warnebring, conducting Haydn's *Surprise Symphony*, with his tone deaf, antithetic brother Amadeus in the audience, while outside is Magnus, Sanna, and crew with the heavy equipment delivering their own surprise, a ground rumbling, percussive musical moment that disrupts the Haydn performance as they enact the antithesis of an enclosed, fee-demanding, musically constrained composition. What remains is to articulate a way to conceive the kind of (re)punctuating of the city that is involved in the film's dialectical, John cage–inspired musical challenge.

Conclusion: Disclosing the Aesthetico-Ludic City

The political effects enacted in *Sound of Noise* (and in various forms of street circus, especially clowning) register themselves in a combination of aesthetic and ludic gestures. What is generated is an aesthetics of politics in the sense that Jacques Rancière identifies: events that are moments of interruption or intervention that put in question ways of being in common, that destabilize the commonsense view of political relationships, and that reorder or repartition sensible experience. How then does the ludic articulate with the aesthetic? Like aesthetic interventions, play introduces moments of indeterminacy in situations and domains that are taken as fixed. Clowning and other playful moments of urban intervention reorient the "'psychogeographic' potential of the urban grid."[89] Such disruptions derail people's usual utilitarian, goal-oriented fulfillment-seeking and encourage new ways of thinking about identities and space and thus new ways of moving/acting together. An aesthetic of play operates "against the normative, the rational, and the ideal [while signifying] . . . the absence of essence [and] . . . excess beyond binary opposition."[90]

Perhaps most importantly (for the theory of music of John Cage and its realization in *Sound of Noise*), the ludic aesthetic of musical anarchism is antithetical to the commodification of music experience. Episodes of play oppose a political economy based on means-ends calculations and experiences valued for their productiveness. Among the places where that opposition has been explored is in Michel Tournier's novel *Vendredi ou les limbes du Pacifique* (*Friday, or the Other Island*), a version of the Robinson Crusoe story that is antithetical to Daniel Defoe's Robinson Crusoe who, though on an island very distant from Defoe's England, labored to reproduce England's version of capitalism.[91] As is noted in one discerning commentary: "Defoe's hero—unlike most of us—has been endowed with the basic necessities for the successful exercise of free enterprise. He is not actually a primitive or a proletarian or even a professional man, but a capitalist. He owns freehold, an estate which is rich but unimproved. It is not a desert island in the geographical sense—it is merely barren of owners or competitors."[92]

In Tournier's novel, Crusoe's companion Friday subverts the order of the island, playfully "destroying almost every aspect of Crusoe's rationally administered island, while at the same time creating a different island, one dedicated to play rather than the duties of administrator and wage earner."[93] Crusoe is at first baffled by Friday's antics but is eventually edified. At moments, "His [Crusoe's] mind dwelt on the ravages caused by Friday in the meticulous ordering of the island [but eventually he appreciated] . . . the *spirit* manifested by Friday, the tricks and devices, the diabolical or impish notions that entered his head, setting up confusion by which Robinson himself was infected."[94] As I've noted, "When eventually Crusoe's bafflement and ambivalence are replaced with recognition, what he is able to discern through Friday's subversion is that his administered island is but one among other possible islands. . . . [Friday's island is] dedicated not to a system of rational exchange but to an order based on expressivity or play, demonstrated by such acts as taking objects that have high exchange value in eighteenth century England and using them to decorate plants and then enlisting them in elaborate rituals of imagination."[95]

Moving from a ludic island to "the ludic city," I want to evoke again Henri Lefebvre's remark about play as "an escape from the localization and 'punctualization' of activities," a foil against capitalism's structuring of productive and consumptive social relations.[96] Seeing play as a counterforce to capitalist structuring, especially as it operates within urban space, Quentin Stevens, in his analysis of the ludic dimensions of city life, notes, "The density and diversity of city life inevitably leads to tensions and contradictions between rational social organization and people's other desires. Noninstrumental playful behavior thrives in continuing negotiation with various forms of discipline, exploration and spectacle which constitute the contemporary city."[97]

Certainly, the antics of the anarchic musicians in *Sound of Noise* reveal the strictures of both concert hall and night club–enclosed forms of musical performance while at the same time demonstrating the potential of the city's varied venues for creative moments in which city noises can contribute to musical composition. What is required, as Magnus and Sanna's drummers show, is to challenge the city's institutionalized "spatial habitus" that "constrains play because it defines 'appropriate' times and places which . . . organize and codify social action."[98] They enact play's dialectical potential while revealing a ludic Stockholm sequestered within the disciplined one, where the latter is represented in the dialectic relationship between the Warnebring brothers, the tone-deaf bother who polices disruptive play (Amadeus) and the other (music-sensitive) brother (Oscar), who conducts (and restrains) musical performance. Ultimately, the anarchic musical ensemble that plays Magnus's composition, "Music for One City and Six Drummers," creates an antisymphonic "symphony for a great city," as against the agents of control they disclose the conditions of possibility for another (ludic) Stockholm.

Finally, I want to emphasize that there is always "another Stockholm" (as is the case with other urban formations). What are required for that otherness to become evident are events of encounter. The disruptive performance of Magnus's composition for six drummers revealed part of the "infinite alterity" in Stockholm's soundscape, an alterity hidden by the conceit that "music" belongs only to certain professional and commercial venues.[99] The effect of the guerilla theater enacted by Magnus's ensemble is not unlike the effects engendered by Wodiczko's prosthesis-wearing immigrants. As they (re)punctuate urban space, they challenge the subjectivities of urban residents unaware of their own lack of singularity. As is pointed out in Maurice Blanchot's conception of the conditions of possibility for community, when "the other intervenes . . . [and] introduces [a] *dissymmetry* [she/he] . . . devastates the integrity of the subject, making its centered and isolated identity collapse, opening to an irrevocable exteriority, in a constitutive incompleteness."[100] Disruptive events by the intervention of others, which punctuate everyday life in urban formations, introducing countermovements to the flows of urban bodies, are the moments in which the incompleteness of community within urban society (and within urban society's subjects) becomes evident.

C.HAPTE.R THR.EE

ARCHITECTURAL PUNCTUATIONS: THE POLITICS OF "EVENT SPACES"

Fred Hampton's Apartment

London, July 18, 2017: As I walked through the Tate Modern Museum's "Soul of a Nation" exhibition (devoted to the way the arts have represented the mid-1960s Black Power movement), my attention was riveted by one display. It was Dana C. Chandler Jr.'s facsimile of the bullet-punctuated door to Fred Hampton's Chicago apartment, testifying to his assassination (along with Mark Clark's) by the FBI and Chicago police in a predawn raid on December 4, 1969 (see figure 3.1).[1]

Hampton and Clark had been targeted as part of the FBI's notorious attack on American left-wing activists. Subsequent forensic investigations showed that the door, along with the rest of the apartment, was punctuated by over ninety bullet holes, all but one of which resulted from "law enforcement" guns.

I was reminded of the architectural theorist Bernard Tschumi's dictum, "There is no architecture without action, no architecture without events, no architecture without program. . . . [and] By extension . . . no architecture without violence."[2] Although Tschumi had less dramatic interventions in mind when he issued that dictum (he used "violence" as a "metaphor for the intensity of a relationship between individuals and their surrounding spaces"),[3] the cast of characters and venue of the assault on Hampton and Clark fit his view of the relationship between architecture and events: "Architecture's violence is fundamental and unavoidable, for architecture is linked to events in the same way that the guard is linked to the prisoner, the police to the criminal, the doctor to the patient, order to chaos [thus] . . . actions quality spaces as much as spaces qualify actions."[4]

There are more recent, ready-to-hand examples of Tschumi's remark about architectural violence, for example the prisons at Abu Ghraib and Guantanamo Bay, used in the "war on terror" by the administration of President George W. Bush after 9/11. As Richard Ross points out, they have a "certain familiarity" in that they mimic other coercive institutions designed for intimidation:

Figure 3.1
Hampton's door.

Both are environments with infinite architectural nuances. Cells, interview rooms, interrogation rooms have a certain familiarity around the globe, and every prison has its segregation cells, isolation areas, "the pit" and "the hole." Architecture is not necessarily an innocent act of creativity. A confessional in a Catholic church and an interview room at Los Angeles Police Department headquarters share the same intimate dimensions. They are both uncomfortably tight spaces constructed to force people together, to extract a confession in exchange for some form of redemption.[5]

Another ready-to-hand example indicates the way the architecture-violence relationship is reciprocal. The political economy of drug use, specifically the crack cocaine epidemic, has been shown to produce an architectural violence. Beginning with the remark, "Within the space of violence is crack," Michael Hays goes on to describe its impact on architecture:

> In my hometown in Alabama, in what used to be downtown, there are seven pawnshops where once there were hardware stores, diners, and pool halls. Downtown is flanked on either side by shopping malls, whose parking lots provide turnarounds for the nightly circuit of cruising cars. The monetary economy of crack cocaine produces as part of its spatialization these nodes of exchange where my grandfather's pistol and my brother's wife's new television set are traded for nightlong highs.[6]

Crucial for the analysis to follow is Tschumi's perspective that buildings are not to be understood merely structurally but as "event spaces" that result from practices of human intrusion. As he insists, "Any relationship between a building and its users is one of violence, for any use means the intrusion of a human body into a given space, the intrusion of one order into another."[7] In the case of Hampton's apartment, the initial intrusion involved habitation, while the second involved homicide. Subsequent to that second intrusion were contending forensic investigations emerging out of alternative subcultures. The law enforcement agencies, the FBI and police, backed to some extent by mainstream media, interpreted the killings and inflected the forensic evidence to point to a just war, a shootout between law enforcement and terrorists. Segments of the black community and Hampton's colleagues in the Black Panther movement saw it as an assassination (supported ultimately by other forensic work). As a *Chicago Tribune* report put it, "the police maintained they were justified in opening fire, but the Panthers saw the raid as a pretext for killing Hampton." Supporting the Panthers' interpretation, "outraged black voters" ended the "career of Cook County State's Atty. Edward V. Hanrahan who [authorized the raid and] was indicted but cleared with 13 other law-enforcement agents on charges of obstructing justice."[8]

If we heed Eyal Weizman's perspective on "forensic architecture [which he describes as] . . . a critical field of practice [whose aim is] to disseminate evidence of war crimes in urban context," Hampton's apartment, like other buildings, "continuously record[ed] [its] environment so that one can read political force" in it.[9] For Weizman, as for Tschumi, "buildings are not static entities; they continually undergo dynamic transformations."[10] After experiencing a violent intrusion, the Hampton apartment's silent testimony yielded the details of the event (virtually all the bullet holes coming from FBI and police weapons). The evidence of its transformation from a mere living space to a space of violent encounter supported the Panthers' version of the event; it suggested assassination rather than "just war." The FBI's firearms examiner reached the conclusion to which the apartment testified.[11] Contrary to the police description of a shootout, evidence showed that "Hampton was murdered in his bed while unconscious."[12] It's a conclusion that the exhibition, "Soul of a Nation," did not want us to forget.

I give Weizman's approach to forensic architecture more attention as I pick up the architecture-violence relationship again later in the analysis. In what follows, I throttle back for the moment and pursue architectural punctuation in general as I pursue Tschumi's approach to buildings as event spaces and explore the diverse ways that materially sedimented events and the practices that animate them have political resonances. To state those political resonances succinctly, I draw here from a statement of the relationship that effectively summarizes my argument: "architecture plays an active role in 'doing politics' [not as] a procedural attempt to reach a good decision or to achieve the perfect 'consensus' [but] . . . rather [as] a substantive move to 'materially refigure' and transfigure the practices, reshape the connections and redistribute . . . agency."[13] I turn now to the re- and transfigurations, which enfranchise oppositional communities of sense, after first exploring the diverse ways in which architectural punctuations operate and the performative, experience-shaping utterances they effectively make.

Architectural Punctuations

Architecture's punctuations exist in two ways. First, as buildings punctuate space, they are distinguished by their designs, which include their vantage points, their modes of access both visually and physically (a function of barriers and partitioning: walls, doors, windows, etc.), their degree of transparency versus opacity (implemented by the materials used), their modes of access to their adjacent environs, and their decorative motifs (which locate their allegiances, histories, and interpersonal and institutional interconnections). Second, buildings are animated through use. Functioning as event spaces, they participate in the organization of action and experience. They are temporally punctuated by the diverse "practices of space" of the bodies that use them.[14] Importantly for purposes of my analysis, Tschumi links the spatial implications of architectural design and the practices through which it is utilized to politics, wondering, for example, about whether the ambiguity of space (which is in between a social product and a pure category) allows it to be "a political instrument in the hands of the state."[15]

Certainly, architecture has macropolitical resonances, which surface in the state's symbolic authority practices, for example in the way the transparency of Berlin's new Reichstag with its pervasive use of glass makes a statement about the transparency of contemporary governmental decision-making. As Andreas Huyssen has pointed out, Berlin's postwar architecture was created to be explicitly "anti-monumental."[16] Norman Forster's Reichstag was designed to provide visibility and ease of access (with its glass dome and spiraling ramps that make the inside visually accessible) to distinguish it from Albert Speer's Nazi-era monumentalism, a design whose opacity (e.g., impenetrable façades) reflected an unaccountable authority structure.

Architecture also has micropolitical resonances, expressed, for example, in the designs of private dwellings whose layouts both affect and reflect the way the household orients itself both to the organization of familial interactions inside and to the interface between the home and what exists outside of it. Heeding Tschumi's reflections on architecture's spatio-temporal manifestations, I explore the various ways that architecture punctuates space and is in turn punctuated by activities as I survey some of the diverse practices that reveal the temporalities of architectural punctuation and examine the macro- and micropolitical consequences of those punctuations.

My illustrations are drawn largely from literary and cinematic texts because they invent and mobilize bodies in ways that demonstrate how architecture functions as event space. Paradoxically, my turn to fictional genres is a turn toward realism. I am in accord with Jacques Rancière's assertion, "Fiction is a structure of rationality which is required wherever a sense of reality must be produced. It is firstly a form of presentation of things that cuts out a frame and places elements within it so as to compose a situation and make it perceptible."[17]

To begin with a simple observation: One of the most familiar ways that architecture punctuates space is through its verticality—exemplified, for example, in a commentary on Thailand's MahaNakhon mixed-use tower, described as a "Pixelated Punctuation Mark on the Bangkok Skyline."[18] The historical conditions of possibility for that tower were construction and design innovations, for example the overhead crane and such people-moving technologies as the elevator, which enabled the development of the high-rise building and was instrumental in the development of "stacked housing,")[19] which now populates urban metropolises.

Standing as a series of urban exclamation points, high-rise buildings have attracted conflicting political interpretations. The architect Louis Sullivan (1856–1924), known as the "father of the skyscraper," thought that his "stark Chicago-style skyscraper . . . would help bring to fruition democracy's promise."[20] Focused on exterior design, he juxtaposed his unadorned buildings to the Gothic buildings on the University of Chicago campus, which he regarded as a materialized "negation of democracy."[21] Sullivan's interpretative approach to his skyscrapers, however, is merely "perspectival"; he emphasizes what the buildings say about the life world in which they are situated. It is an approach in which the built form tends to "recede behind . . . subjective readings" at the expense of recognizing the "practicalities, materialities and events of buildings."[22] That aspect of architecture yields itself to the kind of analysis Albena Yaneva describes as a "slow ethnography,"[23] achieved by one who "strolls the building and wanders around in it . . . extract[ing] speeds from the building, not meanings."[24]

Here I turn to a text that enacts such a "slow ethnography," a Colin Harrison novel that discloses the antidemocratic structures of domination and dynamics of interaction that a skyscraper embodies. In his Walt Whitman–inspired *Bodies Electric*, situated in Manhattan, he has his protagonist, Jack Whitman, express his disdain for the economic dominance located in the downtown high-rise building in which he works: "This is *the* big American media entertainment corporation, many times larger than Disney and Paramount and all the others, the one whose stock is considered a blue-chip growth equity into the next century, and is thus owned by the Japanese and German banks, by all universities and other institutions with huge endowments. . . . Ranked by market value, the fifty-sixth largest publically traded company in the world. Way up high in the thirty-ninth floor. I lived in its heart."[25]

Jack Whitman's "skyscraper" houses a megacorporation, an actor in the global network of international enterprises, which reflects and practices economic dominance rather than democratic proclivities. Doubtless, most of the sky-scraping exclamation points punctuating urban space are icons of an economic reality that dominates lives within the buildings, within the localities in which they are situated, and frequently at a distance as well. Materialized containers of hierarchical structures of management, skyscrapers merely seem mute, appearing as enigmatic façades to the many citizen subjects who hurry past them. Their implicit statements and practices emerge when summoned by (among other things) such fictional dramas as Harrison's novel.

Louis Sullivan was not obtuse to what transpires *within* buildings. As part of his desire to construct democracy, his design work ranged beyond skyscrapers to include an architectural project that manifested a different binary, that between transparency and opacity, realized in his design for the People's Savings Bank in Cedar Rapids, Iowa, where "in the interests of creating a more democratic space, [he] tried to lower the barriers separating bank employee and customers as well as the barrier that divided employees themselves. . . . To this end the offices of bank executives were made as visible and accessible as the spaces used by bank tellers [all] . . . organized around a central area used by the public."[26]

As in the case of his skyscrapers, however, one can discern a difference between the design's aspiration and how it functioned. Certainly the bank's transparency was designed to welcome a clientele. The architecture of consumer seduction can have unintended consequences, however, which is well illustrated in an intricate crime story, the novelist Joe Gores's *32 Cadillacs,* which, like Harrison's *Bodies Electric*, focuses on the way bodies involved in dramatic interactions disclose the way the built environment both contains and enables desired accomplishments

The novel's drama involves a series of encounters between a Roma collective that endeavors to steal thirty-two Cadillacs (to be used for their deceased Gypsy king's funeral cortege) and a team of repo men who, along with a police detective, try to recover them. At one point in the drama, one of the Roma, who is planning to pass a bad check at a bank, takes advantage of the bank's visual accessibility and temporal rhythms: "Rudolph Marino enters the main branch of 'California Citizen's Bank at One Embarcadero (*Now Open Nine to Five Every Wednesday to Serve You Better*) and is able to see all his relevant opportunities."[27]

"Marino scanned the bank officers behind the metal and Formica railing. He chose a pretty early-40s roundfaced woman with pouty lips. She wore floral perfume and pink-tinted glasses that magnified her eyes into a slightly surprised expression. She did not wear a wedding band. Her nameplate said Helen Wooding."[28] As I have noted elsewhere, "The bank laden with signs and spaces organized to seduce a clientele and governed by a rigid temporal structure (fixed opening and closing hours and consistent durations for check clearing), turns out to be an easy mark for someone prepared to be the seducer rather than the seduced."[29]

Gores's theft drama also exposes an aspect of architectural punctuation that exceeds the visibility-opacity binary; he treats accessibility versus impenetrability. That binary becomes especially apprehensible if one follows the careers of successful thieves. As Geoff Manaugh points out in his *Burglar's Guide to the City*, the thief sees the city as a "world where criminal opportunities [are] hidden in the very architecture of the metropolis."[30] Referring to one the most (in)famous burglars, Leonidas Leslie (operating in the nineteenth century), he writes, Leslie recognized that "the best way to commune with architectural space was breaking into it."[31] Although the buildings he hit were designed for legitimate activities, Leslie's architectural sagacity rendered them as designs for the illicit user (the events of theft) as much as for the licit ones. The concept of event space bears on burglary as much as it does on licit activities because a thief's ability to defeat a building's security requires her/him to assess its temporal rhythms as well as its spatial layout. Accordingly, the master jewel thief (and former building manager) Bill Mason wrote in his memoir *Confessions of a Master Jewel Thief* (2003) that he found it easy to "bypass a lot of security" by being attentive to less-used spaces—the "service corridors, . . . the internal hinterlands" and marginal rooms such as maintenance areas that residents rarely visit—and to heed the temporal rhythms of the building: "Every building had its rhythms . . . [moments with] fewer guards on patrol or residents taking out garbage."[32]

Familiarity with the spatio-temporality of buildings also facilitates violent crimes. Historically, "the house plan [has been] an intrinsic feature in detective fiction"—for example, the key role of the "floor plan" of houses featured in Agatha Christie's crime novels, whose detectives turn the plans into event spaces by recovering the comings and goings of residents and visitors.[33] Subsequent crime story writers have followed Christie's practice of making architecture a main protagonist in their own dramas. For example, buildings are main characters in the crime novels of Qiu Xiaolong, who continually makes architecture one of the protagonists in his contemporary Shanghai-situated stories. In his *When Red Is Black* (2004), for example, a main protagonist is a *shikumen* apartment complex in which the crime occurs.[34] Evolving since 1949, *shikumen* (literally "stone gate") multiple-unit buildings are two- to three-story structures featuring straight alleyways surmounted by stone arches and a front yard situated behind a high brick wall. The conditions of possibility for the design of these buildings were the development of iron and concrete construction—famously analyzed in detail by the architectural historian Sigfried Giedion[35]—which made possible an "industrial standardization" of dwellings, resulting in the "materialization of new forms of [collective] life."[36]

In the case of violent crime, however, the building's material structure is less important than the comings and goings of its inhabitants and commercial visitors. A perpetrator's opportunity for committing murder requires familiarity with the building's spatio-temporal punctuations: its access points (e.g., its front versus back door entrances) and the temporal rhythms of bodies moving within and without the structure. In the novel, the *shikumen* building and the murder victim are figured as similar, history-worn protagonists. The victim, Yin, a disgraced writer, suffered because of the strictures on writers imposed during the Cultural Revolution. She is described along with the other residents as one "covered by the dust of the past, just like the *shikumen* building," which is part of Shanghai's long-term architectural history.[37]

Once the building is positioned as a main protagonist, it emerges as a complex event space whose architectural features shape the repetitive movements (inside and outside) that are the conditions of possibility for both committing the murder and for finding witnesses to help solve it.

For example, as detective Yu, who has the primary responsibility for solving the crime, watches the building, he sees "an elderly woman . . . pushing open the black-painted door . . . with one hand, carrying a chamber pot in the other . . . [a] familiar sight."[38] And the comings and goings of street merchants—a "shrimp lady" at the front entrance ("an important witness . . . [who is] familiar with the *shikumen* building and with the habits of the other residents") and a "green-onion-cake peddler at a rear entrance"[39]—are spatio-temporal architectural features that yield the witnesses relevant to solving the crime.

The way the building's openings and partitioning shape the moments and interactions of residents and nonresident suppliers ultimately constitutes the way the drama emerges in the *shikumen*-as-event space, for example, when entrances and exits are accessible: "Both the front and back doors of Yin's building were locked during the night. The front door, latched from inside, did not open until around seven, and then at around nine thirty in the evening, it was closed again. As for the back door, people who went in and out through it, either early in the morning or late in the evening were supposed to lock it behind them."[40] Also important are common spaces and the rhythms of their use, for example, the *tingzijian* room, near the murder victim's apartment.

Having reflected on how some socially situated types—writers, thieves, and murderers—think *about* architecture as they negotiate its intricacies in their projects and, as aesthetic subjects, explicate through their actions the ways in which architecture shapes some interpersonal experience, I want to reverse the emphasis and explore how architecture thinks as it shapes some of the conditions of possibility for experience by turning to cinema and an episode in John Ford's most famous western, *The Searchers* (1956).

How Architecture Thinks: A Telling Cinematic Moment

The uncanny appeal of the opening scene of John Ford's *The Searchers*, which begins with a framing shot aimed at the prairie from inside the dark interior of the Edwards family home, has provoked considerable commentary,[41] in part because interiors have both architectural and psychological resonances, and in part because such shots are the "archetypes" that "provoke in the addressee a sort of intense emotion accompanied by a vague feeling of *déjà vu* that everyone yearns to see again."[42] That opening scene

Figure 3.2 *Searchers* image.

is the first of the film's three inside-out shots, taken from dark interiors toward the landscape outside[43] (this one from behind Aaron Edward's wife, Martha [Dorothy Jordan], who looks out toward the prairie watching her brother-in-law, Ethan, approach [see figure 3.2]). The way the scene is shot makes "the house itself . . . a camera pointed at nature."[44]

Describing that scene elsewhere, I wrote: "The opening scene of *The Searchers* . . . is both cinematically powerful and narratively expansive. It is shot from inside the cabin of Ethan Edward's (John Wayne) brother's cabin, providing a view of a vast expansive prairie, from which Edwards is approaching . . . observed by his sister-in-law from her front porch, which, architecturally, plays a role in designating the house as a refuge from outer threats." I went on to reflect on the kind of architectural statement made by front porches, quoting a lyrical passage in a novel by Alessandro Baricco, who describes the porch as being: "inside and outside at the same time . . . it represents an extended threshold. . . . It's a no man's land . . . the idea of protected place—where every house, by its very existence, bears witness to. . . . One could even say that the porch ceases to be a frail echo of the house it is attached to and becomes the confirmation of what the house just hints at: the ultimate sanction of the protected place, the solution to the theorem that the house merely states."[45]

Architectural Thought-Worlds

The conceptual burden of that John Ford moment (and Alessandro Baricco's reflection on porches) is that as architecture thinks and speaks, it also "calls for thinking."[46] It is a call that Baricco heeded in the midst of his novelistic drama about a city and is the call I am heeding as I focus both on what architecture *says* about the organization and dynamics of the life world and *how* it plays a role in apprehending and shaping that world. To proceed with that analysis, I turn throughout this investigation to various media genres—especially literary and cinematic—that actualize the ways architecture thinks and speaks as it participates in the conditions of possibility for individual and collective experience. Before providing those illustrations, however, I want to explore the architecture-thought relationship with an emphasis on architecture's ideational role in both affirming and contesting the dominant "thought-worlds" within which architectural designs and their realizations have been developed. Architecture "becomes cognate to mind" as it orchestrates the events involved in relations between inner and outer worlds.[47]

I borrow the concept of a "thought-world" from the historian of late antiquity, Peter Brown, who points out that contrary to the conceits about exclusivity within the early history of Christendom, Christianity departed slowly from paganism while incorporating many of its perspectives. Although there "were strenuous attempts to avoid what Christians regarded as the polluting effects of pagan practices, . . . 'in the ancients' thought-worlds potentially exclusive explanatory systems coexisted," a coexistence that was architecturally actualized. As Brown notes, "the public culture of ruling elites in the age of Constantine did not represent themselves in terms of Christian but rather in terms of pagan cosmology: [among other media] 'on the mosaics in their villas and the ceremonial icons in the imperial court.'"[48]

A more elaborate analysis of the relationship between architecture and the thought-worlds (articulated by theological-oriented philosophies) is undertaken in Erwin Panofsky's treatise on the Gothic cathedral, in which he demonstrates how its architecture constitutes a realization of the scholastic thought-world. While the prior Romanesque design, responsive to "prescholasticism's" thought-world, afforded no space for a reasoning subject (it "conveys the impression of a space determinate and impenetrable, whether we find ourselves inside or outside the edifice"),[49] the Gothic design actualized a "perspective interpretation of space"; it was designed "with reference to the very process of sight," creating a viewing subject with a "comprehensive picture of space" (in contrast with the Romanesque design's "isolated solids").[50] Specifically, the design of the Gothic cathedral was shaped by scholasticism's "mental habit,"[51] a commitment to contentious reasoning, an "all embracing . . . unconditional clarification" in the face of incommensurate forms of authority (a pluralistic set of reflections on dogma).[52]

Given the visual orientation that Panofsky ascribes to Gothic architecture, which enfranchises a *viewing* subject situated in a contentious terrain of competing forms of authority, the architecture of the Mormon Tabernacle in Salt Lake City provides a striking contrast. The Tabernacle is designed with a different kind of clarity in mind, an acoustic clarity aimed at facilitating a form of music that functions the way Jacques Attali famously figures it, as a "tool for the creation and consolidation of community."[53] Although Attali's insistence that "the entire history of tonal music" involves "an attempt to make people believe in a consensual representation of the world" is belied by many aspects of the history of musical composition and its reception,[54] his position fits the purpose behind the Tabernacle's design well. In contrast with the visual orientation of the Gothic cathedral, the Mormon Tabernacle "was designed first and foremost as a musical instrument." Shaped as "a medium of listening" to accommodate a *listening* subject—with the "recognition of the role of the performing arts in forging community"—the "primary concern of the Salt Lake Tabernacle is not visual but sonic control; here architecture functions as a machine for the manipulation of sound."[55]

Architecture and the Politics of Subjectivity

In both cases, architectural design connects bodies and buildings, anticipating the way subjects employ their senses to *apprehend* their environment. Subjects do more than apprehend their environs, however; they move about in them, turning designs into "event spaces."[56] To elaborate what architecture as event space implies requires an appreciation of "architecture as dynamic . . . defined as the sum of a figure walking through a space and the space itself."[57]

Certainly, the most pervasive design-induced events involve consumption, for much of contemporary architecture is commercially oriented; it seeks to capture the attention of and redirect moving bodies. Rather than venues of worship, they are (as one sociologist refers to shopping malls) "cathedrals of consumption."[58] Instead of evoking the ideational reflections of a viewing subject (the Gothic cathedral) or the communal allegiance of a listening subject (the Mormon Tabernacle), the purpose is to provoke desire. In short, architecture's commercial design aim is enticement, as it participates in the construction of the consuming subject.

As Walter Benjamin suggested in his observations on the Paris arcades, the history of shopping is among other things a history of commercial design, and doubtless contemporary shopping malls, which constitute a major commercial punctuation of space, are its most exemplary current realization (even though their peak is now long past).[59] The many films whose dramatic action takes place in shopping malls provide testimony to the pervasiveness of mall-punctuated land- and cityscapes throughout the United States.[60]

The ways that such films mobilize their subjects and demonstrate how malls function as event spaces is exemplified, in Paul Mazursky's *Scenes from a Mall* (1991). In the film the mall as setting (Los Angeles's Beverley Center) performs as a major protagonist. Its visual and aural summonses shape the itinerary of the other protagonists, a shopping couple, while at the same time operating somewhat independently from the interpersonal narrative about Deborah Feingold-Fifer (Bette Midler) and Nick Fifer (Woody Allen), whose fraught interactions reflect a troubled marriage. It's a setting freed by the camera's framing and tracking shots "from its service to the story,"[61] even as its images and sounds accompany and to some extent direct the characters' movements (e.g., Nina Rota's music accompanies and animates their bodily comportment at a moment when Nick and Deborah are headed down an escalator, and various displays in store windows are inviting them both into the stores' interiors).[62]

To return to a more abstract and comparative perspective on malls (which the film addresses and animates), the architecture of the contemporary shopping mall participates in the design orientations of both the Gothic cathedral and the Mormon Tabernacle in that it is involved in fashioning both a seeing and listening subject, which is in motion rather than contained within a functionally singular space. As a result, the design challenge of malls involves capturing attention and redirecting that motion into the interiors of stores. Containing many stores under one roof, the visual technologies of the mall are a legacy of the consumer revolution initiated by development of the modern department store, which as William Leach points out, employed "color, glass, and light," the technologies involved in display strategies aimed at provoking consumer desire. The most significant event in that provocation was the invention of the department store window (credited to the author of *The Wizard of* Oz, Frank Baum); "it amplified the visual, transforming the already watching city person into a potentially compulsive viewer."[63]

Notably, the effect of the sonic can be as important as that of the visual in directing the flow of consuming bodies. As Jonathan Sterne points out, "In places like the Mall of America, music becomes a form of architecture."[64] "The use of programmed music in a shopping mall is about the production and consumption of consumption."[65] The productive force of the music derives significantly from its participation in the design of the space within which it operates as it inflects "the contradictory flows of movement throughout the mall."[66] As Sterne puts it, "Programmed music can be said to territorialize the mall: it builds and encloses the acoustical space, and manages the transitions from one location to another" (for example, in the way the "soundtracking . . . serves to structure the hallway as a transitional space . . . of movement").[67]

In the case of such commercial structures, architecture's punctuating visual and aural organization commands movement and directs its flows (with visual enticements and aural motion-encouraging rhythms). In this sense, architecture's commands are in accord with Paul Virilio's characterization of a modernity in which the former operation of power as a "*constraint to immobility*" (operating within prerevolution aristocracies) became an "*obligation to mobility*."[68] Nevertheless, there are architectural punctuations (in the form of physical barriers and enclosures) that inhibit movement rather than command it.

For purposes of illustration, I turn to Tomas Alfredson's 2011 film version of the John le Carré spy novel, *Tinker Tailor Soldier Spy* (1974), in which much of the drama occurs within buildings that utilize a variety of architectural barriers to access. To recognize the way architecture functions within the film, we can heed the Russian director Sergei Eisenstein's cinematic practice in which he endeavored to "find practical answers to the problem of how to film a building, how to transform it from a passive setting of the action, into a major agent of the plot."[69] Among the answers Eisenstein got (after reading—"with the eye of a filmmaker"[70]—the way August Choisy described the Parthenon in his *Histoire d'architecture* from the point of view of someone walking around it) was the need for a "montage effect," which requires an emphasis on "the sequence."[71] So instructed, Eisenstein made architecture one of his major cinematic protagonists by filming its role in narrative sequences, which Alfredson does as well in *Tinker Tailor Soldier Spy*.

Architectural Protagonists in *Tinker Tailor Soldier Spy*

For a description of the drama of le Carré's spy story, David Denby's brief synopsis is adequate: "In 'Tinker,' le Carré tells us very little about how treason begins, but he creates a fictional account of how it might be shut down. As all the world knows, the meek-mannered cuckold George Smiley, roused from retirement and disgrace, uncovers a mole in MI-6. (the Circus) by setting traps so intricate that only a spy could fall into them (funny, in its way)."[72] Alfredson's film narrative manages that aspect of the plot well. Quite apart from the specifics of the narrative drama, however, is the way buildings, especially MI-6's headquarters, serve as protagonists. They are among the most significant "event spaces" in the film, which not surprisingly accords well with Tschumi's concept of event space because Tschumi's perspective on architecture as event space was inspired by his attention to cinema.[73]

While the MI-6 building is the main architectural protagonist, several other buildings participate in the plot as well: two homes (those belonging to Control (the head of MI-6) and Smiley), a safe house, a sequestered space of brutal interrogation, and a hotel room. In the novel version of the story, the MI-6 building, which houses "the Circus," is described as located in London's West End above a nondescript shop near the corner of Shaftesbury Avenue and Charing Cross Road. Thereafter, the story is dominated by its character-operatives, whose action trajectories are delivered in nonlinear sets of flashbacks, with the story beginning well after Control has died, leaving Smiley with the task of finding the mole spying on behalf of Russia.

In contrast, Alfredson's film version, with its camera continually recording images of buildings and their interior details and moments of use, has architecture functioning as protagonists along with the operatives. Openings and closings dominate the building shots, but the very first opening is a door to Control's (John Hurt) home, which is ambiguously both a residence and a workplace. The operative Jim Prideaux (Mark Strong) is ushered into the study, which is used in this moment as a space outside of MI-6 headquarters to keep the meeting and conversation secret from other operatives because the summons to Prideaux (who is being sent to Budapest) is connected with Control's attempt to find the mole that is allegedly located at a high level within "the Circus."

During this encounter, as in the rest of the film's interpersonal moments, the camera pays at least as much attention to buildings as it does to people. Moreover, the bodies-buildings relationship is edited with a dual rhythm, making use of what Noël Burch refers to as two kinds of cinematic space: "To understand cinematic space, it may prove useful to consider it as in fact consisting of *two different kinds of space:* that included within the frame and that outside the frame . . . [where] screen space can be defined very simply as including everything perceived on the screen by the eye."[74] Off screen, space is registered when, for example, "a character reaches it by going out a door, going around a street corner, disappearing behind a pillar or behind another person, or performing some similar act. The outer limit of this . . . segment of space is just beyond the horizon."[75]

The on-screen–off-screen dynamic to which Burch refers is enacted within the film's buildings, often when characters pair off and take leave of other colleagues to have private conversations. At the MI-6 building, those seeking privacy tend to move to the roof, a venue that contrasts with the building's conference room, where the entire group of high-level operatives meet. To convey the way the different rooms work, the shots of collective and paired conversations are taken from distances that reveal the structural partitioning that enables the different conversational events. Ultimately, if we heed the rhythms of the cinematic montage, we are apprised of the connections among the important events spaces: Control's and Smiley's (Gary Oldman) homes, the safe house in which the conspirators belonging to a group known as "Witchcraft" meet, the sequestered space of incarceration and torture where Prideaux is interrogated after being captured by Soviet operatives, the hotel room that Smiley and his associate Peter Giulam set up to work on finding the mole, and the parliamentary office of Oliver Lacon (Simon McBurney), the vice-minister in charge of intelligence, whom Smiley keeps apprised of the investigation.

The other and doubtless more significant architectural exploration involves lingering, long takes of the opening and closing of portals in the MI-6 building and tracking shots of the movements of personnel and files, which as a whole testify to the interactions of bodies, buildings, and intelligence materials that constitute the structures and dynamics of interaction among them, shaped by the building's partitions and moving parts. Those shots display the role of the architecture of everyday intelligence work (the roles of structure and temporal punctuations in the event space of the MI-6 building). That the aim is to show an architecture of hypersecurity is in evidence early in the film; as the credits are run, the camera lingers on a metal fence topped by sharp spikes around it, along with barbed wire on top, as Smiley and Control leave the building and are seen through a metal grating, and are then shown passing through a turnstile.

Figure 3.3 Briefcase in dumb waiter.

To show the parallel security attached to intelligence materials, there is a cut back to the building as the camera follows a briefcase bulging with papers being placed in a dumb waiter, shown closing, descending, and then reopening in the basement where the papers are to be secured (see figure 3.3). Ultimately, the film version of *Tinker Tailor Soldier Spy*, with its image commentary, discloses what the novel version, with its emphasis on human protagonists, neglects—the architectural agency of the event spaces involved in the macro- and micropolitics of the British intelligence operations during the Cold War.

Re- and Transfigurations of Event Spaces: The Micropolitics of Resistance

Railings: Welcoming Risk

I begin with a simple architectural object, the railing, whose design aim is safety. Its purpose is risk prevention, specifically to prevent falls as people ascend and descend staircases. While the foot traffic that takes advantage of this feature is the daily flow of bodies headed up, down, and past the railing-equipped staircases, there is a counterflow that, rather than moving past those installations, engages in their repetitive use. It is a flow of skateboarders transfiguring the stairways into a different kind of event space as they mount the railings on their skateboards, slide down to perfect an acrobatic leap, and continually re-ascend to repeat the performance. They use the railings for something that is the reverse of their design purpose, to heighten risk. And insofar as the performances involve a gathering of skateboarders, they reveal an "underlying cooperate ethos in [their] repeat performances of the stunt for one another in skateboard parks or on stair railings." Using the architectural feature to engage in something other than more familiar mainstream security-oriented activities, they perform a "precarious dance" and a "derivative sociality."[76] It is a ludic politics that functions "[b]eyond the telos of cognitive decision-making that drives collective action toward the norms of perfectible decision-making machinery [and] . . . opens what can be done together that elicits a visceral response [and assembles a temporary community of sense] . . . that takes in excess and yields a moment of joy."[77]

Hotels: Repartitioning Space

There are different yields from the trans- and refigurations of the built environment in more complex structures. They tend to involve a more elaborate politics of resistance than the extraction of pleasure associated with risky skateboarding moves. To approach that more elaborate politics, I turn first to hotels because they provide an opportunity for assessing both macro- and micropolitical uses. The former is best understood as "hotel geopolitics," which includes the symbolic and material effects of the spread of U.S.-based as well as other hotel chains worldwide. The development of the Hilton Hotel franchise, for example, was conceived in part as a Cold War project, an anticommunist statement made explicit in remarks by Conrad Hilton: "We feel that what we are saying about liberty, about communism, about happiness, that we as a nation . . . mean these hotels as a challenge . . . to the way of life prescribed by the communist world."[78] In addition to their power-projecting discursive participation in geopolitical contention, international hotels have been sites for housing diplomatic delegations, which have attracted high levels of surveillance by intelligence agencies (e.g., "a system of surveillance code-named 'Royal Concierge' by the British secret service)[79] and of warfare (for example, when Beirut's Holiday Inn "became a strategic base for armed militias to target the city below").[80]

In contrast with "hotel geopolitics" is the micropolitics of hotel architecture, which becomes comprehensible when one heeds the disparate flows of bodies into and around hotel space—the surrounding public, the tourists booking rooms, and the hotel's service personnel. The way hotels spatially manage those flows is summarized well by Sara Fregonese and Adam Ramadan:

> The conditional relation of hospitality is manifested within and without the hotel, and represents *the* defining characteristic of hotel space . . . guests are screened, controlled and charged and welcomed into certain spaces: public areas like the entrance hall, reception corridors, elevators, restaurants, and private areas like guest rooms and function rooms. At the same time guests are restricted from accessing other spaces such as service areas [and] the hotel must . . . maintain a controlled openness to the outside—to the potential customer—while being able to screen, monitor and subtly control those who enter [because] the open door allows the outside inside.[81]

The details of that spatial management is a major feature of the dramatic narrative in Stephen Frears's feature film *Dirty Pretty Things* (2002), which turns its primary architectural protagonist, London's fictional Baltic Hotel, into a complex event space in which, as the film narrative proceeds, it is transfigured from a space of control and coercion to one of empowerment. Because the camera lingers on London's buildings while following the fates of its characters, the film is among other things a story of bodies and buildings. The film drama opens and closes at one of London's Heathrow International Airport's terminals, where at the outset of the film, Okwe (Chiwetel Ejiofor), a Nigerian refugee and medical doctor (working illegally without a valid passport or visa), is soliciting passengers for the cab he drives during the day, while in the conclusion is there to see off his friend Senay (Audrey Tautou), a Turkish refugee, as she departs for the United States.

The other important buildings in the film—aside from the Baltic Hotel, where Okwe works as a night clerk and Senay (early in the film) works as a maid—are Okwe's cab company (run by a Caribbean immigrant), a morgue, where Okwe's friend Guo (Benedict Wong) works, an apartment which he shares with Senay (they use it in separate shifts), a sewing sweatshop where Senay is sexually exploited later in the film, and a hospital, where Okwe sneaks in disguised as a janitor in order to steal medicines, first to help refugees without access to health care and later to get them for an operation at the end of the film (in order to participate in the hotel manager's [Sergi López] illegal organ harvesting business, which he runs in the hotel at night).

The drama's major issue begins when Okwe discovers a human heart clogging one of the hotel toilets. Because of his illegal status, he cannot do anything about his discovery (as his friend Guo explains: "Okwe, you are nothing, you have nothing. . . . just help the people you can"). Once

Okwe's medical background is discovered by Senior Juan (the hotel manager), he and Senay are offered illegal passports (one of Senior Juan's side businesses) in exchange for Okwe's medical service as an organ harvester. Although Okwe initially refuses, he changes his mind when he discovers that Senay is about to exchange a kidney for a passport. Instead of harvesting Senay's kidney, however, he drugs and extracts Senior Juan's kidney, delivers it to a waiting driver in the hotel basement, collects the fee, and along with Senay is driven to Heathrow Airport by Guo, where he sees Senay off to the United States with her illegal passport and then calls Nigeria to tell his young daughter he is coming home.

As a drama, the film is about a significant political event, one in which two disempowered refuges (with the help of a group of marginal people: a prostitute who works in the hotel at night, a doorman from somewhere in Eastern Europe, and a Chinese immigrant who works in a morgue) are transfigured from victims into political subjects, forging a temporary oppositional community of sense, which acts effectively to overcome a precarious situation.

I want to focus, however, on the way the Baltic Hotel, as the primary event space in the film, becomes a major protagonist, affording the opportunity for the power transfiguration featured in the drama. Although the camera follows the characters during their fraught exchanges with Senior Juan and the desperate tactics through which they barely avoid two immigration agents who continually threaten them, it also foregrounds the Baltic Hotel. There are many framing shots of it from outside and many framing and tracking shots within that explore its internal partitions, which separate its guest and service areas. Throughout the film, the footage of the hotel emphasizes the way it manages the boundaries between hospitality and security. Recalling Fregonese and Ramadan's earlier description about the separation between guest and service areas, the difference between the guest and service areas in the film is color-coded. The guest areas appear in bright red and gold colors while the service areas, the basement where the workers' lockers are and the garage where deliveries are made, are seen through a more subdued blue and green filtering (see figures 3.4 and 3.5).

As for how the largely immigrant hotel staff appears: "Hotel workers are treated as unseen objects of the multiple desires and fantasies of managers, clients, and co-workers."[82] Notably, the *way* they are "unseen" is owed in part to the hotel's social positioning. In contrast with the hotel's guests, whose invisibility (as Siegfried Kracauer famously puts it) is a matter of controlled impression—"The . . . hotel lobby . . . allows the indi-

Figures 3.4. + 3.5 Baltic Hotel basement and Baltic Hotel lobby.

Figure 3.6 Baltic Hotel garage.

vidual to disappear behind the peripheral equality of social masks"[83]—the invisibility of the hotel's immigrant workers is a matter of both their inability to rise above the normative standards of social recognition and the spatio-temporal partitioning of the hotel's spaces.

Temporality is also crucial to the hotel as protagonist. What goes on in the Baltic Hotel is dramatically different at night than during the day. One difference is a common aspect of hotel experiences; a sex worker, Juliette (Sophie Okonedo), meets her clients there at night and, as she puts it in a conversation with Okwe, she "doesn't exist" (she is not officially present). Dramatically different with respect to the hotel-as-event-space is Senior Juan's organ harvesting business, which goes on in otherwise-vacant rooms at night. After Okwe and his team reverse the power situation and harvest Senior Juan's kidney, a telling follow-up scene takes place: Okwe, accompanied by his operating team, descends to the dark, underground parking garage, where they hand over the kidney, packed in ice in a box. A well-dressed white Englishman accepts it and wonders aloud who they are. Having expected Senior Juan to make the delivery, he asks, "How come I've never seen you before?" Okwe responds, "Because we are the people you do not see. We clean your room, iron your clothes, and suck your cocks" (see figure 3.6).

As it turned out, their invisibility, owed in part to architectural partitioning, has been a primary resource, along with the solidarity they have forged. Using their lack of social recognition and the ways in which the built environment has afforded "transitory spatial zones" throughout the city and hidden-from-view areas within the hotel to meet and plan, they are able to evade Senior Juan's coercive power. Ultimately, their transfiguration of a space of hospitality, which the Baltic Hotel features during the day, is a micropolitical event in which the hotel-as-event-space is reconfigured. As I described it in an earlier reading of the film:

> By reorienting the room [where Okwe operates on Senior Juan] along with other spaces throughout the Baltic . . . in order to mount a political challenge to the hotel's dirty business. . . . Okwe and friends repartition the hotel, turning it from a place of business (whether welcoming touristic bodies or exploiting those of refugee/immigrants) into a space of political engagement . . . [a] repartitioning [that encourages] . . . a rethinking of the presupposed organisation of political space.[84]

Apartments: Queering the Building

Queer theory is not only about politicizing sexual orientation but also about resistance to institutionalized norms in general. With respect to the latter, "queer" tends to be used "as a verb, as action within . . . networks of norms [and thus] . . . to name queer as an action implicates us in a search for oral and political agency that resistance is supposed to name."[85] That understood, the Wachowski Brothers' film *Bound* (1996) queers the *film noir* genre (and the building in which the action takes place) by having its main female protagonists refigure the space of an apartment building, enacting a "queering of architecture" and at the same time disclosing the "fluidity of various layers of identity" that tend to be repressed.[86]

Like traditional *film noir* crime stories, *Bound* features a *femme fatale* whose body and habits are objects of camera scrutiny. And also like the traditional *femme fatale*, the protagonist Violet's (Jennifer Tilly) heterosexual moments are not about erotic investment but are a cover for a temporal investment, a deferral to fool a gullible male, Caesar (Joe Pantoliano), a mafia money launderer with whom she shares an apartment where she exchanges sexual favors for room and board with him and his associates (while hatching an escape plan). In this respect, she bears comparison with the traditional *film noir femme fatale*, who is an "unabashedly independent and ruthlessly ambitious [woman] using her seductive charms and her intelligence to liberate herself from the imprisonment of an unfulfilling marriage, gaining power over the *noir* hero by nourishing his sexual fantasies [while] her own interest is only superficially erotic."[87]

The film's drama begins when a lesbian ex-con, Corky (Gina Gershon), moves into the apartment next door as a temporary hire with the task of refurbishing the apartment. Violet, who first spies her when they share a brief moment of public space (the building's elevator), is immediately attracted to her and conspires to initiate erotic encounters, which begin in Violet's apartment and are later repeated in Corky's. Their erotic connection begins when Violet invites Corky to her apartment to help find a ring, which she has (purposely) lost down a sink drain. As the two begin touching and then groping, with Corky in control in this initial encounter (Violet later becomes the aggressor), a telling event takes place.

They abruptly separate as Caesar enters the apartment. On seeing Corky, who looks very masculine (in leather and jeans, in contrast with the very feminine and [hetero-]sexily attired Violet), he shouts, "What's this; what the fuck is this." After a closer look, he recognizes Corky as a lesbian and excuses his outburst, saying, "It's fuckn' dark in here." Caesar's remark has a double resonance; in addition to referring to "the *film noir* genre, it reflects the blindness in his perception of Violet. He is unable to imagine a woman who dresses in outfits with heterosexual appeal and acts seductively toward men as one who is actually attracted to women. With respect to Violet's dominant persona, Caesar is always in the dark.

A similar perceptual issue afflicts Corky's view of Violet. Shortly after their erotic connection begins, Corky expresses contempt and jealousy about Violet "having sex with men." Violet responds that she isn't having sex with men, to which Corky responds, "I hear you, thin walls, remember?" Violet replies, "That wasn't sex." "What the fuck was it?" asks Corky. "Work," replies Violet. Apart from what Violet's response reveals about the film's pedagogy about the plasticities of identity (especially Violet's mobile subjectivity), the role of the wall evoked in the conversation is central to how the film thinks. From the very outset, architectural features create the conditions of possibility for the way the characters affect and connect with each other. A closet is the focus in the very first scene, as well as in a later one, when a bound Corky is thrown into the closet by Caesar after he discovers the women's plot to rob the mafia and have Caesar blamed for the missing money. Like the wall that separates Violet and Corky's apartments, however, the closet does double duty. It represents the initial sequestering of Violet's lesbian identity.

Another important architectural scene is shot in the elevator, where Corky rides up with Caesar and Violet and the women exchange their first glances (a seductive look by Violet and a curious one by Corky). Although that scene initiates the complexities of the triad, it is clear the elevator plays a role; it's a public access space that has created the possibility for the first encounter. And significantly, included in that scene is an overhead

Figure 3.7 *Bound* elevator scene.

shot of the three bodies, showing the structural triad as a preview for the dramatic interpersonal perceptions and actions to follow (see figure 3.7).

However, the dramatic narrative in which Violet ultimately grabs Caesar's gun and shoots him, freeing the women for their escape with the money, doesn't capture what I have suggested as "the film's most significant, micropolitical aspects,"[88] the primary one being the wall separating the two apartments. The film's camera work brings the role of the building's partitions into focus on many occasions with many long takes of the wall shown from Corky's side (see figure 3.8).

Crucially, there are many shots panning the technologies that make the wall permeable, for example plumbing pipes and phone lines, along with the wall's thinness and thus permeability to voices heard through it. Henri Lefebvre has captured the significance of the technologies that make buildings permeable: "One might almost see it [the building] as the epitome of immovability, with its concrete and rigid outlines. . . . Now a critical analysis would doubtless destroy the appearance of solidity . . . stripping it as it were of its concrete slabs and its thin non-load-bearing walls, which are really glorified screens . . . [the building] would emerge as permeated in every direction by streams of energy which run in and out of it by every imaginable route: water, gas, electricity, telephone lines."[89]

Certainly, the camera is telling us that the apartment building has shaped the events that take place within it. Beyond that, however, is the way the women's plot unfolds. Violet and Corky take advantage of the

Figure 3.8
Corky by the wall.

wall's permeability to transfigure the building's event space from one of money laundering (disguised as a form of domesticity) to one of liberation, as Violet's amorous-life-as-business becomes amorous-life-as-mutual trust, that is, to an affective and action-enabled way of being in common (at one point, Corky has explained that such a dangerous plot requires even more trust than does an erotic relationship). Edified by the transfigurations in both *Dirty Pretty Things* and *Bound*, I underscore the politics of architectural re- and transfiguration in what follows as I analyze another drama in which a wall is prominent and return to the issue of architectural violence in a geopolitical venue (the Israel-Palestine border area), where architecture-as-violence is opposed by an architecture of resistance.

A Violent Event Space

The Violent Architectures of Occupation and Destruction

The controversies surrounding architecture in the long-running Israeli-Palestinian conflict have asserted themselves within clashing cartographic histories, geopolitical and sacred. The crux of that clash became apparent in September 1996 when a violent conflict ensued after the Israeli prime minister, Benyamin Netanyahu, opened a new gate to the ancient tunnel that connected the Israeli sector by the Western Wall and passed under the al-Aqsa Mosque and the Muslim sector of the city. Reviewing that conflict and looking into the interpretive practices through which architecture has been presumed to present itself as political reality, Daniel B. Monk analyzes what he refers to as "the career of architecture in the prehistory of the present conflict" (while at the same time questioning the "normative presentations of architecture's political self-certainty").[90] Certainly, monumental architecture is central to the conflicting allegiances in the region, inclining Monk to characterize the Israeli occupation as aesthetic and to investigate the (interpretation-mediated) career of architecture that has been continually featured in accounts of the conflict, even though a reliance on such concrete appearances can be misleading.

Although architecture remains an active force in the conflict, it now has a different modality and an undeniably violent effect. The architectural history that postdates the "career" to which Monk refers involves a dialectic of violence featuring encounters between the forces of occupation and securitization mounted by the Israeli military (the IDF) and the counterforce of Palestinian resistance. Quite apart from the loosely integrated violent tactics of various Palestinian commando forces, a resistance involving spatio-temporal ingenuity has been underway since the period of Israel's Separation Wall, whose construction was completed in 2006. The wall and a series of checkpoints radically partition Palestinian territories structurally and temporally, imposing difficult travel restrictions within Palestinian territories, as well as between them and Israel. That violent architectural imposition has had the effect of rigidifying what had for decades been a "frontier" with a more "elastic morphology."[91]

Israel's passive geometry of separation—the wall and check points—has been supplemented with a more active geometry, a set of search-and-destroy tactics, which Eyal Weizman describes elaborately (after a set of ethnographic interviews with Israeli forces). For example, examining the 2002 Israeli attack on the West Bank City of Nablus, he learns from the Israeli Commander, Aviv Kochavi, that the army's tactics involved an "inverse geometry . . . defined as the reorganization of the urban syntax by means of a series of micro-tactical actions [in which] soldiers avoided the streets, roads, alleys and courtyards that define the logic of movement through the city, as well as the external doors, internal stairwells and windows that constitute the order of buildings; rather they were punching holes through party walls, ceilings and floors, and moving across them through 2100 meter pathways of domestic interior hollowed out of the dense and contiguous city fabric."[92] Given the overwhelmingly destructive capacity of the Israeli air force, along with the destructive tactics of the military on the ground, the armed Palestinian resistance has been forced underground, so much so that much of the economy of Gaza has resulted from tunnel building by private contractors.[93]

Architecture of Resistance

An encounter of cartographies characterizes the way Palestinians regain mobility to make life livable in response to the architectural violence they face. One map, drawn and used by the IDF, is the one that has ordered the Israeli strategies of isolation, incursion, and destruction on the ground and from the air. The Palestinian cartographic response is both structural and temporal. Structurally, it has sought to restore some of the elasticity that the wall and system of checkpoints has effaced. As the Palestinian architect Yara Sharif puts it, the design problem involves the creation of a more "elastic space born from the will to connect—a space of resistance that keeps on changing with the . . . interventions [that] respond to [an imposed] instability through the tactics of an emergent architecture, which in its nature, might seem ephemeral, yet is quick in its effects."[94]

Employing Henri Lefebvre's concept of "counter spaces," Sharif refers to the need to "step above and underneath the exhausted surface of Palestine . . . [to evade the way Israel is] . . . eating away slowly and quietly at the Palestinian landscape."[95] She points out that as the Occupation's checkpoints divide Palestinians from each other, the Palestinians refigure the spaces around them; they are "transformed by the everyday behaviour to try to create spaces of possibility. . . . Playing with lines on the map has created new lines. Palestine is no longer the city and the village—it is also the in-between, the dead spaces and the margins, in which people perform wait, remember and resist. It's the new route that its people create, the tunnels we dig under the wall and the sewage pipes we walk through every day."[96]

Through such countermapping and refiguring, Palestine becomes a resistant event space as (in Sharif's terms) "'non-places' [are] being made in everyday life into real places."[97] Sharif thus effectively conveys the way Palestinians have met the architecture of occupation with a counterarchitecture, which involves (among other things) redesigns that create possibilities of mobility that the Separation Wall and checkpoints stymie. The countering of the Israeli-controlled opening and closing of border gates—open at 7:00 am and closed at 7 pm[98]—requires temporal design strategies. For example, unable to move effectively within the "complicated lines" that define the spatio-temporal rhythms of the occupation, young Palestinians looking for job opportunities within Israel have to use the darkness and various "hidden spaces," which they refer to as "rabbit holes." Meeting "usually at two or three o'clock in the morning [groups of young men] gather at agreed points and sneak through together. . . . to reach the other side of the wall."[99] Ultimately, through such tactics (which as Michel de Certeau famously points out, involves the use of time by people who cannot control space),[100] Palestinians activate "micro-space events" to transform the border areas into an alternative event space: "Playing with Israel's imposed borderlines has thus created further lines on the map. By putting together . . . micro-scale events, Palestine is reshaping the dead spaces and urban voids in which people wait, remember and resist. The intensification of the borderlines does not leave any alternative but to occupy the margins, which in turn creates a new spatial quality and intensity to the 'dark points' on the map."[101]

Conclusion: Animating the Micro-Events of Resistance: Hany Abu-Assad's *Omar*

Recalling Eisenstein's remark that cinema can turn a passive setting into a major agent of the plot, I turn to Hany Abu-Assad's film *Omar* (2013), in which the Separation Wall is one of the film's primary agents/protagonists. Moreover, through the way the film interarticulates action and setting, as it mobilizes an aesthetic subject involved in the microevents to which Sharif refers, we can better appreciate her descriptions of the dynamics of architectural resistance (which are enacted by Abu-Assad's eponymous protagonist, Omar). Omar (Adam Bakri) is part of the uprooted world that the Occupation has created, a subject effectively exiled in his own homeland, living in a space of space-punctuating barriers—mainly the Separation Wall and a series of checkpoints—that impede his relationships with his fiancée, Nadia, his friends, and his fellow political activists.

The drama is punctuated several times by its paradigmatic scenes of Omar repeatedly scaling of the Separation Wall. Those moments, along with one in which he is harassed and brutalized by Israeli soldiers at a checkpoint, reflect the collective Palestinian experience of the architecture of occupation; "The Wall," as Ana Cristina Mendes points out, "is presented in *Omar*, as the ultimate visual expression of domination, a dynamic that plays itself out continually in a context of asymmetric power dynamics of an unequal access to visual rights . . . a site of a continuing coloniality of power [but also] . . . of a playful vacillation between revealing and concealing and hence the site of adaptive ambivalence and radical potentiality."[102] Mobilizing its primary aesthetic subject, who must cope with the barriers to movement, *Omar* (which is part of a developing po-

Figure 3.9 Omar and the wall.

litically oriented "Palestinian national cinema") discloses a "structure of feeling . . . a collective ontology of Palestinians which is one of constant negotiation of the tension(s) between mobility and immobility."[103]

The opening scene suggests the radical potentiality. While the first image shows Omar at the wall in shadow, seemingly dwarfed by its enormity (see figure 3.9), he is later shown rapidly scaling it, hand over hand, as he uses a rope to pull himself over it with impressive athleticism. When he is seen climbing over the top, a siren goes off and shots are fired as he descends on the other side and runs through alleys and crooked streets toward his fiancée's house.

By the end of the film, however, an exhausted Omar, who has been imprisoned, turned into an informant by the tactics of the Israeli military, separated from his fiancée, and spurned by his former friends, is barely able to climb the wall. Only after an elderly citizen shouts encouragement and gives him a boost is he able to slowly make the ascent. That moment of Palestinian solidarity is what seems to remain of collective cohesion, given the way the architecture of occupation has sundered the Palestinian life world.

To return to Weizman's critical practice of forensic architecture, aimed at disseminating evidence of war crimes in urban contexts, it is clear that what the diminution of Omar's efficacy (the shift that the film shows of his transformation from a healthy, exhilarated, and hopeful body to an exhausted one) is a result of the Occupation, which constitutes a continuing war crime, "produced," as Weizman puts it, "by a multiplicity of military agents using a network of different technologies and apparatuses, run by political, institutional and administrative logics."[104] Although the architecture of resistance that Sharif describes shows how Palestinians manage a degree of mobility in the face of the territorial rigidities and separations that the Occupation imposes, critical investigations and testimony from outside of the culture of the Occupation is an essential political response. That is the critical move involved in Weizman's practice of forensic architecture. In response to the technologies of the Occupation, which sequester and immobilize people and impede the sharing of information and access, are the techniques of forensics, which "make objects reveal information by subjecting them to additional force. To be analyzed, structures often have to be cut apart. . . . [forensics is thus] the art of object-interrogation, the inquisitions of things and buildings."[105]

Like Abu-Assad's film, forensic architecture turns what appears to be materialized stasis into a dynamic and dialectic of force relations. Like the film, it helps to construct an oppositional (global) community of sense by providing some of the resources necessary for witnessing and judging. To summarize the relationship between architecture-as-event-space and forensic architecture: what constitutes an "event" is subject to durational contestation. The forensic interventions in Weizman et al.'s forensic architectural practice extend event space with counterinvestigations, involving "counterforensics"[106] that challenge official accounts. The "events" in event spaces are continually susceptible to forensic inventions that turn what political and policing officials portray as routine legal interventions into human rights violations. Although the current Israel-Palestine encounter involves a force of arms, an architectural dialectic is very much at the center of the conflict.

CH.AP.TER FOU.R

IMAGE PUNCTUATIONS: FROM THE PHOTOGRAPHIC TO THE CINEMATIC

Photographic Punctuation

In his famous essay on the photographic image, André Bazin writes, "photography . . . embalms time."[1] Doubtless he selects that figuration because he viewed "the plastic arts ontologically . . . as a defense against [the death-assuring] passage of time." Photographs "snatch" [death] from the flow of time, to stow it away neatly . . . in the hold of life."[2] In contrast with how photography punctuates time by arresting it, cinema as Bazin conceives it overcomes photographic punctuation. Rather than halting duration, "cinema . . . no longer content to preserve the object, enshrouded as it were in an instant . . . delivers baroque art from its convulsive catalepsy. . . . [so that] . . . the image of things is likewise the image of their duration."[3]

Bazin also lends photography an epistemological punctuation because of the way it is situated temporarily with respect to other arts. As an "event in the history of the plastic arts," he writes, it has "freed Western painting, once and for all with its obsession with realism [for]. . . . Only when form ceases to have any imitative value can it be swallowed up in color. . . . So the person of Cézanne, once more regains possession of the canvass."[4] I turn to color punctuation—in the work of Cézanne, among others—later in this chapter. First, I want to question the radical distinction that Bazin makes between the painter's and photographer's "hand," with which he implies that photography is wholly mimetic, an art in which "nature" is the "justification."[5]

For that purpose, I turn to Teju Cole's commentary on the photography of the South African Santu Mofokeng, whose images are marked by his compositional and stylistic work. They abound in "deep shadow and blur"—for example, an unclear image of body parts on a train, captioned "The Drumming, Johannesburg-Soweto Line form Train Church, 1986" (see figure 4.1)[6]—and in unusual spatial composition (for example, a funeral scene shot from a great distance with a "seemingly fallow space" between the photographer and his subject [figure 4.2]).

Cole suggests that the details of the funeral procession, "a hearse and a crowd of marchers" along with "a nearby bus, behind which are two

Figure 4.1 Soweto line image.

women, who might be walking slowly or trying to catch up with the main party, seem to have less significance than what is around them . . . the great expanse of the landscape [so that] the photo comes to feel less like an image of a funeral than an image of this space."[7] He goes on to identify Mofokeng's "ability to evoke a space" in which "the main event is almost too small to be seen." Conveyed by Mofokeng's "hand," creating a blur by "shooting at a low shutter speed, without a flash or a tripod" and composing a "spaciousness" that renders the details difficult to apprehend, is an "intimacy with this . . . world . . . a world that isn't insubstantial but that is elusive to the uninitiated or to outsiders."[8]

As Cole discerns, Mofokeng's photographic practice has political resonances. In the context of the apartheid world in which his art is fashioned: " . . . the harsh interrogative light of an unjust political reality," the "dreamlike . . . effect of Mofokeng's photographic compositions . . . offers . . . knowledge of a more secret sort."[9] Contrasting shadows and blurs to that "harsh interrogative light," Mofokeng achieves his political effect by rendering things difficult to apprehend (and his "hand" continues its interventionist role in the darkroom, shaping moods and affects after the images are recorded). I want to pursue the Mofokeng event—his

Figure 4.2
Funeral procession.

politically attuned photographic intervention into "South Africa's historiography"[10]—a bit further because it provides a threshold for much of the analysis to follow.

Mofokeng's photographic method is closely linked to its political impetus. As Patricia Hayes points out, "while his Afrapix [an anti-apartheid documentary photography collective] colleagues were chasing police and protests and producing sharp realist images of unassailable clarity for local and international consumption, Santu Mofokeng was, in his own phrase, 'chasing shadows' [he was experimenting with] effects of a fractured viewpoint, arising specifically in Africa [in order to] offer some possibilities for thinking about photography."[11] The political effect of such a methodological shift, which "opens up uncertainties and emphasizes different things,"[12] is captured in part by Kaja Silverman's suggestion that such "aesthetic work," which has the effect of displacing us from the geometrical point (i.e., the center), allows us "to see in ways not dictated in advance by the dominant fiction,"[13] and *apropos* of the political concern animating Mofokeng's method, alerts us to "other people's memories."[14]

To achieve that alert, Mofokeng had to resist the "figurative givens" and "psychic clichés" of the global image economy.[15] After exploring and rejecting what he called a "politics of representation"[16] that portrayed South Africa's black assemblage only in terms of their victimization, he strove for "an alternative representation of black life" by showing everyday scenes of "normal" life, predicated on a "counter narrative to the dominant images of townships as places of violent struggle."[17] Moreover, rather than pandering to a global audience of voyeurs of the violence associated with South Africa's apartheid struggle, Mofokeng's ideal viewers are township dwellers. He constructs scenes designed to be understandable to a black South African community of sense. As astute commentators (Cole, among others) have discerned, the form Mofokeng has chosen constitutes the political sensibility his images convey. In constructing scenes that are blurry and occasionally shrouded in smoke or mist, Mofokeng deliberately sought to "occlude rather than expose" the black South African life world because for him the violence of apartheid existed not in what immediately meets the eye. Rather, as he states, "The violence is in the knowing" of those who have been oppressed; they are his intended viewers.[18]

Because there are ambiguities, distortions, and disturbances in what "immediately meets the eye"—the punctuations in Mofokeng's images (the parts of bodies on a train, seen unclearly, and the "fallow" space in his funeral image)—I want to elaborate their implications by turning to an insight provided by the art historian Georges Didi-Huberman, who in an analysis of Vermeer's paintings, distinguishes a "detail," which allows for "*seeing* well something that is hidden," from a "patch," "a part of a painting which ostensibly interrupts . . . the continuity of the representational system of the picture," and "exists only as a result of not seeing well."[19] As my chapter progresses, I connect such *aporias* of vision, owed to disturbances of representation, to a micropolitics of sense, to the way such disruptions of transparency create the openings for persons and collectives (e.g., Mofokeng's township dwellers) to (re)negotiate the meanings of politically relevant experience as they recognize themselves and their relationships in new ways. To launch that analysis, I visit the conceptual legacy that shapes Didi-Huberman's reading of Vermeer's canvasses, developed in Roland Barthes's meditations on photography.

Barthes's Punctums

Much of the conceptual practice with which Didi-Huberman distinguishes patches from details is owed to Roland Barthes's oft-cited distinction (which I mention in the Introduction) between a photograph's *studium* and its *punctum*. Briefly, a photograph's *studium* is the content that one grasps as a result of being familiar with the context of its referents, for example, a well-known historical scene that the viewer recognizes by dint of her/his familiarity with the image's historical connotations. In contrast is what Barthes refers to as "the second element," which "will break (or punctuate) the *studium*. . . . it is this element which arises from the scene, shoots out of it like an arrow, and pierces me. . . . This second element, which will disturb the *studium* I shall therefore call the *punctum;* for *punctum* is also: sting, speck, cut, little hole."[20]

In maintaining the distinction between the two elements, Barthes juxtaposes the photographer's representational intention (the photograph's *studium*), with which the viewer is encouraged to enter into a "harmony," and the non- or extra-representational elements that Didi-Huberman figures with disharmonizing temporal tropes—for example, likening a painting's patch to Barthes's *punctum* by suggesting that it creates a "catastrophic commotion in present time" and noting that the *punctum* operates as a "symptom of time."[21] With such temporal references, Didi-Huberman captures the implicit durational aspect of photographic images central to Barthes's treatment of the photographic aesthetic. For Barthes, "time . . . functions as a punctum."[22]

Walter Benjamin uses a different expression for a similar effect. He refers to the way the viewer of the photograph "feels an irresistible compulsion to look for the tiny spark of chance of the here and now."[23] Similarly, the photographic image invariably provoked Barthes to address his own duration, the "question why is it that I am alive here and now,"[24] and what might succeed the here and now: "Each photograph always contains this imperious sign of my future death."[25] Thus the concept of the *punctum*, which Barthes conceives as an element that evokes death-contemplating time, resonates with Bazin's death-preoccupied ontological approach to the photographic image.

While the temporal *punctum* that shoots out of [the photograph] like an arrow and "pierces" Barthes is highly personal, artists who have a hand in creating images with the two elements—referential and extrareferential—often achieve effects with the potential to impact trans-individual, collective communities of sense, for example, Mofokeng's punctums, which evoke the trauma of the historical period of apartheid that haunts the postapartheid present for many South Africans.[26]

In what follows, I explore those transindividual effects, turning to other artistic genres to elaborate their political resonances. As I do so, I offer a broad and multigenre view of the punctum effect by treating it as punctuation that holds in tension two contrasting effects. On the one hand, there is the arrest of the viewer/subject's process of recognition, a disruption of her/his attempt to incorporate what is seen into something expected-to-be-seen. On the other hand is the opening created by such a disruption—a space for oppositional communities of sense to achieve consolidation and to have their experiential world rise above the threshold of recognition so they can emerge as politically invested countercollective subjects. I begin with an example from architecture, which provides a material realization of the punctuations with which I am concerned.

Architectural Punctums

Recalling Barthes's string of synonyms for the *punctum*, which include a "cut" and "little hole," I focus in this section on the deconstructive architecture of Gordon Matta-Clark, whose work radically reorients the way a viewing subject experiences a building. During his brief working years (he died at age 35 from pancreatic cancer), Matta-Clark sought out abandoned buildings and attacked them with power tools, making cuts and holes. Regarding his architectural deconstructions as "anarchitecture,"[27] he challenged the perspectival stasis implied in modernism's functional approach to buildings. Juxtaposing his anarchitecture to "Louis Sullivan's dictum 'form follows function,'" for example, he punned, "form *fallows* function."[28]

One of the main results of Matta-Clark's anarchitectural design work (or antidesign work) is the way he turned buildings into vision machines. As his friend and occasional assistant, Ned Smyth, puts it, "Gordon would cut slits or shaped holes in the walls, leading from one room to another until you could see through the entire apartment." He liked especially to create views looking out windows "through a long horizontal cut [which] could expose the passage of the elevated subway."[29] The cuts he made—for example, the circles he carved "into the abandoned shell of a town house in the working-class section of Paris [near the] Pompidou Center"—had the effect of "creating a sense of physical and visual instability, opening up unexpected views." Thus, the cut of a "big, eye-shaped opening in the back wall of a warehouse along the West Side piers in Manhattan allow[ed] a blazing light to spill into the cavernous interior. . . . the cut out portion is suspended by chains in the warehouse space, giving a powerful impression of its weight and scale."[30]

Conceiving a critical intimacy between photography and architecture, Matta-Clark's *Splitting* project in Englewood, New Jersey, of jacking up a house until it split in the middle and then cutting through it with a chainsaw was exhibited along with a photomontage (see figure 4.3). Describing the importance of the photographic documentation "as a correlate of his physical installations,"[31] Matta-Clark spoke of the importance of seeing a project from multiple positions in order to capture the narrative process of the "piece being made. . . . What's happened is that I've become systematically interested in the way of doing photographs . . . , working with photographs and trying to overcome some of the clichés that have been developed dealing with multiple images."[32] The correlating photo documentation is important for Matta-Clark because he viewed his cut-

Figure 4.3 Gordon Matta-Clark's split house.

ting punctuations as a form of "expressive interpretation"[33] (an activist hermeneutics)—for example, "I dig a deep hole [in the basement of 112 Greene St in New York] . . . so that a person could see the actual foundations, the 'removed' spaces under the foundation, and liberate the building's enormous compressive, confining forces simply by making a hole."[34] Such holes served to disclose the latent behind the manifest.

While there is a hermeneutic dimension to Matta-Clark's anarchitecture, its aim is clearly not mere passive interpretation. Toward the end of his working life, he evoked the expression "Marxist hermeneutics" to note that his activities "combine the inwardly removed sphere of hermeneutics and interpretation with the material dialectics of a real environment."[35] The political effects of Matta-Clark's work, however, involve more than simply demonstrating "the real." A political sensibility emerges from the way he redeems what has been forgotten with his attention to seemingly minor fragments—for example, the kind of punctums that occupy Didi-Huberman's analysis—"patches of dirt and asphalt," and "streaks of color" which "draw attention to the city's forgotten corners" and thereby redistribute the saliences of the objects in the life world in ways that can redeem neglected or uncoded segments of communal attachment.[36] That redistribution accords with Didi-Huberman's previously noted analysis of the nonrepresentational aspects of artistic canvasses, to which I return with a focus on Vermeer's color-as-punctuation.

Patches of Color in the Canvasses of Vermeer

Didi-Huberman begins his commentary on Vermeer's color patches with the simple observation that "what painting shows is its material cause,"[37] making it evident that to suggest that a Vermeer scene is mere depiction is belied by how the work is made. Some art historians "give primacy to the referent,"[38] for example, Svetlana Alpers's position in a commentary on Vermeer's *View of Delft* that Delft is the cause of Vermeer's painted view of it. To challenge that position and elaborate the role of paint's nonrepresentational effects, especially the role of color patches, Didi-Huberman turns to Marcel Proust, who saw his practice as a writer as "the opposite of [merely] describing" and quotes from "the famous passage of *La prisonierre* [the captive]," which deals with Vermeer's *View of Delft*. In the passage, "Proust is concerned with *matter and layers of paint*."[39] "At last he came to the Vermeer . . . and, finally, the precious substance of the tiny patch of yellow wall. His dizziness increased; he fixed his gaze, like a child upon a yellow butterfly that it wants to catch, on the precious little patch of wall. 'That's how I ought to have written,' he said. . . . I ought to have gone over them with a few layers of colour, made my language precious in itself. . . . He repeated to himself: 'Little patch of yellow wall with a sloping roof, little patch of yellow wall.' "[40] As Didi-Huberman points out, Proust is pointing to "something very real *at work* in the painting, almost a form of dazzlement . . . an effect of paint at work not as a descriptive sign but as coloured matter."[41] Didi-Huberman goes on to elaborate other color punctuations in Vermeer's canvasses, for example, a "patch of red paint in *The Lace Maker* which unsettles representation."[42]

How can we pursue the implications for political thinking of such moments ("intrusive flashes of color")[43] in Vermeer's canvasses? Didi-Huberman provides an avenue of pursuit; he refers to "*partial intensities* in which the usual relationships between local and global elements are overturned,"[44] for example, "a burst of colour in the foreground" of Vermeer's *The Lacemaker*, which distinguishes a "zone altogether more salient than all the details to be found or looked for between the lace maker's fingers."[45] With such chromatic punctuations (often a "patch of red"), Vermeer unsettles and even "tyrannizes representation."[46] In short, color punctuation in Vermeer's canvasses renders the perception of space unstable. The "intense representational voids" which "are frequent in Vermeer's work" function very much like the cuts and holes in Matta-Clark's anarchitectural projects. They encourage reflection on the relationships between subjectivity and space by disrupting representation. The color patches are Vermeer's political analysis–enabling punctums.

Color plays a similar role in other media genres, especially cinema, to which I give extended treatment. Before turning to cinematic illustrations and their political effects, however, I want to explore the way color can express a temporality that situates and often resituates the relationship between images and subjectivity by examining one of the most exemplary colorists in the history of painting, Paul Cézanne, whose chromatic method evokes the dynamics of visual interpretation, as the modern viewing subject (which Cézanne helped to invent)[47] comes to terms with the scene.

Cézanne

The art historian/critic Meyer Schapiro describes Cézanne's nonrepresentational method concisely: "The visible world is not represented on Cézanne's canvass. It is re-created through strokes of color." Distinguishing that method from the Impressionist approach to painting, whose legacy Cézanne eschewed, Schapiro adds, "The strokes of high-keyed color, which in Impressionist paintings dissolved objects into atmosphere and sunlight, forming a crust of twinkling points, Cézanne applied to the building of solid forms."[48] Contrasting Cézanne's view of *L'Estaque* with Claude Monet's *The Beach at Sainte-Adresse*, Schapiro writes that whereas "in Monet's canvass, a peculiar diluteness or greyness prevails in all these colors," in Cézanne's "picture the large divisions of the landscape are re-enforced by tones of a great span of intensity and hue. The sea is a full blue robustly paired with orange in the foreground. . . . These great differences in intensity also suggest depth."[49] Similarly, Maurice Merleau-Ponty discerned that in Cézanne (as contrasted with Impressionists), "The object is no longer covered by reflections and lost in its relationships to the atmosphere and to other objects; it seems subtly illuminated from within. . . . the result is an impression of solidity and material substance."[50]

As is the case in Vermeer's canvasses, Cézanne's contain "patches" of color. In Cézanne's case, however, the patches are not isolated disruptions to representation. Rather than being (what Didi-Huberman calls) "catastrophic commotions," his "distinctive blocky strokes" are interconnected. His canvasses are proto-cinematic, because in addition to recovering the material depth of objects, they *modulate* the changing perspectives through which the painting can be viewed by pluralizing the painting's spatial organization: "Graduated sequences of hues, dark and light, warm and cool, situated first by regular blocky strokes, then by freer more irregular ones, become the abstract designators of position. Through color difference, otherwise known as color interval, they build the space."[51] To appreciate how *modulation* (a term Cézanne himself applied to his technique) operates, Norman Turner likens the modulating transitional moments from color to color in Cézanne's canvasses to Richard Wagner's melodic structures in which "music written in one key departs it to step into another through modulation."[52]

Just as the organization of Wagner's music involves an appeal to emotions—with "semitone progressions" (that avoid the traditional sonata form's "repeats and returns"), he develops a "chromaticism . . . with systematic modulations that greatly undermine or completely remove any sense of a secure harmonic base. . . . in other words, the harmony expresses feeling"—Cézanne assembles "little sensations" chromatically as he "marches from color to color," "swept along on the tide of feeling."[53] Thus akin to the modulations of Wagnerian music, Cézanne's color modulations register changes of salience or value. As Turner puts it, "Each change of value strides with a change of hue."[54] Crucially, the dynamism of the modulations suggests that the punctuating color strokes articulate another, more fundamental punctuation, *time* (which as I have noted is Barthes's primary photographic punctum).

Importantly, for purposes of the analysis to follow, the temporality that results from Cézanne's color modulations resonates with the temporality of the painting's reception. The filmmaker Wim Wenders, alert to that connection, as it is created in Cézanne's *Mont Sainte-Victoire* canvass (figure 4.4), says, "the painter has painted the perception of the mountain"; what he opens up is "the reflection of the condition of seeing the mountain."[55] The Cézanne effect thus involves a rhythmic encounter between the creating brush strokes and the rhythms of viewer reception. As Jonah Lehrer suggests, "Cézanne was trying to return to the start of sight. . . . The slowness of this method forces Cézanne to focus on simple things,"[56] which produces a corresponding slowness in the viewer's process of recognizing a scene. As Lehrer puts it, "The mind easily invents the form that Cézanne's paint barely insinuates. Although the Mountain is almost literally invisible—Cézanne has only implied its presence—its looming gravity anchors the painting. We don't know where the painting ends and we begin."[57] As "Cézanne's art exposes the process of seeing, . . . he forces us to see, in the same static canvass, the beginning and the end of our sight."[58]

As for how Cézanne's approach creates such an effect, Cézanne would begin a painting "as if there is no independent, closed, preexisting object, given to the painter's eye for representation, but only a multitude of successively probed sensations."[59] As a result, Cézanne's processes of *building* (Schapiro's term) the picture required a "slowness"[60] that is homologous with the dynamic through which the viewer moves from initially being affected by the scene to making sense of it, a sequence suggested by Merleau-Ponty's remark that Cézanne depicted "matter as it takes on form."[61] It is a chromatic practice in which "the experience of chromatic phantasy exceeds the forms of spatio-temporal intuition."[62]

In terms of its effects on reception, it initiates a narrative of experience that is well captured in Simon O'Sullivan's Deleuze-inspired account of the temporal dynamic of art encounters in general in which the effects produced by sensations initiated in the encounter with the artistic work constitute the "dark precursors" of the subsequent conceptual actualizations of what has been encountered.[63] That process, which Cézanne achieves with the chromatic palette of blotchy brush strokes, operates in the way some directors apply color in their films. To appreciate that intermediality as we move from the canvass to the screen, however, we have to recognize as well the temporality-effected decentering of perception in Cézanne's canvasses, which are a departure from the static spaces rendered in Impressionist works. In a passage that links Cézanne's temporal effect with Gilles Deleuze's analysis of cinema's time-images, George Heard Hamilton notes that what distinguishes Cézanne from his contemporaries' creations of "static space seen instantaneously" is his "record[ing] of the experience of continuous movement through space in time [because] his paintings change without ceasing [making him] the first modern artist to create an image of time" (see figure 4.4).[64]

The absence of a stable center in Cézanne's paintings displaces the viewing subject from a single viewing focal point and thus accords with one of Deleuze's insights about the way cinema resists the stability of perceptual centering: "cinema does *not* have subjective perception as its model because [in accord with the 'continuous movement through space and time' in a Cézanne canvas] the mobility of its centers and the variability of its framings always lead it to restore vast acentered and deframed zones."[65] That restoration operates in Cézanne's canvases as well, which

Figure 4.4 Cézanne's *Mont Sainte-Victoire.*

include not only what is immediately in front of the viewer but also "the peripheral retinal sensation simultaneously."[66]

Recognizing that effect, Rainier Maria Rilke identifies Cézanne's practice as a continual "beginning at a new center."[67] It is an effect that is especially pronounced in films by directors that employ multiple cameras instead of relying on one that deploys a perpetual master shot—for example, Robert Altman in *Nashville* (1975) in which he avoided what his editor, Sid Levin, calls "the classic style . . . the conventional use of master, medium and close-up shots." Instead, there are "three or four different master angles of the same sequence, each with a variation in camera angle."[68] In what follows, I transition from the way Cézanne's slow painting practice situates viewers and challenges the phenomenology of subjective perception to an example of "slow cinema," two of the color films of Michelangelo Antonioni, in which I note the way they effect the viewers' need for reflective reception, which requires attention to color and time sequence punctuations.

Cinematic Punctuations: Antonioni

Red Desert

The writer Peter Handke reports that he learned to see landscape by following Paul Cézanne's artistic path through *L'Estaque*, noting that Cézanne's "colors and forms alone sufficed to do [his subject's] honor";[69] "thanks to Cézanne," he writes, "I was standing amid the colors of the open country between Aix-en-Provence and the village of Le Tholonet, and that I saw even the asphalt highway as color."[70] Handke indicates as well that because Cézanne was loath to bring his color-oriented aesthetic to industrial landscapes, "When refineries sprang up around *L'Estaque*, he stopped painting there."[71]

In contrast, Antonioni was not put off by industrial landscapes. In his *Red Desert* (1964), he "painted" the film, adding color to a factory's structure and the trees and grounds nearby as well. As he reports, "I want to paint the film as one paints a canvass; I want to invent color relationships, and not limit myself to photographing only natural colors."[72] Rather than disparaging the industrialization of Italy and regarding industrial landscapes as wholly unaesthetic, Antonioni maintained an ambivalence toward industrial modernity, seeing its potential for alienation and estrangement and at the same time recognizing its potential for artistic intervention: "It's too simplistic to say . . . that [in *Red Desert*] I am condemning the inhuman industrialised world which oppresses individuals and leads them to neurosis. My intention was to translate the poetry of that world, in which even factories can be beautiful. The lines and the curves of factories and their chimneys can be more beautiful than the outline of trees, which we are already too accustomed to seeing. It is a rich world, alive and serviceable."[73] Nevertheless, despite their different preferences for venues, Antonioni shared Cézanne's perspective on how color can be employed to convey the dynamic emergence of space and character. They both painted their worlds in order to capture the intensities through which objects, landscapes, and personalities emerge.[74] For both, color works within composition. Merleau-Ponty, describing Cézanne's approach, writes, "If the painter is to express the world—the arrangement of his colors must carry with it this invisible whole."[75] And Antonioni writes (referring to the painting of landscapes and buildings in his *Red Desert*),

"I'm forced to modify or eliminate colors as I find them in order to make an acceptable composition."[76]

There is yet another important similarity between Cézanne's canvasses and Antonioni's filming of *Red Desert*. Like Cézanne, Antonioni captures the process of seeing. In *Red Desert,* that process is staged by beginning each scene "out of focus—then a head, upper body, or even in one case a foot, will suddenly move into the frame, in focus, organizing the space, making sudden visual sense of things for the viewer."[77] But what is the subjective context of that visual sense? Because Antonioni was both enthralled and disturbed by the industrialization of Ravenna's landscape, where he painted and filmed *Red Desert*, he has his main character, Giuliana (Monica Vitti), who is ill at ease, struggle to make sense of her industrial surroundings. As Pier Paolo Pasolini has famously pointed out, *Red Desert* has two protagonists. One is Giuliana, through whom Antonioni "looks at the world by immersing himself in his neurotic protagonist, reanimating the facts through her eyes."[78] The other is the "real protagonist . . . style. . . . Antonioni's 'poesis' with which he allow[s] the camera to be felt."[79]

What is felt, however, abounds in contradiction. Where Handke, as I have noted, draws a subjectively attuned lesson from painting after heeding what he terms "The Lesson of [Cézanne's] Mont Sainte-Victoire" and is thereby able to come to terms not only with landscapes but also with other media (for example, Friedrich Hölderlin's epistolary novel, *Hyperion* [1797], which he "finally understood [because he] was able to look on its words as images"),[80] Antonioni draws on painting (and paints) to express ambivalence and contradiction.[81] Swatches of color added to the scenes he films are (like Vermeer's color patches) his punctums; they are interruptions of "the continuity of the representational system."[82]

As Antonioni has suggested (in a criticism of what he regarded as Hitchcock's unrealistic suspense narratives), "Life is also made up of pauses";[83] rather than creating Hitchcockian suspense, Antonioni continually suspends the dramatic action while organizing his filming to create an ambiguity as to whose point of view shapes the scene. The slowness of his filming thus results from his endeavor to focus on details rather than drama. Accordingly, the "chromatic dissonance"[84] with which his *Red Desert* is continually punctuated (with clashing color coding, attuned to who is dominating the scene and in what mood) expresses both his cinematic style and his ambivalence about industrial modernity, which is also articulated through Giuliana's struggle with making sense of the scopic field with which she is confronted. In a scene in which she is with her paramour, Corrado (Richard Harris), she says, "I feel my eyes tearing up. What should I do with my eyes? What should I watch?" As for Antonioni's ambivalence:

> The feelings in the film evinced in its dramatization are . . . fundamentally contradictory and intractable, [for] . . . on the one hand, Antonioni would say, the world created by the advance of technology is undoubtedly *beautiful* [an aesthetic to which he contributes with color, having for the first time ventured away from black and white films]. . . . On the other hand, . . . this new world is very close to hell. A wasteland is a wasteland after all, . . . and if a "new beauty" has been born, . . . the phenomenon is shot with poison."[85]

Antonioni articulates much of that ambivalence by giving his *Red Desert* a painterly patrimony that extends beyond its punctuation with pictorial tableaux. The film's color hues and architectural foci delivered in many framing, zoom, and close-up shots evoke a variety of art historical styles: the monochrome, color-muted style of Giorgio Morandi, the "deserted agora of Giorgio de Chirico,"[86] and the color patches of Mark Rothko. Interspersing shots of an industrial landscape full of ugly monochrome voids with aesthetically pleasing pictorial moments, spaces and buildings suffused with added color, *Red Desert* articulates a contradiction between beauty and sublimity.

As for its articulation through Giuliana, there are cinematic punctuations: blurry images, colors, and fallow spaces, which operate within the cinematic grammar to evince her (and also the viewers') estrangement with images. The film's opening scenes accordingly exercise all three punctuating forms. One is an implicit time image that delivers a dynamic of perception. While the credits run, the factory world is a blur before the landscape, buildings, and people become distinct. Thereafter, the figures—initially workers, some on strike, walking around the factory, and then Giuliana and her son Valerio slowly approaching the factory area—are seen mostly from a distance, rendering the scene like Mofokeng's funeral procession photograph in which (as noted earlier, quoting Cole) the figures "seem to have less significance than what is around them: ' . . . the great expanse of the landscape [so that] the photo comes to feel less like an image of a funeral than an image of this space.' "[87] As in the rest of his film corpus, Antonioni uses space to create "a sense of tension between the landscape and the human figures."[88] Figures and buildings punctuate Antonioni's cinematic space, serving as "point[s] of anchorage" in the landscapes, while many of the scenes are devoid of

Figure 4.5 Giuliana and Valerio.

people to emphasize the extent to which that anchorage is what turns space into place.[89]

The third punctuation throughout *Red Desert* is, of course, color. When Giuliana and Valerio appear, they punctuate the initially monochrome landscape with color: Giuliana in a green coat and Valerio in a brown one (see figure 4.5). Their color difference anticipates a tension between them (enacted by Valerio, who at one point feigns paralysis), and the intrusion of their colored coats hints at their lack of ease within the industrial modernity in which their husband and father, Ugo, functions as a plant manager. Antonioni's color intrusions are thus not "ornamental, atmospheric or emotional factors"; "they are," as Pascal Bonitzer puts it, "veritable *ideas*."[90]

Once Giuliana is introduced, her path throughout the film narrative is also color-differentiated. The sharp colors that abound within and outside the factory—dark greens, blues, and reds—give way to earth colors and pastels within the spaces and rooms where the film story takes her (for example, her store, where she shows Corrado sample pastel green and blue color patches on the wall, and the beach they visit, where the sand is pink). Like the blurry moments, when the world of Ravenna is hard to see, the softened color-coding reflects Giuliana's inability to extract "coherent meaning out of a confused visual field."[91]

As a drama, the interpersonal narrative involves a love triangle, which begins when a traumatized Giuliana walks into the petrochemical plant complex and is introduced to her husband Ugo's old friend Corrado, who has come to try and recruit workers for an overseas commercial venture. After Corrado is apprised of the basis of Giuliana's nervous behavior—her husband Ugo (Carlo Chionetti) ascribes it to the trauma of an auto accident—Corrado, attracted to her and intrigued by her plan to start a retail business in a small shop she has acquired, visits her and takes advantage of Giuliana's postaccident inability to respond to her husband's amorous advances.

Because the romantic narrative pales in comparison with the complex industrial or technologically sublime landscape and the forces it imposes on the characters (emphasized with color-coded images), Corrado is better thought of as a "chromatic character" than a paramour. As William Arrowsmith suggests, "[Corrado exists in] . . . a point midway between Giuliana and Ugo, modulating easily between their poles [able to move easily] between the violent noise and bright colors of the refinery to the secretive silence of Giuliana's hideaway. . . . Corrado with his reddish hair and pastel greens, his shades of straw and stone, is immediately admissible into Giuliana's world, without jar, as Ugo is not."[92]

Ultimately, akin to the slow process with which Cézanne built his scenes, Antonioni's "slow movie" creates a homology between the tasks of the viewers and his characters. His camera articulates an image-oriented (cinematic version of) "free indirect discourse," which "in literature . . . presents speech or writing or thought of a character in the character's own language, without using quotation marks."[93] In its cinematic realization, free indirect discourse operates as a "semi-subjective image" that "implies two perceivers who exist independently of the image itself . . . the character. . . . [and an] other [that] is sometimes the filmmaker and sometimes the audience."[94] In accord with the "semi-subjective" image (a concept credited to the film theorist Jean Mitry),[95] which is pervasive in *Red Desert* (among other films), Deleuze identifies a "cinema of seeing" (a cinema genre to which I return in the conclusion), in which the viewer is unsure of what she is seeing.[96] In *Red Desert*, Antonioni patiently draws the viewer into a world in which his characters are raising the same question for themselves. Antonioni's cinematic poesis makes seeing as unstable for the viewer as it is for his characters.

How then can we derive a political sensibility from *Red Desert*? Certainly a micropolitics of subjectivity is explored in the film, which can be approached within two alternative conceptual frames. First, given Giuliana's anxiety about managing a confusing scopic field, a Lacanian focus on the gaze suggests itself. Lacan identifies the gaze as "that which performs like a phantom force. . . . In our relation to things, in so far as this relation is constituted by the way of vision, and ordered in the figures of representation, something slips, passes, is transmitted, from stage to stage, and is always to some degree eluded in it—that is what we call the gaze."[97] As Lacan explains, the gaze, as opposed to the eyes, reflects the reciprocal force within the scopic field. It is disruptive to the subject, whose sense of being in control of her/his perceptions is undermined because the field has no definitive center, an effect that Antonioni achieves with the "semi subjective" camera—filming from points of view that do not wholly coincide with his characters' perceptions. As he has said, "I no longer want to employ the subjective camera, in other words the camera that represents the viewpoint of the character."[98]

Once we recognize that perception is unstable and that Antonioni's filming of the spaces of Ravenna emphasizes the aesthetic ambiguities of its milieu (making the film's psychological moments pale in comparison with the force field within which the characters have their encounters), our reading of the film must move toward a Deleuzian rather than a Lacanian perspective. Resisting a psychological emphasis in which perception controls the way the film thinks, we have to recall Deleuze's insistence that "cinema does *not* have subjective perception as its model because the mobility of its centers and the variability of its framings always lead it to restore vast acentered and deframed zones."[99] With a focus on the decentering of selfhood, we are encouraged to entertain an immanent rather than a transcendent view of the subject. Instead of assuming that subjects have experiences, we have to recognize that subjectivity is epiphenomenal to experience. "In an immanent tradition," as Patricia Pisters summarizes it, "the subject is not *a priori* given, but perception and experience form it. It is by the multiplicity of perceptions that the 'I' is formed. . . . In an immanent philosophy [Deleuze's], the subject is in constant formation, always changing through multiple encounters."[100]

Given such a philosophical framing, how does *Red Desert* assert a critical perspective on those encounters? As I suggested in the treatment of Matta-Clark's deconstructive architecture, a political sensibility emerges from the way he redeems what has been forgotten with his attention to seemingly minor fragments—for example, the kind of punctums that occupy Didi-Huberman's analysis—"patches of dirt and asphalt," and "streaks of color" which "draw attention to the city's forgotten corners" and thereby redistribute the saliences of the objects in the life world.[101] Similarly, we must observe a political sensibility in *Red Desert* emerging through the fragments and shades and streaks of color that punctuate the film. Because colors deliver varying degrees of intensity, and compositions that utilize them organize those intensities to articulate a politics of experience, we need an elaboration of the intensity-politics relationship to appreciate more fully how *Red Desert* and other image-oriented texts think. I reserve that consideration for the chapter's conclusion.

I turn now to one of Antonioni's later color-infused films, *The Passenger* (1975), because its combination of intense color-coding and architectural exploration, along with a more spatially extensive geography, provides another (in this case, more spatially complex) cinematic text that thinks about the micropolitics of subjectivity. Crucially, *The Passenger*, like *Red Desert* (and indeed the whole of Antonioni's work), replaces "'traditional drama with a kind of *optical drama* lived by the character.'"[102] Antonioni thinks his way through the film by having his visual choices constitute the dramatic ones.[103]

The Passenger

As in *Red Desert,* Antonioni has one of his characters provide a metastatement about how the film is working. At one point, the reporter on assignment to interview rebel leaders in Chad, David Locke (Jack Nicholson), whose story of malaise and ultimate death is the main narrative, says to the "girl" (Maria Schneider) with whom he is traveling, "we translate every experience into the same old codes," a line that reflects the trajectory of his identity migration. Seeking "to escape the tyranny of the co-ordinates of his present existence [and] . . . re-open his life to new experiences," he steals the identity of a deceased man, Robertson, who is sharing his hotel in Chad, and feigns taking on the man's business as an arms dealer.[104] When the girl with whom he ends up traveling asks, "What are you running away from," he bids her to get the answer by positioning herself backward in the front seat of his rental car so she can observe what they are leaving rather than where they're headed.

He tellingly alerts the viewer to how his gradual disappearance as Locke is cinematically accomplished by referring not only to how people appear and disappear in the life world but also to how it is accomplished in cinema. At a point in the film, when the girl who joins him in the corridors of Antoni Gaudí's famous Palau Güell, says, "People disappear every day," Locke responds, "Yes, every time they leave the room." Locke's observation accords with Noël Burch's identification of "two different kinds of cinematic space" (discussed in chapter 3). As Burch puts it, "To understand cinematic space, it may prove useful to consider it as in fact consisting of *two different kinds of space:* that included within the frame and that outside the frame," where one segment outside the frame is involved when "[a] character reaches it by going out a door, going around a street corner, disappearing behind a pillar or behind another person."[105]

That moment inside and outside the frame is played out in two key scenes in the film: the first during the process in which Locke trades his identity for a man named Robertson and the second when Locke's drama of identity disappearance is emphasized by moments in which he and the girl go through a series of cinematic disappearances, as in that same scene from the Palau Güell, where they are shown moving in and out of sight behind pillars as their dialogue about disappearances takes place.

Rather than simply filling in the film narrative in the usual descriptive way (by following Locke's action trajectory throughout the film), I want to elaborate the film's complex temporalities by summoning texts that provide ways of locating and conceptualizing its two temporal layers. The primary or surface layer is Locke's personal story as a television reporter who, frustrated by his inability to successfully prepare a documentary about a guerilla war in the African country of Chad, decides to trade in his life for Robertson's, who has died in an adjacent room in the hotel where they are both staying. During Locke's identity theft, Antonioni's camera keeps moving from room to room in the hotel they have shared. He uses the architectural partitions, shooting from one room through a doorway into another, and through a window into a room. The building's partitions effectively "double the camera's framing"[106] of the action as Locke steals the dead man's passport and clothes and then manages to convince the desk clerk (who seemingly cannot distinguish between the two white men) that "Locke" had died and he, "Robertson," is reporting the episode. The rest of the film drama carries Locke, masquerading as Robertson, toward his death in a desert hotel, shot by counterrevolutionary agents who think he is Robertson.

Certainly Don DeLillo's famous line (spoken by the character Gladney in his novel *White Noise*), "All plots tend to move deathward," fits the narrative trajectory of David Locke's story, as does Ira Jaffe's characterization of such "slow movies" in which "the plot and dialogue . . . often gravitate toward stillness and death."[107]

Because of the way the temporal structure of Locke's story unfolds as he seems to be planning his own death, however, we have to turn to a more extended death-plot framing, which I suggest is Shakespeare's *Hamlet*, especially the way the story is explicated by Jacques Lacan. Others noting the pervasiveness of mirrors, both actual and implied, see the film as susceptible to a Lacanian reading—for example, Jack Turner: "The film works as a powerful psychological allegory that fits the framework of

Lacan's primary matrix (Imaginary, Symbolic, Real)." "Because Locke has come to dislike the self he sees in the mirror," Turner suggests that, "Much like a patient Lacan discusses, he has 'come to the end of his tether' [and seeks to] 'excuse his own impotence,' . . . [and similarly] Locke is impotent in completing his assignment in the desert, impotent in communicating with the Africans"[108]

Nevertheless, recalling my remarks in my reading of *Red Desert* that "the film's psychological moments pale in comparison with the force-field within which the characters have their encounters," I also want to resist quarantining this film drama in a wholly psychological frame, in part because Antonioni imposes an image economy rather than a psychic one (his sequence of shots and their dispositions enact ambiguous perspectives on selfhood that resist a psychic-centered reading of the narrative progression) and in part because the film provides an elaborate historical framing that transcends Locke's singular fate. The second temporality, a historical-geopolitical one that I discuss below, is understated yet available through a variety of moments and objects subjected to long takes.

To begin by pursuing the individual story: Rather than seeking to psychoanalyze Locke, my turn to Lacan's reading of *Hamlet* helps me to map the color-coded and spatially punctuated temporality of Locke's deathward march, as (like Hamlet), "he wants to breathe in the suffocating air of fate in one deep breath."[109] Rather than foregrounding and dwelling on the psychology of Locke's death wish, however, Antonioni's film exposes the way subjectivity emerges from encounters. Lacan's reading of Shakespeare's *Hamlet* suggests itself for two main reasons. First, because Antonioni creates Locke's traveling companion as an object rather than a subject—she is doubtless unnamed because she serves as an object of encounter—and second, because when Locke decides to adopt Robertson's identity, the shots of the identity change show him hesitatingly deciding to wear another man's colors (figure 4.6).

In his lecture on *Hamlet*, Lacan references both reasons. He constructs Ophelia as an object, beginning his lecture with the heading, "The Object Ophelia," and proceeding to suggest that Ophelia "becomes one of the innermost elements in Hamlet's drama, the drama of Hamlet as the man who has lost the way of his desire . . . [a] drama of an individual subjectivity."[110] The other main encounter with Robertson evokes an especially pertinent reading of Hamlet by Lacan, who describes "the final act" in which Hamlet enters the tournament on the side of the King, when his uncle and stepfather remarks, "He thus wears another man's colors."[111]

Beyond those two notable and *apropos* insights, Lacan's reading of

Figure 4.6 Locke by another man's colors.

Hamlet also helps us recognize the ongoing temporal punctuations in Locke's emerging and ambiguous subject formation as his geographic odyssey imposes deferrals on his ultimate object of desire, death. As his analysis of *Hamlet* proceeds, Lacan locates Hamlet's relationship to the object of desire as "the relationship of the subject to time," noting that Hamlet is constantly "suspended in the time of the Other throughout the entire story until the very end."[112] Recalling the noted tendency for Antonioni to privilege what he calls "pauses" (or as Michael Tawa puts it, "radical suspensions of movement and time")[113] rather than dramatic suspense, Locke's Hamlet-like deferrals of his journey toward death are isomorphic with the way Antonioni constructs plots. There is a coordinated cinematic and character/subject pause (shot #65)[114] that is especially telling, the point just before Locke decides "to wear another man's colors." Locke adopts a Hamlet-like pose, staring at Robertson's dead face in a scene reminiscent

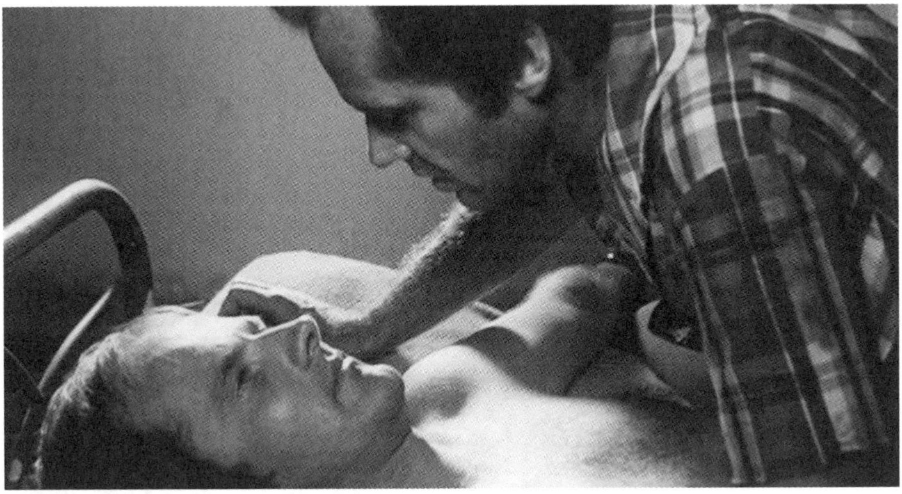

Figure 4.7 Locke and Robertson.

of Hamlet's contemplation of the skull of the dead Yorick (see figures 4.7 and 4.8). Crucially, like Hamlet, Locke keeps hesitating—for example, hesitating before placing the call that will start him on a road that extracts him from his past as he becomes Robertson. Throughout the individual drama, the narrative is occupied by Locke's Hamlet-like temporality, which (quoting Lacan) proceeds toward "the hour of his destruction," after following his "unrelenting movement . . . toward that hour."[115]

Apart from the deathward narrative that defines Locke's personal story are the color punctuations that announce his presence in places in which he appears obtrusive. His ill-at-ease presence as the film opens is conveyed by the chromatic dissonance between his light blue Land Rover and a boy in the street wearing a yellow shirt. As the film progresses, bright red colors repeatedly punctuate scenes—for example, the point at which (after leaving the Gaudí building) Locke enters a bright red Avis car rental agency, which recalls an earlier Avis car rental scene in which the Avis employee was wearing a red "We Try Harder" button. In contrast with the reds that accompany his various encounters (for example, he exchanged his red and white plaid shirt for Robert's light blue one when he switched identities) is the desert, in which his initial frustrations began when his Land Rover was mired in the sand. It is a vast monochrome landscape with a dull pinkish hue, against which Locke's changing colors stand out.

The other relevant cinematic practice that accompanies Locke's story involves space. Antonioni's landscape shots introduce a disjuncture and

Figure 4.8 Hamlet and Yorick.

thus tension between the spaces and characters. And given the frequency of unpeopled scenes, the characters (often color-coded) and buildings (whose colors contrast with the monochrome landscapes) that punctuate the film make the tension especially available to the eye. Locke's increasing absence from himself is given a surcharge with the spaces from which he is either absent or seen from a distance. Moreover, although there are strong emotional resonances in the personal narrative, especially those attending Locke's identity struggle, resulting first in the theft of another's identity and then a distancing from the romantic relationship he had begun with the girl, the narrative works with both affective intensities articulated as color punctuations and by connecting affects deployed with spatial shots rather than with "affection images" (moments when "the subject perceives itself" registered in close ups).[116]

As Leo Bersani and Ulysse Dutoit point out in their reading of Jean Luc Godard's *Contempt* (1963), the film is less focused on "the psychic origins of contempt" than on "what contempt does to cinematic space."[117] Similarly, rather than a lot of close-ups that call attention to affect, Antonioni organizes space to show how characters are being affected—for example, following Locke's hesitating moves as he decides to become Robertson with shots from other rooms and creating extended spatial distance and architectural barriers between Locke and the girl's movements in moments when they're becoming estranged.

So much for the temporal unfolding of the personal drama: the transcendent temporality to which I have referred pertains to the African venue of the film. It is a space with a history of colonial violence in which weapons technologies have played a major role. Accompanying the slaughter that the weapons have enabled have been legitimating (Eurocentric) discourses that have allocated the violence to noble causes. To develop that part of the film's focus, I read the relevant images along with Sven Lindqvist's account of a journey (his own), which, like Locke's, begins with him traveling in a monotonous desert scene in which "hour after hour the white desert pours past: stone and sand, stone and gravel, gravel and sand—all gleaming like snow."[118] Both Locke and Lindqvist are men "in transit in the desert," but one of them is on "a borrowed mission" (Locke), while the other (Lindqvist) is on his own.[119]

While Locke's story locates him in the violence of the postcolonial present—his uncompleted task was to document an antigovernment guerilla movement in the (largely) desert state of Chad—Lindqvist's has a greater historical sweep, to recover the violence of European exterminism during the colonization of Africa. As he pursued the writer Joseph Conrad's journey (which eventuated in his novel *The Heart of Darkness*), Lindqvist, figuring himself as a fictional character (like all who write "I," even as he arrives at "knowledge," "step by step, proof by proof"),[120] recovered Africa as an event space of European cruelty. He describes such details as the effects of European weapons technology on large-scale slaughters, pointing out, for example, the effect of the invention of the breech-loading rifle: "The art of killing from a distance became a European specialty very early on. . . . At the battle of Omdurman, the entire Sudanese army was annihilated . . ." without there being a single English casualty.[121]

Like Lindqvist, Locke associates himself first with media coverage of violence on the African continent (in his vocation as a journalist) and subsequently with the arrival of weapons in Africa through the borrowed identity of an arms dealer whose commodities are to feed a local rebellion rather than a colonial or imperial initiative. Nevertheless, in constructing the arms trading vocation of the Robertson character, Antonioni is inserting his drama into a historically violent event space that transcends Locke's story. The history of Chad, an active staging place for the slave trade, is a history of atrocity and colonial domination. Rather than explicit historical references, however, Antonioni provides subtle image clues, object punctuations that, as Alain Robbe-Grillet explains (noted in the Introduction), are the way to translate literary assertions into images.[122]

For example, early in the film narrative, cigarettes are objects testifying to the history of colonial domination. The Africans with whom Locke comes in contact at the outset of his journey eschew reciprocity. In response to his queries about how to find places, they say either nothing or give cryptic directions that fail to help him. In two instances, it is cigarettes that are the telling object punctuations. Men wordlessly ask him for cigarettes by merely gesturing with two figures, raised in a cigarette-holding position, followed by no gestures of gratitude after they receive them. The implication appears to be that in light of Europe's past violent domination (extractive without return), they are owed a lot, but nothing white men give can obviate the historical debt accumulated over centuries.

Aside from those subtle clues is one provided by an object-image that refers to more contemporary violence: Western interference with African self-determination. While Locke is in Robertson's hotel room, completing the process in which he assumes his identity, there is a close-up shot of a book on the table beside Robertson's bed whose title reads in part, "de Lumumba aux colonels" (referring to Patrice Lumumba, the Congo's anticolonial independence leader, murdered with the assistance of western agents in 1961). And significantly on top of the book, partially obscuring its title, is a photo of Locke's wife Rachel, implying that Locke's personal drama is more important to him than the continuing violence that is a legacy of Africa's colonial past he has been covering. Also testifying to his insensitivity to atrocity is a flashback to Locke's earlier footage of a government execution of a rebel leader that is shown as merely "a voyeuristic newsreel . . . display[ing] no analytic or moral responsibility of any kind. And in [an] interview with a witchdoctor, Locke's voice and manner hint at the underlying condescension of the colonialist attitude."[123]

The main historical/colonial punctuation throughout the film, however, is color. With respect to the colonial temporality, the significant colors are black and white. It becomes evident that whiteness is now so irrelevant in the film's main black African venue that Africans are no longer attentive to white faces. Locke is able to impersonate Robinson in the hotel with a mere change into different-colored clothing. In other moments—the key encounters in Locke's personal story—it is flashes of red that are the key punctuations. During the moment when Locke is affixing his picture into Robertson's passport, for example, the red nozzle of a glue bottle separates the two passports in the frame. And at the end of the film when Locke is at the Hotel Gloria where he is killed, he is shown wearing a bright red shirt. At those two moments, "bright red colors repeatedly punctuate scenes." The color punctuation in Antonioni's films, like those in Vermeer's canvasses, are, as I have suggested, "intrusive flashes of color" with "implications for political thinking" that Didi-Huberman helps us to approach when he refers to such patches of color as "*partial intensities* in which the usual relationships between local and global elements are overturned."[124] In the conclusion, which retrieves the political resonances in the image trajectory I have provided, I want to fulfill my earlier promise to provide an elaboration of the intensity-politics relationship as it applies to the dynamics of subjectivity, articulated in image-oriented texts.

Conclusion: Intensities and Political Thinking

I begin by adding some conceptual depth to the image compositions I have illustrated throughout the chapter, emphasizing both the way the compositions think and the way they provoke reception. Rather than foregrounding abstract conceptualizations on the philosophies of experience within which the reception of the image compositions can be located, however, I want to stick close to the textual trajectory that has marked my analysis thus far. To evoke a lesson from what Michel Foucault referred to as his "choice of method" at the outset of his lectures on *The Birth of Biopolitics*: "instead of deducing concrete phenomena from universals, or instead of starting with universals as an obligatory grid of intelligibility for certain concrete practices, I would like to start with the concrete practices and, as it were, pass these universals through the grid of these practices."[125] Accordingly, I work from specific images to the more abstract conceptualizations to achieve the political significance of image punctuations.

To commence, I return to the politically pregnant photographs of Santu Mofokeng, whose details are noted in the Teju Cole commentary from which I quoted. One of Cole's words stands out: *intimacy*. As he writes, "The spaciousness and blur of Mofokeng's pictures come ultimately with this intimacy with this 'gossamer' world" (where *gossamer* is Mofokeng's word for the spirituality imminent in the black South African life world, manifested in church services). To ascend to a more theoretical level, the "intimacy" to which Cole refers—and elaborates by noting that it's a world "that is elusive to the uninitiated or outsiders"—I turn to the concept of assemblage, which Deleuze and Guattari use to conceive the way bodies form collective attachments through their shared capacity to affect each other. Mofokeng references that capacity and its effect on black

South African self-recognition when he remarks that his intended viewers are black South Africans who can recognize the violence of apartheid in the photographs. As he puts it (to repeat an earlier quotation), "the violence is in the knowing."[126]

Mofokeng's photographic practice effectively locates him as what Antonioni Gramsci identifies as an "organic intellectual" (one who "speak[s] for the interests of a specific class").[127] His image-thoughts participate in evoking and helping to assemble a black South African community of sense. Cole's commentary broadens the political resonances of his photographs, providing a sensibility that extends beyond Mofokeng's constituency. For example, he links the political aesthetic of Mofokeng's photographs with the work of Roy DeCarava (with whom Mofokeng studied):

> When Mofokeng left South Africa to study at the International Center of Photography in New York in 1991, through a scholarship named for Ernest Cole, he attended Roy DeCarava's workshops. It was a meeting of minds. The point is not that DeCarava was an influence—Mofokeng's voice was established before he met DeCarava—but that both artists found productive use for stylistic reticence and literal obscurity. Perhaps no photographer since DeCarava has kept as much faith with shadows as Mofokeng has. Mofokeng's work did not seek to demystify the townships just as DeCarava's did not seek to explain Harlem.[128]

What I want to suggest is that this moment in Cole's commentary points to a politics of artistic encounter, which (in Deleuze and Guattari's terms) speaks to the capacity of bodies (individual or collective) to form assemblages with other bodies to create a shared community of sense while at the same time preserving what distinguishes each body.[129] Cole's analysis of photographic art shows how disparate communities of sense have had artists who help unite them by making their oppression visible. In so doing, he provides the reader with an appreciation of a model of a politics of aesthetics that is not ordinarily understood, the significance of blurs, shadows, and fallow spaces that impose interpretive unease in the uninitiated viewer while affirming a shared sensibility among those whose life world is on display.

In addition to conveying the pedagogy of Cole's commentary, however, I want to emphasize what it is in Mofokeng's photographs that enabled Cole to achieve the critical reception he passed on to his readers. At the outset of his commentary, Cole confesses that he was unable initially to appreciate what Mofokeng was conveying. As he puts it,

When I first encountered [Mofokeng's photographs], some 15 or so years ago, I didn't understand them. Something about them seemed unfinished, imprecise or wrong. They looked like good ideas for photographs that never quite made it into actual good photographs. When I sought out a pictorial record of apartheid, classic photojournalism that lived up to the idea of the "decisive moment" seemed a better way to go. . . . [for example] . . . I could turn to photographs by David Goldblatt, which showed—through photographs of people, landscapes and buildings—both the infrastructure of South Africa and the lived experience of people under Apartheid. Most of Goldblatt's photographs were well lit, in focus and direct, with emotion kept to a minimum. I loved their form of witness. I still do.[130]

Cole returned to an examination of Mofokeng's photographs, admitting that in comparison with the more direct and lucid photographic approaches to apartheid victimization, his "understanding of Mofokeng came more slowly."[131] It was Mofokeng's punctums, the ambiguities and obscurities that disrupt the viewer's usual receptive expectations (making it unclear what "meets the eye") that encouraged Cole to suspend his preconceived expectations of issue-relevant images and reconceive how the images think. As Cole came to recognize, Mofokeng did not merely record a people's life world; he composed it to enfranchise an experiential knowledge that effectively recomposes a "people," a people that had been composed, alternatively as unworthy of shared citizenship (by a structure of domination) and as victims (whose liberation is a function of the critical knowledge practices of outsiders).

The slowness to which Cole refers in his coming to appreciate how Mofokeng's images work is matched in what I have noted as the Cézanne event, a slow chromatic application that allows a scene to emerge while at the same time creating a viewer reception that has no secure or central location. Cézanne creates an opportunity for the viewer to slowly acquire the sense of a scene as his canvass registers the way that he (the painter) "initially encounters the world as an infra-pictorial chaos, from which the canvass will arise."[132] Then given the way the composition-as-form has taken shape, he robs the viewer of her scopic sovereignty, because, as I have noted, there is no center from which the viewing subject can adopt a secure position. Nevertheless, while that robbery is disruptive, it is also enabling. It frees the viewer/subject from the viewing anchorage that the history of painting from the Renaissance on has created.

The Cézanne event is thus the creation of a novel (visual) subjectivity, one toward which Peter Handke gestures when in his novella "The Lesson of Mont Sainte-Victoire," he mobilizes his wandering protagonist, who "found himself at home with colors,"[133] in the landscape in which Cézanne built the scene with the chromatic strokes that Handke calls "proposals."[134] Cézanne animated "a thing-image-brushstroke-dance"[135] that resonated for Handke's protagonist as he (the protagonist) interconnects "the mountain and me, the pictures and me . . . setting them down side by side as unconnected fragments,"[136] until he achieves a momentary self-possession as subject-in-process. The durational effect of Cézanne's "proposals" yields a durational subject seeking to "hold [his] story together,"[137] as Cézanne's interconnected, chromatically built intensities attune him to his mobile subjectivity.

Handke's commentary on his protagonist's encounter with a landscape that takes on intensities and saliences, when mediated by Cézanne's chromatic renderings of it, accords with the way critically oriented perspectives in general suggest that subjectivity follows experiences of encounter (in this case, as a mediated encounter with a landscape). *The Passenger* animates such an encounter as its protagonist strives to become a different subject (wearing another man's colors). The film exposes the way subjectivity emerges from encounters with both spaces and persons. And crucially, the most salient encounters are marked by the colors with the highest intensities. Moreover, the color markings with their varying intensities guide the viewers who (much like the desk clerk in the hotel where the identity change occurs) have to come to terms with the significance of what they're seeing.

Recalling Giuliana's lament in *Red Desert,* "What should I do with my eyes," viewers of *The Passenger* have to struggle to position themselves throughout the chromatically and spatially changing narrative sequences. They too must struggle with what there is to see as they're confronted with what Deleuze famously calls a "cinema of seeing," in which (as I have noted) the continual question for the viewer is, "What is there to see in the image?" (as opposed to a cinema of action, in which the question the viewer is asking is, "What are we going to see in the next image").[138] Like Locke, the film's protagonist, their position as (viewing) subjects is insecure and in process throughout the film. And like Cézanne's painting, cinema as I have already pointed out (quoting Deleuze) also has "vast acentered and deframed zones," in its case a result of the "continuous movement through space and time."[139]

What then are the implications for a micropolitics of subjectivity of the textual hopscotch of image practices I have treated throughout this chapter (with special emphasis on chromatic shifts)? The first step to address those implications is to recognize a grammar that locates subjects as object-effects of encounters. It is a recognition well captured in this line from a Peter Handke poem: "then, someone crawls out from under a thicket in the park and becomes a suspicious subject."[140] That line references the way subjectivity emerges from the outside, resulting from practices of recognition. To treat what emerges within, we can follow the Deleuzian narrative of aesthetic experience and presume that prior to making sense of themselves, their world, and others, potential subjects are located in a "field of intensive forces, vibratory or rhythmic forces that prolong themselves." They first experience themselves "in a chaos of pressures . . . and waves of forces that affect [them]."[141] The writer Karl Ove Knausgaard (despite his expressed diffidence about his ability to read philosophical texts) understands that Deleuzian, experience-subjectivity narrative well. After witnessing and hearing a flock of migrating birds in formation outside his home, he reexperiences the "affective tonalities"[142] of that moment after returning to his kitchen: "Within me the migrating birds are living a life of their own. I'm not thinking of them, but they are there, in the stream of sensations and feelings which at times freeze into images. Not clear and distinct images, as with photographs. . . . What kinds of feelings? I ask myself now, as I write this. I know them so well, but only as feelings, not as thoughts or concepts."[143]

Like Cézanne's canvasses, which follow and evoke that progression from sensation to subsequent thinking, the two Antonioni films I have analyzed also generate intensities derived from the films' "affective tonalities," which include such cinematic punctuations as sound or silence, spaces with figures or devoid of them, and especially colors as the subject/protagonist is experiencing himself and the viewers are making sense of his identity trajectory toward a different subject position. Crucially, the chromatically constructed, affective tonalities resonate for the contemporary film viewer, who experiences a way of seeing that Antonioni's film (and indeed much of contemporary cinema) has created. It is a cinema less oriented to a dramatic narrative and more focused on the way its punctuations (what Antonioni refers to as "pauses") reveal how subjects make sense of themselves. As Antonioni has stated, *The Passenger* "is about the relation . . . of the individual with himself—"[144] and (I want to add) it registers the way that sense of one's self becomes apparent to others.

There is a moment in the film that gestures toward that registering. Rachel, Locke's presumed widow, and Knight, a publicist and former media colleague, assemble Locke's past career by creating a made-for-television program about Locke's reporting ventures with footage from his reports. There is a point, however, at which Knight has a "problem assembling a portrait of David Locke from the footage at his disposal."[145] At a simple narrative level, the suggestion is that Locke's achievements are ambiguous. I want to suggest, however, that the difficulty is captured with the word *portrait*. Locke-as-subject cannot be located in a static frame that fixes the self because he is a mobile subject. Instead of collecting a subject's acts to paint his portrait (as if, for example, he was assembling them to generate a biopic), Antonioni chromatically marks the encounters through which Locke's identity odyssey is shaped, using more vivid colors (especially reds) to identify the most salient moments and paler hues to note the less salient ones as the story of the subjectivity dynamic unfolds. As each crucial moment in that dynamic is chromatically marked for degrees of salience, the viewer is presented with a subject who, like Lacan's version of Hamlet, is struggling to create himself while caught "in the time of the Other." He must flee those who can recognize him as Locke—his wife Rachel and colleague Knight, who look for him after realizing he's alive—as well as those who think he is Robertson (both rebels who seek assurance about his deliveries and government agents who are after him for aiding the antigovernment rebellion).

To ascend from the concrete details (the sequence of shots and their objects) of Antonioni's film to its conceptually elaborated implications, I suggest that Locke's struggle to become a subject, while stuck "in the time of the Other," is a universal affliction because identity is not an attribute of a person or individual, it is a relationship. Knausgaard puts it simply, "The wisest person knows the 'I' is nothing in itself."[146] To lend that ontology of the "I" toward which Knausgaard gestures more complexity (in order to appreciate the subjectivity drama in Antonioni's *The Passenger*, as well as in some of the other visual texts I have analyzed), we have to displace the concept of the individual with that of *the process of individuation.*

Individuation, a concept developed by Gilbert Simondon and adopted (albeit in somewhat reoriented form) by Deleuze is a "transindividuality" that refers to a "double movement." First, there is an individualization, "the generation of an individual from a preindividual being to its physical existence," and second, there is the "movement . . . through which individuals continue to exist [in a] series of individualizations that corresponds to an individual's action in an environment and with other individuals."[147] That second movement articulates a relational ontology, one in which subjectivity involves reciprocal modes of recognition between subjects in formation. What I want to add to that relational ontological is the effects of disruption, moments when an artistic intervention (for example, Mofokeng's photographs) interrupts the usual process of relational forms of individuation (specifically in the case of black South African subject formation), an interruption as the subjects-as-victims are reconfigured as knowing subjects. It is a substitution in which the photographic work has a double movement: first bringing bodies together in mutual recognition as a salient assemblage in touch with who they have been and who instead they might be, and second, a movement evoking a relationality aided by the photographs' dissemination, for example, commentaries on them (e.g., Cole's), which generate recognition outside the assemblage.

It is such artistic interventions that constitute what Rancière refers to as "aesthetic breaks."[148] Among those I have analyzed, which reorient the micropolitics of subjectivity and create the conditions of possibility for new aesthetic (and often "dissensual") communities of sense, are Mofokeng's photographs and Matta-Clark's anarchitectural projects. They are artistic challenges that destabilize reigning structures of intelligibility and exemplify a politics of aesthetics because they reveal the existence of alternative "sensory worlds."[149]

HOLOCAUST PUNCTUATIONS: HANDKE, KERTÉSZ, AND SEBALD

Literary Punctuation

In my discussions (in the Introduction and chapter 4) of Roland Barthes's analysis of *punctums*—attention-getting arrests that disrupt one's attempt to incorporate images easily into thematic interpretations—I have emphasized how they lend a temporality to photographic images. In this chapter, I adapt the temporal structure of punctuation to literary texts, beginning with an illustration of a novel whose punctuation style articulates the nature of a helter-skelter narrative that challenges reader reception. Laszlo Krasznahorkai's *War and War* has an unusual punctuation rhythm. It contains (as I have noted elsewhere) "long sentences that frequently comprise entire chapters."[1] That punctuation style is also a feature of the manuscript described within the novel; the manuscript was brought to New York by Krasznahorkai's protagonist, Korin, an archivist from Hungary, and posted on the Internet. At one point, Korin describes the rationale for the manuscript's punctuation structure: "There is an order in the sentences: words, punctuation, periods, commas all in place. . . . and yet the events that follow in the last chapter may be characterized as a series of collapses . . . for the sentences have lost their reason, not just growing ever longer and longer but galloping desperately onward in a harum scarum scramble—*crazy rush*."[2] As the novel's long sentences also gallop in "a harum scarum scramble," they have the effect of drawing the reader "toward the consciousness of the archivist character," a "vertigo inducing sentence structure"[3] that matches the delusional testimony of Korin, who throughout the novel is trying to comprehend the kaleidoscopic imagery rushing past him in the hyper-intense environment of the New York metropolis. Just as in Barthes's work, in which photographic punctuation functions as a symptom of time because *punctums* lend photographs implicit durations that affect viewer reception, literary punctuation also articulates time. It conveys the durational features of the novel's narrative and non-narrative moments and their effects on reader reception.

Time's immanence in literary punctuation is well captured in Rancière's analysis of what he calls "fictions of time" (noted in the Introduction).[4] Commenting on the epistemological force of literary fiction (which he designates as "avowed fiction"), Rancière writes,

> Literary fiction—or avowed fiction in general—is not so much the object that social science has to analyse as it is the laboratory where fictional forms are experimented as such and which, for that reason, helps us understand the functioning of the forms of unavowed fiction at work in politics, social science or other theoretical discourses. It does so because it is obliged to construct what is at the heart of any fictional rationality but easily can be presupposed in the forms of unavowed fiction: time, which means the form of coexistence of facts that defines a situation and the mode of connection between events that defines a story.[5]

The political force of the fictional responses to the Holocaust that are my concern are articulated precisely by temporalities that inhere in the structure of literary texts, the "form of coexistence of facts" that the writers compose. What then is the force of the *occasion* for the writing?

The Event

The Holocaust stands as an alarming punctuation mark in modern history. It is, in Imre Kertész's words, "an absolute turning point in Europe's history, an event in the light of which will be seen everything that happened before and will happen after."[6] While the event's omnipresence shows up as a shadow force in the policies of nation states, its more vivid realizations exist in the arts, for example, in remembrance museums (most notably in Daniel Libeskind's Jewish Museum in Berlin), in scores of feature and documentary films, and in modern fiction. My examination of its fictional realizations accords with the writer Imre Kertész's insistence that fiction is "a form more truthful,"[7] and that as a creative act, it affords the best paths to remembrance. Kertész's remarks resonate with Rancière's view (quoted in chapter 3) that, "Fiction is a structure of rationality which is required wherever a sense of reality must be produced. It is firstly a form of presentation of things that cuts out a frame and places elements within it so as to compose a situation and make it perceptible."[8]

Featuring three European writers—the Austrian Peter Handke, who struggled with a national patrimony that was hospitable to Nazi exterminism, the Hungarian Imre Kertész, who wrote to take back an identity that had been violently usurped, and the German W. G. Sebald, who embarked on a journey of detection, articulated through a fictional character whose life is disrupted and occluded by the Holocaust—I analyze the ways their distinctive styles challenge traditional and institutionalized understandings of the event. Exemplifying the mission that Maurice Blanchot famously ascribes to critically self-conscious literature, their texts "interrupt the purposeful steps we are always taking toward a deeper understanding and a surer grasp upon things."[9] Like Blanchot's writing, their texts are "directed not toward any inner confirmation—not a kind of central, unshakable certitude—but toward an outer bound where it must continually contest itself."[10] In response to how the apotheosis of that necropolitical event has punctuated history, they re-open the event's significance by (re)punctuating the writing practices through which its intelligibility has been traditionally figured. Their writing "punches a hole" in the "instituted knowledges" that have been brought to bear on the Holocaust.[11] In implicit and distinctive calls for political thinking, their texts perform a never-consummated task of sense-making in response to an event for which words can only hover in the vicinity of that historical catastrophe without definitively capturing it. As Kertész puts it, the Holocaust is an "unseizable reality."[12]

Nevertheless, it is primarily with words that the significance of events is negotiated. As is the case with Kafka (to whose writing style all three are indebted), the writers I analyze have distinctive ways with words. In many places in their texts, one finds what always hovered in Kafka's prose: "behind the formulas of common speech [among their fictional protagonists] a space suddenly opens up where words reverberate and sprout meanings, acquiring an intensity that at times is paralyzing."[13] Resisting definitive closure on how the Holocaust is to be understood, the writers whose words I interrogate are involved in proposing rather than capturing. No matter the writing genre, fitting words to events is an ambiguous and contestable task. Every attempt invites normative collision, a situation that has characterized diverse writing genres dedicated to both cultural formations and historically specific events. I turn here to one such illustration, an exemplar of the tragic disposition, which famously attracted Nietzsche's approval. For him, as I have noted elsewhere, "The purpose of the tragic art is the affirmation of irreconcilable forces, not the revelation of a primordial truth."[14]

Words and Events

Dramatizing a tense political moment in his play *Seven Against Thebes* (treated briefly in the Introduction), Aeschylus has Eteocles, King of Thebes, whose brother Polynices is surrounding the walls of the city with a rebellious army, address his citizens: "Townsmen of Cadmus, speech must be fitted to the times."[15] As the play proceeds, it becomes evident that the fit cannot easily be achieved because Greek society embraces conflicting ontologies within which words have alternative significance. The normative collision the play stages imperils the possibility of fitting speech to the occasion. As I have noted, "the collision between different and irreconcilable normative terrains or spheres of justice" is articulated as contending inscriptions on the shields of the defenders of the city and on those of the attackers.[16] The ensuing battle therefore involves a clash of codes as well as arms.

Similarly, fitting speech (or writing) to the event of the Holocaust (in any genre, fictional or biographical), is a politically fraught venture. Some (most famously Theodor Adorno)[17] have suggested that putting the event into words or representing it artistically is either impossible or ethically obscene. As Vivian Liska points out, "The claim about the necessity of silence, of emptiness, of interrupting the world-stream as an act of opposition against soothing representations and biased discourse, was initially put forward by the first post-war generation of survivors. It mirrors the sensibilities and demands of a 'damaged life' (Adorno), whose deep traumatization made any harmonious lyrical speech seem barbaric and every narrative dishonest."[18] She adds, "Not surprisingly, silence as a literary mode could not endure. . . . gradually an awareness arises that talking about absence and the impossibility of words itself turns into speech. And, unnoticed at first, one finds oneself in the midst of dialogue and conversation."[19] As for art after Auschwitz, Rancière insists that "to show Auschwitz, art is the only thing possible, because art always entails the presence of an absence because it is the very job of art to reveal something that is invisible, through the controlled power of words and images, connected or unconnected."[20]

In the case of art's images, "fictions of the real"[21] are what Claude Lanzmann (discussed in the Introduction) says he provides in his documentary film *Shoah*. Similarly, Peter Forgács creates fictions of the real in his hybrid films (combinations of home movies and newsreels that record footage of some of the ordinary lives that were ultimately swept up and extinguished in the Holocaust).[22] Lanzmann's and Forgács's moving images *show* how the Holocaust persists in personal recollections and archives, respectively, while writers, rejecting silence as "a literary mode" (explicitly in the case of Imre Kertész), have insisted that in the face of such a catastrophic experience, one *must* write. In Kertész's case, he wrote in order to recover his selfhood and "trust in the world."[23] At a minimum, to participate through writing in the shaping of the Holocaust's future anterior (how it will-have-been) is to enter a contentious literary terrain.[24]

The three writers I address have entered that terrain with strong wills to expression. That will in Handke's case is articulated as a desire to create a science of peace; in Kertész's, it is to take over his naming after that function had been brutally usurped; and in Sebald's, it is to find a way of (re)creating a historical record that will lend the event biographical depth, resurrecting it from abstract to lived time (to what Claude Romano calls an "inner temporality").[25] Each of these three writers provides a distinctive, singularly motivated "poetics of Holocaust remembrance."[26] And the poetics for each of them unfolds within subject-focused narrative genres. The protagonists in their texts are in the process of becoming (in M. M. Bakhtin's phrase, they are "axiological yet to be").[27]

As a result, they are alerted to the ethical demands of the past on their presents as they heed the temporal imbrication of the spaces through which they pass while their self-fashioning unfolds. Following Bakhtin's concept of the "chronotope" (a version of time immanent in the prose of literary genres),[28] in the texts that occupy my attention, the characters demonstrate an "ability to *see time*, to *read time*, in the spatial whole of the world . . . to perceive the filling of space not as an immobile background, a given that is completed once and for all but as an emerging event—this is the ability to read in everything *signs that show time in its course*.[29]

Peter Handke

For Peter Handke, the world is a series of "event spaces."[30] At the outset of his novella "The Long Way Around," his protagonist, Austrian geoscientist Valentine Sorger, is dwelling in an "Indian Settlement" in the "Far North," a nameless place whose landscape he temporalizes, experiencing it as an "episodic space." Its episodes are a function of the way the sunlight and flora give the landscape alternative appearances at different moments during the day.[31] It becomes evident that in those momentary events, Sorger is finding solace from what he later refers to (obliquely) as the violent event of the Holocaust, which as an Austrian he regards as a painful part of his patrimony. He describes his "forefathers" as "violent monsters," and seeks to shed a self that he fears is a "replica of [those] death-cult masters."[32]

The novel is punctuated by Sorger's passage through the spaces in which he intermittently dwells as he moves through them. Their various characteristics are articulated through the ways they are situated in the world of names. Names, Handke implies, obviate one's ability to experience a space as more than a mere cliché. For example, Sorger's first move is from "the episodic [or experiential] space" of the "Far North" to "The Pacific Coast," which the text designates as "Space Prohibited." Rather than directly experiencing the vicissitudes of climatic and geological events there (as he had in the Far North), Sorger instead finds himself in a space of mere names, exemplified, for example, by a street sign that reads "Northern Lights Boulevard."[33]

Earlier in the story, before he leaves the "Indian village" in the "Far North" (during the initial period of his dwelling on "the Other Continent"), Sorger discovers that his "science" is inadequate to an understanding of the landscape he is investigating. Unconvinced by its knowledge protocols (its "linguistic formulas"),[34] he substitutes a phenomenological or experiential understanding, having recognized that his presence as an affected subject with a fraught history is involved in the meaning of the space. Infusing his observations of the temporality of the northern landscape with his personal temporal trajectory, Sorger constructs himself as a durational subject who at one point sees himself "fusing [his] individual history with the movement of the northern autumn, the landscape was in turn transformed by this human history into a temporal vault in which this self-forgetful man, without a destiny but also with a sense of loss . . . was still present."[35]

As his experience of the space transpires, the affective ties he has developed for the landscape—for example, in "his surprising affection for the river"—allows him to feel "his own story."[36] As a result, Sorger's investigation becomes the occasion for a personal exploration. As a becoming subject, Sorger arrives at an ethos by heeding the subjective effects of his spatial encounters. Crucially, his desire to evade his national patrimony shapes the autobiographical scripting of the self that is involved in the becoming process. His *Slow Homecoming* is an allegorical narrative whose grammatical shifts (which I treat below) reveal the novella's "two frames of reference, a 'story' and a 'commentary' about the story."[37] The interaction of the two frames constitute the novella's sense-making as a "philopoesis,"[38] a strategy in which the philosophical frame (articulated as a conceptual commentary) interferes with the personal story's affects and percepts, yielding a literary critique of violence (to which the protagonist, Sorger, refers as a "science of peace").

Desiring to achieve that "science of peace," Sorger has to overcome two levels of violence, a macro level (the event of the Holocaust) and a micro level, the world of names that rigidifies the spaces he traverses as he seeks to achieve a mobile subjectivity oriented toward discovering his potential for self-fashioning. He begins to realize that potential by initially appreciating the resistance to naming in his Far North settlement, which contrasts with the world of names he encounters once he leaves to return home. As he begins to recognize that his selfhood is the ultimate object of his discoveries, Sorger is able to experience the vivacity of a life world, which reveals itself when it is no longer screened by the naming protocols that have been the customary means of place identification (for example, he is able to connect with himself while passing through Denver, once he experiences it as more than simply the "Mile High City").

By shedding the coercive force of names, Sorger is increasingly able to appreciate the way a subject can fashion a home in the world. In one of his later encounters, for example, one in which he experiences the world of colors (in the collection's second novella, *The Lesson of Mont Sainte-Victoire*), observed during his journey through the "route taken by [the painter, Paul] Cézanne, leading eastward from Aix-en-Provence to the village of Tholonet," he finds himself "at home with colors."[39] His discovery is aided by mediating his landscape gaze through his observations of the landscape paintings of Paul Cézanne: "Yes, it was thanks to Paul Cézanne that I was standing amid the colors of the open country between Aix-en-Provence and the Village of Tholonet."[40]

The gratitude that Handke is expressing is owed to a confrontation of two events of becoming. Cézanne's Mont Sainte-Victoire canvasses capture (in Lyotard's words) the "event-ness of the given"; he offers "the world in the process of becoming" perceptible.[41] And Handke encounters that space-becoming-perceptible while undergoing his own experience as a becoming subject. Cézanne's capture of such a dynamic of spatial perception serves as validation for the subjectivity dynamic Handke is experiencing in his encounter with Cézanne-mediated space-as-event.

Along with such spatial punctuations that proceed throughout the three-novella narrative of Sorger's journey "homeward" (meant both geographically and phenomenologically) are the grammatical punctuations through which Sorger becomes alternatively a subject and object of his experiences as he tells the story and comments on it at the same time. At times, Sorger is an "I": "In my naïve country I couldn't even conceive of belonging to the country and its people,"[42] and a possessive "my" (e.g., in the vicinity of Mont Sainte-Victoire, he says, "I was going through a period of transitions; a year without fixed residence. . . . decided, in part by the development of my story."[43] At times, especially early in the "story," he is a "he" (the novella begins, "Sorger had outlived several of those who had become close to him"),[44] and at the point at which he is returning to Europe, having successfully become the primary object of his observations, he becomes a "you": "In the night plane to Europe it was as though you, my dear Sorger, were taking your 'first real journey,' the journey on which, so it is said, a man learns what his own style is. . . . You no longer knew who you were. Where was your dream of greatness? You were no one."[45]

It is at that point that the dominant micropolitical theme of the story becomes evident, Sorger's continuing attempt to achieve control of his subjectivity by wresting it from its shameful association with his Austrian patrimony. Rather than stating that political problematic directly, Sorger deploys it on spaces and on other bodies. With respect to the latter, there is an exemplary encounter between Sorger and a cat that suffers from the kind of imposed subjectivity that it is Sorger's desire to transcend. In one of the novel's most lyrical as well as critical passages, Sorger is holding the cat while describing (in the German language, within which he feels at home) the various ways cats have been identified. Lifting the cat, he says, "Now say something. Stop pretending, you sanctimonious quadruped, you parentless monster, you childless thief. . . . Absurd beast . . . satanic creature of the night, slavishly available metaphor."[46]

Time is a constant punctuation in Handke's narrative. Wanting to rid himself of his own slavishness (to his national origin), specifically to take possession of a self that can substitute a *time* of peace for his former association (as an Austrian) with a *time* of violence, he realizes "that history is not a mere sequence of evils which someone like me can do nothing but despise—but has also, from time immemorial, been a peace-fostering form that can be perpetrated by anyone (including me)."[47] To manage that perpetration, Handke's aesthetic subject and alter ego, Sorger, becomes nomadic, not only by traversing spaces but also by engaging in what Gilles Deleuze famously calls "nomad thought," thought with which one can "evade the codes of settled people."[48]

While for Deleuze, nomad thought is an anti-state "war machine,"[49] for Handke, it's an antistate peace machine. His nomad thought is nevertheless in accord with Deleuze's notion of "nomadic ethics," which promotes "transformation in opposition to the normative protocols of Kantian universalism" and serves to "empower . . . modes of becoming."[50] On the road (physically as well as conceptually), Handke/Sorger contrasts with sedentary "[w]riters who are firmly located in the *polis*."[51] Traversing spaces, he is part of a flow that no one nation-state's allegiance demands can contain. Seeking to be at home with himself, the thought Handke achieves is a "counter-habitation,"[52] an articulation of "the kind of critical consciousness that resists settling into socially coded modes of thought and behavior."[53]

Handke had addressed that kind of critical consciousness with another traveling/becoming subject in an earlier novel, *Short Letter Long Farewell*, in which the traveler (a writer) experiences a destabilization of identity (also on the "other continent"):

> "This is my second day in America," I said stepping off the sidewalk. "I wonder if I've already changed. . . . for the present I had left my old environment behind me; in my new environment I was still incapable of being anything more than a someone who made use of public conveniences.[54]
>
> As I have put it elsewhere (in response to that passage), "Here is an identity in flux . . . yet [it] comes to rest. . . . The narrator, partly because as a traveler he is especially aware of the instability of identities, becomes an attentive reader of his environment and recognizes that all realities within which subjects take up residence are in some way scripted."[55]

As has been the case throughout his oeuvre, Handke punctuates each of his protagonist's encounters by giving them a dual force; first, there is the nature of his character's perception of things, followed by a commentary on what the perception reveals about the instabilities of identity and about the ontological investments revealed about the subject, as the experience of instability produces a drive toward self-fashioning. For example, at the very outset of Sorger's story, he is in what is described as both a "laboratory" and a "dwelling" (where "dwelling" implies more than mere living space; it also suggests that he is situated not only in a knowledge venture but also in an ontological project). Alternatively observing things through microscopes and binoculars, his vista of things is first described, "sunset light and the hovering woolly-white seeds of the dwarf poplars." Then the vista becomes "an after-work corridor, as it were to 'his' beach."[56]

The perceptual situation is followed by the ontological investment. Handke's style therefore differs markedly from dialog-oriented writing, for example, Dostoevsky's novels, which are wholly dialogic and thus unpunctuated by conceptual commentary. Within Dostoyevsky's texts, there is no other "conceptual persona"[57] observing from the outside. As Bakhtin puts it, "Not a single element of the work is structured from the point of view of a non-participating 'third person.' . . . there is no place for them compositionally."[58]

In contrast, what is accomplished by Handke's punctuating style is access to the dynamic through which subjects become objects. Grammatical shifts articulate that dynamic as Handke composes his stories by punctuating his subject's experiences with commentary from the outside. Once alerted to the forces that render their subjectivity as a relationship with what transpires around them, Handke's protagonists become open to change or *transformation* (Handke's preferred term). That insight about subjects-as-objects appears in one of Handke's poems, "Changes During the Course of the Day" (written from an ironic perspective of a subject becoming objectified):

> And when the car makes a sudden stop in front of me—I become an obstacle.
> Then I am seen by a figure in the dark—and become a figure in the dark.
> And when I am observed through binoculars—I am an object.
> Then someone stumbles over me—and I become a body.
> And when I am stepped on—I become something soft.
> Then I am wrapped up in something—and become a content.[59]

While his poems have a "monologically sealed off" subject—a "single person hegemony over his own language"[60]—in the novels, Handke accomplishes an ironic distance to treat the subject-as-object by dividing his subjectivity with frequent grammatical switching.

There is similar grammatical punctuation in Imre Kertész's writing (even though his primary form of punctuation is accomplished with ironic tropes). In his case, to simultaneously create perspectives from the inside and outside, he has sentences in which the subject pronoun is a third person, followed by an (I), explicitly in *The Union Jack* and symbolically in his other novels.[61] In addition to the grammatical punctuations, Kertész's writings are philosophically punctuated. He acquired a philosophical distance from his personal experience after his period as an adolescent in the concentration camps, where, as is the case for all camp survivors, he survived because of an "accident": "survival was an exception, a flaw in the Nazi machinery."[62] To make sense of that experience, he not only wrote but also immersed himself in Western European philosophical texts (some of which he translated into Hungarian). Those texts, especially Kant's three critiques, inflected the way he retrospectively understood his camp experiences.

Imre Kertész

While the main concept that punctuates Handke's Holocaust-inspired writing is peace, for Kertész, it is life. For example, questioned (in his *Dossier K*) by a fictional interviewer about his solution to maintaining his sanity (while many succumbed to "Jewish self-hatred"), he credits his post-Auschwitz mental survival to his decision to become a writer: "As a writer I was able to treat my cares as the raw material of my art. And even if that raw material looks fairly cheerless, the form is able to transform it and turn it into pleasure, because writing can only come from an abundance of energies, from pleasure; writing—and this is not my invention—is heightened life."[63]

Like Handke, Kertész liberated his thinking through a territorial migration that enlightened him about "life." He moved for some time to Berlin, "not for the architecture but for the life—the air of culture and freedom," which contrasted with the situation in his native Hungary.[64] Noting that his first and most important novel, *Fatelessness*, is about the Holocaust but is set in Hungary in the sixties and seventies, he is asked, "Which historical episode exerted more of an influence on how he novel came to life," to which he responds,

> Well, I wrote the entire novel during the Communist period. . . . my first challenge was to create a language, a form, and finally a *sujet*. I wanted to examine the particular existence, the experience of life within a totalitarian system. It was not at all clear to me how to go about that stylistically. I had to forge a language from scratch, one sufficiently strong and precise, I didn't want to add to all the white noise around the topic.[65]

Kertész was thus addressing "life" in two registers—his life as a survivor and the life world within which his surviving was taking place. As for his ultimate stylistic choices, the writing situation he faced is akin to what the painter Francis Bacon faced. As Gilles Deleuze suggests, it is wrong to assume that the artist "works on a white surface." Rather, "everything he has in his head, or around him is already on the canvass, more or less virtually, before he begins his work."[66] To avoid what Deleuze calls the "psychic clichés and "*figurative givens*" in painting genres, the artist must "transform" or "deform" what is "always already on the canvass."[67]

Similarly, as Kertész implies, he was not faced with blank pages; he was writing not only to fill the pages but also to clear away the clichés of "Holocaust Culture" as a representational practice—for example, the happy ending stories: "You think of Steven Spielberg in the United States, or the 'negative' approaches: people talk about the Holocaust and inhumanity . . . well, . . . it was of course humans who were responsible, so I'm not sure it makes much sense to talk about inhumanity."[68]

In his drive to recover *his* humanity through writing, Kertész sought to overcome an imposed facticity. His identity plight bore striking resemblance to Frantz Fanon's, whose most inspired writing was also in reaction to an imposition. In his chapter "The Fact of Blackness," Fanon refers to the way he is identified by "others"—as a "Dirty Nigger!" Or simply [as a] "Negro," an experience of being "an object in the midst of other objects," of being "sealed into [a] crushing objecthood."[69] Similarly, Kertész was confronted with the fact of Jewishness. He and his parents—more or less nonobservant Jews—had thought of themselves simply as Hungarians. As the Nazis' noose began to tighten around Hungary's Jewish population, however, their Jewishness was increasingly imposed. Thus, early in *Fatelessness*, Kertész's protagonist, György (Gyuri) Köves, observes an alteration in the family's attentiveness to their surrounding ethnoscape, which they had formerly ignored: "A while ago we took little notice of the neighbors, but now it has turned out that we are of the same race, which calls for some exchanging of views of an evening on the matter of our changing prospects."[70]

The dispassionate mood of that passage is maintained throughout the novel as Köves finds himself struggling to make sense of a fate that is perplexingly assigned to him. Rather than challenging its injustice, Kertész describes it from the point of view of a naïve character being swept along by events in which others impose a disparaged identity on him. At each stage of the tightening carceral network, Köves has no ability to assert a personality. He cannot act from "propensities" of his "character" or "individuality . . . but solely from the situation, which commands the terrain like a foreign power."[71] He merely tries to adapt, described in passages that are "saturated with irony."[72] For example, at the historical point at which Jews are forced to wear yellow stars, rather than bitterly lamenting the symbolic violence that requirement entails, Köves calmly reports his growing libidinal interest in a girl his age who, he says, "has a long neck and is already starting to round out under her yellow star."[73] And when his father is sent off to a forced labor camp, Köves, who had been largely innocent of Jewish ritual, is drawn into a prayer session by his Uncle Lajos:

I was a bit put out by not understanding a single word of what we were saying to God, since I had to recite to Him in Hebrew, a language unknown to me. In order somehow to keep up, I was therefore increasingly obliged to watch Uncle Lajos's lip movements, so in actual fact out of the whole business all that remained with me of what we mumbled was the sight of those mostly wriggling, fleshy lips and the incomprehensible gabble of a foreign tongue.[74]

Of course, the consequences of an imposed Jewish subjectivity—his being interpellated as a Jew by his Uncle Lajos—pale in comparison with what follows from his experiences in three concentration camps, Auschwitz, Buchenwald, and Zeitz, where within the violent purview of the Nazi death machine, he is a "Jew" and accordingly subjected to forced labor (where he nearly dies from malnutrition and illness). Both the benign and violent interpellations that afflict Köves are, like all imposed subjectivities, "misinterpellations" (if we accept a model of the subject that is multiple). Köves's experience, though extraordinarily harsh, is nevertheless universal. As James Martel points out (in his reinflection of the Althusserian concept of interpellation), "we have never been the subjects we thought we were. . . . we are not in fact utterly determined and controlled by those identities we receive."[75]

Moreover (and very much fitting the experiences of Kertész's Köves), (mis)interpellations can be experienced as accusations. As Martel puts it, "interpellation itself is inherently a form of accusation . . . a form of address that occurs within a preestablished field of guilt," which is a common reaction among those oppressed.[76] In response to accusations, however—for example, being designated as part of "the whole Jewish rabble" (at the point at which he is rounded up with other Jews destined for transshipment to Auschwitz)—rather than feeling guilty, Köves is bewildered. At that moment, he simply tries to make sense of his captors' "indecipherable babble of commands," saying: "I didn't even know offhand which way I was supposed to turn, and all I remember is that in the thick of it I felt a bit like laughing, in part out of astonishment and confusion, a sense of having been slap in the middle of some crazy play in which I was not entirely acquainted with my role."[77]

Shortly afterward, in contrast with the chaos of the initial roundup, Köves is relieved and admiring of the orderliness with which the German soldiers, "the sole anchors of solidity and calm in the whole tumult," manage "with elegant hand gestures to indicate directions" during the organization of the journey to the Auschwitz.[78] And once in the camps, he remains calm. Rather than lamenting the (mis)interpellations that have afflicted him, robbing him of control over his "fate," he makes the best of his circumstances, admiring the orderliness the Nazis' organization of the concentration camps' daily operations and finding "peace" in difficult circumstances by maintaining a studied passivity: "As for work, I no longer strove to give the appearance of it. If people did not like that, at most they would beat me, and even then they could not do much harm, since for me it just won some time: at the first blow I would promptly stretch out on the ground and would feel nothing after that, since I would meanwhile drop off to sleep."[79]

Nevertheless, *Fatelessness* and Kertész's subsequent novels push back against the injustice of Köves's stolen fate. It is irony rather than bitter recrimination, however, that punctuates Kertész's fictional version of his experiences, carried out through a trilogy of novels (*Fatelessness* was followed by *Fiasco* and *Kaddish for an Unborn Child*). Although the novels all display an ironic detachment, they manifest an intensity that Kertész achieves by punctuating the texts with strings of adjectives. In *Fatelessness*, Kertész has Köves explain his literary posture to a man whom Köves encounters on a train while headed home to Budapest. After the man admonishes the conductor for demanding a ticket from one who has suffered in the camps, he asks Köves how he is feeling and seeks to solicit the "horror" story he presumes that Köves is positioned to tell: "Did you endure many horrors?" To which I replied that it all depends on what he considered to be a horror. No doubt he declared . . . I had undergone a lot of deprivation, hunger, and more than likely they had beaten me . . . to which I said: Naturally. "Why my dear boy . . . do you keep saying 'naturally,' and about things that are not at all natural?"[80]

Unsatisfied with a story that reveals no sense of horror, Köves's interlocutor follows him off the train and continues to press for an explanation of his seemingly disengaged way of recounting his experience. Köves then explains to him (and to the reader) how he (Köves) naturalized the camps in his day-to-day management of his experience and, accordingly, how he (Kertész) comes to terms with the experience thereafter (a key passage that needs to be presented at length, as the novel's intensity builds, punctuated with adjective strings, and its temporal punctuation is shown to be homologous with the temporality of Köves's/Kertsez's camp experience):

> After a brief reflection I came up with "Time." "What do you mean time?" "Time helps." "Helps with what?" "Everything," and I tried to explain how different it was, for example, to arrive in a not exactly

opulent but still, on the whole, agreeable, neat, and clean station where everything becomes clear only gradually, sequentially over time By the time one has passed a given step, put it behind one, the next one is already there. By the time one knows everything one has already understood it all. And while one is coming to understand everything, a person does not remain idle: he is already attending to his new business, living, acting, moving, carrying out each new demand at each new stage. Were it not for that sequencing in time, and were the entire knowledge to crash in upon a person on the spot in one fell swoop, it might well be that neither one's brain nor one's heart would cope with it.[81]

Just as Köves strove to manage his life in the camps, Kertész sought to manage a novel in which Auschwitz could be brought to life: "everything had to come into being through the magic of language and composition,"[82] a work of fiction but nevertheless, he says, "an equivalent of my experiences . . . a work of art [in which he manages a switch] from the personal to the objective and the general."[83] In constructing the novel, Kertész manages a dual temporality, Köves's, who (as Kertész recollects his own experience) "had a spot of trouble with time; while living it, it seemed interminable to him, but when he thought about it as the past, it seemed practically nothing, a duration that might be fitted into a single hour," and his own, a life in which he had incorporated his past "as the material of [his] experiences" happening "a second time, with much more reality" as he composes it.[84]

The trajectory of Kertész's life is also "from the personal to the objective and the general," inasmuch as having instructed himself with the reading of philosophical texts (as well as those from artistic genres), the story he creates of Köves/Kertész is always already conceptually mediated. Reading Schopenhauer, for example, "had the abiding merit of leading me to Kant."[85] Kantian philosophy's impact on Kertész's novelistic reconstruction of the camp experience is unambiguously evident by the time he wrote *Kaddish for an Unborn Child*, in which he introduces the character "Teacher," who helps Köves stay alive when he becomes too infirm to pick up his own food ration. Seeking to explain why Teacher "did what he did" to "keep Köves alive"—which was against his own survival interests, since he could have taken the extra food ration for himself—Köves turns to Kantian transcendentalism, saying:

There *exists* a pure concept, untrammeled by any foreign matter, such as our body, a notion which lives in a uniform image in our minds, yes

> an idea whose . . . inviolability, safekeeping, or what you will was for him, "Teacher," the *sole genuine chance* of saying alive, without which his chance of staying alive would have been no chance at all, simply because he did not wish and . . . was *unable* to live without preserving this concept intact in its pure, untrammeled openness to scrutiny. . . . *this* is what there is no explanation for, since it is not rational as compared with the tangible rationality of an issue of food rations.[86]

Kantian philosophy provided Kertész with his second freedom: the first was his liberation from the camp; the second was his embrace of Kant's distinction between the sensible and the supersensible. While the former locates the self within the domain of nature, the realm of necessity, the latter locates the self in the domain of freedom. Thus, as Kertész emerged as a writer, his account of his camp experiences is mediated through his reading, not only of German philosophy (e.g., he refers to Nietzsche and Heidegger as well as Kant)[87] but also of literature and a variety of artistic and cultural genres.

With respect to literature, his writing style has a strong affinity with Kafka and Camus, whose protagonists (e.g., Kafka's various versions of "K" and Camus's "Stranger") display an ironically expressed curiosity about and satirical constructions of the banal, unreflective authority structures that victimize them rather than lamenting the injustice of their suffering. With respect to artistic genres, his writing bears signs of his familiarity with detective fiction, exemplified in his later novel *Detective Story*, in which there is a critical speculation about the identity ambiguities afflicting the minds of characters in crisis. And there are also reflections on the influence of music, especially Wagnerian opera, by his protagonist in *The Union Jack* (Kertész admits in *Dossier K* that his literary compositions are musically inspired).

Apart from all the stylistic and ideational mediations that punctuate Kertész's writing, he ultimately saw his writing task as a problem of temporal punctuation. He strove to articulate novelistic time with biographical/historical time. Hence, in response to a question he poses to himself in *Dossier K* about the biographical accuracy of a conversation with two old men, Fleischmann and Steiner, in *Fatelessness*, he writes:

> Pure fiction, although it's possible we really did talk about something of the kind. As I have said already, the figure of Gyorgy Köves more closely resembles the person who wrote the novel than the person who actually lived through it. For the person who wrote the novel the situation was important, the cathartic moment when Köves doesn't just

realize but is able to interpret his fate, and in the novel this had to occur in novelistic time and place that happen to be in the presence of the two old codgers.[88]

Thus Kertész, like Handke's Sorger, was a becoming subject. While Sorger's ascension to self-possession emerges through encounters with land- and cityscapes, Kertész's emerges through his apprenticeship in philosophy and literature. That apprenticeship helped him "survive his survival." Having felt the kind of shame common to survivors, "he had to formulate his shame deftly and give what he had formulated lasting form. In other words, he had to become a good writer."[89]

Edified by Kertész's valorization of writing, which turns the micropolitics of an individual's experience into a macropolitical pedagogy, so that a catastrophic historical event can re-emerge critically refigured with significance beyond the experience of the individual, I turn to a similar contribution that summons the Holocaust through an individual's exemplary experience, W. G. Sebald's *Austerlitz*. It's a novel figured as a journey of detection, which also turns a micropolitics of survival into a macropolitical re-punctuation of the event of the Holocaust. The most immediate similarity between the writing projects of Kertész and Sebald turns on a motivation to achieve a rescue involving names. Kertész rescues himself through writing in order, as I have noted, to take control over naming himself. Sebald's novel *Austerlitz* involves a variety of rescues. However, "Of all the rescues that the novel poses, the most difficult may be this one: to restore to Jacques Austerlitz the individuality of his name and experience, to rescue the living privacy of the surname."[90]

W. G. Sebald

As is the case with Handke and Kertész, Franz Kafka haunts Sebald's compositions, in part because Sebald shares with Handke and Kertész an identity displacement that provides the kind of space from which Kafka wrote, the "margins," which, as Deleuze and Guattari suggest, "allows . . . the means for another consciousness and another sensibility."[91] The other sensibilities enacted by the three writers are articulated through their stylistic debts to Kafka. Handke's attentiveness and debt to Kafka is most evident in his early novel *The Anxiety of the Goaltender During the Penalty Kick*, in which the protagonist/murderer's name is the allusive name, Joseph Bloch, which combines the names of the two accused men in Kafka's *The Trial*, Joseph K and Block. There is also a stylistic debt, a tendency, especially pronounced in *Slow Homecoming*, to use some names and omit others (e.g., in "The Far North, where Sorger and his scientific cabin mate, Lauffer, reside, and there is also 'the Indian woman'). Moreover, just as Kafka articulates paradoxical temporalities—combining "repetitious and singular events" throughout his story "The Burrow"[92]—Handke combines the episodic time that repetitively shapes his daily peaceful experience of the landscape in the far north and the singularity of the event of the Holocaust that violently haunts his experience of his Austrian heritage in "The Long Way Around."

Kafka likewise inhabits many of Kertész's compositions, not only because like Kafka, the author's name and his protagonist in *Fatelessness* are both Ks (doubtless Kertész has Kafka in mind in his naming practices) but also because Kertész's heavily ironic descriptions of persons and places and, most importantly, his protagonists' accounts of their situations are Kafkaesque. His protagonist, Köves, like Kafka's Joseph K, is innocent but prevented from making an effective case with his oppressors. He is like so many of Kafka's oppressed characters (e.g., Karl Rossman in his *Amerika*), (mis)interpellated subjects who, although effectively defenseless, describe their experiences in dispassionate and ironic phrases that make the oppressive authorities they describe appear bizarre. And as in the case of Handke's *Anxiety*, aspects of Kafka's *The Trial* inhabit Kertesz's *Fatelessness*. The previously noted moment when Köves, unable to understand Hebrew while joining his Uncle Lajos in prayer, is baffled by the words and has his gaze fixed on "the sight of those mostly wriggling, fleshy lips," is likely influenced by a moment when Kafka's K cannot understand the Italian or French of his interlocutor and says, "It was no use watching his lips for clues, since their movements were covered by the bushy moustache."[93]

Although all three writers reference Kafka in their texts, only in Sebald's case is Kafka the focus of separate and extended critical commentary. Just as Handke had reacquainted himself with an important influence on his observations, the canvases of Paul Cézanne, by traveling through one of Cézanne's routes, Sebald reacquaints himself with Kafka by rereading his travel diaries while traveling, noting how he, Sebald, has been on the same route and has stayed in some of the same places as Kafka.[94] And in a commentary on Handke's play *Kaspar*, Sebald discusses the Kafkaesque effects in Handke's works.[95] There are also Kafka effects that punctuate Sebald's prose throughout his *Austerlitz*, in which at one point his eponymous protagonist mentions that a neighbor who had read

Kafka's diaries told him about a character in one entry, a bow-legged man with his name, Austerlitz.[96]

Perhaps the most evident Kafka effect, however, derives from Sebald's interest in the way Kafka treats characters with allegorical references to a bestiary (e.g., his mention of Kafka's story about an ape in "Report to an Academy").[97] Tellingly in *Austerlitz*, Sebald's protagonist comes to terms with himself the way Kafka often did, through animal protagonists, in his case especially with moths. In a conversation with the narrator, Austerlitz refers to his Great Uncle Alphonso's practice of observing moths for hours and reports Alphonso's remarks about "how each of these extravagant creatures had its own character."[98] He writes of his uncle's fascination with the way their appearances challenge human's perceptions, leading him to appreciate the fragility of one's grasp of reality:

> The trails of light which they seem to leave behind them in all kinds of curlicues and streamers and spirals . . . were merely phantom traces created by the sluggish reaction of the human eye, appearing to see a certain afterglow in the place from which the insect itself, shining for only the fraction of a second in the lamplight, had really gone. It was such unreal phenomena. . . . the sudden incursion of unreality into the real world, certain effects of light in the landscape spread out before us, or in the eye of a beloved person, that kindled the deepest feelings.[99]

The moth allegory situates a character whose "trails," which at the outset of the story exist as "merely phantom traces," obscure not only an individual biography but also a historical experience common to many that were within the reach of the Nazis' ethnic cleaning apparatuses. Sebald's story, a complicated, nonlinear narrative of the recovery of Austerlitz's patrimony, achieves its main dynamic through conversations over a span of thirty years with the unnamed narrator, who first meets Jacques Austerlitz in Antwerp's Centraal Station, where the first of many of their conversations takes place. Sebald achieves an ironic distance by placing himself in the text as Austerlitz's interlocutor, encountering him at various stages of Austerlitz's voyage of self-discovery. After their first encounter, the *story* (Sebald insists that he is a prose writer rather than a novelist)[100] is punctuated with photographs and observations about architecture, music, cinema, and the history of painting, all in the service of the multiple temporalities that situate an exemplary life dedicated to self-discovery.

To sketch that life briefly (as Sebald invents it): Sent to the U.K. through a rescue effort known as the *kindertransport* (when the U.K. accepted roughly 10,000 Jewish children from Germany, Austria, Czechoslovakia, and Poland prior to the outbreak of World War II), Jacques Austerlitz lost his name and became Dafydd Elias, the adopted son of an austere Calvinist Welsh couple with whom he learned little of his origins. He attends Oxford, where he studies to become an architectural historian and doesn't begin facing the way the Holocaust had claimed his parents' lives and his search to learn the details of their fates until he is middle-aged.

The story's complex web of temporal and geographical punctuations through which Austerlitz's dislocation is composed (the fundamental misinterpellation that historical events have imposed on him) gives the reader a similar sense of dislocation. Like the visitor to Libeskind's Jewish Museum (treated in the Introduction), who is deprived of a main narrative pathway (there is no simple linear narrative of self-discovery to follow), Sebald's text builds a world of disjunctive temporalities, condensed in monuments, buildings, and cityscapes and conveyed in a multitude of artistic media genres that his protagonist interprets to provide disparate clues about the dynamic force field in which he, Austerlitz, recovers his origins. As the personal recovery is underway, the text recovers the historical significance of the names and events that "Austerlitz" signifies: a family name, a famous battle, and a word that resounds with a tonality similar to the name of the extermination camp at Auschwitz.

Throughout the story, Austerlitz provides a commentary on time that effectively represents the way layers of temporality are woven into the story. At one point, he says that "time itself has been nonconcurrent over the centuries,"[101] and adds (in accord with my suggestion that all historical events will-have-been, i.e., they come back with different boundaries and significance when summoned within different thought worlds): "I shall find that all moments of time have co-existed simultaneously, in which case none of what history tells us would be true; past events have not yet occurred but are waiting to do so at the moment when we think of them."[102] In addition to continually referencing Jacques Austerlitz's time consciousness through his utterances, which mimic the structure of the story itself, Sebald locates temporality in artistic genres that disclose and animate interacting temporal layers—in photographs, in buildings, in paintings, in films, and in urban formations, making the story as a whole a poesis of time that links biographical and historical levels. At the same time, Sebald's composing of a "literary time"—well characterized by one commentary as "a poetics of suspension: a poetics that suspends portions of chronology, succession, comprehension, and closure"[103]—imposes on the reader the need to discard the historically received narratives through which events are ordinarily recognized and replace them with a need to reflect.

Of the variety of artistic genres that punctuate Sebald's thought-provoking, nonlinear narrative, photography is the most pervasive, intervening in many moments of the text. The photos express Roland Barthes's previously noted linkage between photography and time. Their presence in Sebald's narrative animates Barthes's suggestion that photographers are "'agents of death. Whether or not the subject is already dead, every photograph is this catastrophe,' . . . an effect . . . surely heightened when we look at photographs of victims of the Nazis."[104] Moreover, if we observe that Sebald's text bears comparison with an essential aspect of the temporality of realist novels, especially those focused on family histories and thus shaped by a "genealogical imperative," that is, a locating of events in a "dynastic line that unites the diverse generations of a genealogical family,"[105] we can recognize an important function that the photographic punctuations effect. Because Sebald's text recovers a genealogical line that has been violently interrupted, the disruptive interspersing of photographs serves to mime the family's historical disruption, while at the same time exploiting the photograph's (Barthean) death connotations, their necro-testimonies.

Competing for space with photographic punctuation are the architectural observations that punctuate Sebald's text. They provide many of the layers of historical time within which Austerlitz's story is situated. At the outset of the story, the narrator's imagination of animal- and peoplescapes is evoked as he interarticulates a bestiary with the architecture of Antwerp's Centraal Station. After visiting Antwerp's zoo, the "Nocturama," whose animals ("denizens") and interior have become confused in his mind with his "memories of the *Salles des pas perdus*," the name of the waiting room of the nearby station, which he describes as he looks up "at the façade of that fantastical building,"[106] he proceeds to note the station's origin, "constructed under the patronage of King Leopold II." He then describes "a vertiginous Negro boy seated upon his dromedary in an oriel turret to the left of the station façade, a monument to the world of animals and naïve peoples of the African continent." That experience leads him to "the passing thought" of "the last members of a diminutive race which had perished or been expelled from its homeland, and that because they alone survived they wore the same sorrowful expression as the creatures in the zoo."[107] He thus temporalizes the station, turning it from silent materiality into a testament to the history of Belgium's colonial atrocities. Such renderings of materiality into temporality are continuous throughout the story as Sebald extracts duration from matter.

After Sebald's nameless narrator emerges from his reverie about the way his visit to the Nocturama evokes the station's testimony to Belgium's colonialism, he has the narrator's conversations with Austerlitz pick up the architectural commentary that punctuates the story thereafter. They are conversations dominated by Austerlitz, who reports that he is involved in "investigations into the history of architecture and civilization." Importantly, at their first encounter, the architectural venue the narrator/interlocutor finds Austerlitz investigating—the *Salles des pas perdus*—is a "waiting room," which serves as an allegory for the two interarticulated aspects of the text.

On the one hand is Austerlitz's life on hold, suspended between the present and past, as he seeks to recover the story of his name and the fates of his mother and father, and on the other is the author's text, a concatenation of suspensions, temporal fragments that situate the reader in a back and forth whirlwind journey that proposes that one comprehend the event of the Holocaust through a "postcatastrophic temporal consciousness"[108] in which the past keeps altering the present. In this sense, Sebald's text accords with a Bergsonian insight: "the most profound paradox of memory: the past is 'contemporaneous with the present' that it *has* been."[109] And crucially, a body caught within the contracted moments of past and present is more than a mere "punctiform instant in time";[110] it is a durational trajectory, a search that covers a wide variety of geographic locations each of which punctuate the way the text constitutes the future anterior (the will-have-been) of the event of the Holocaust.

Above all, the primary punctuations in Sebald's story are the two bodies, two durations that mark the material world that is, has been, and will have been. Thus, as their conversational encounters proceed, buildings and rooms become "event spaces" that mark historical change as they testify obliquely to the Holocaust's fracturing of historical time and "civilization." Exemplary in this respect is a visit by the narrator and Austerlitz to a house, which during the "war years" had been requisitioned "for use as a convalescent home."[111] And tellingly, much of the architectural focus is on railway stations, for example, the one that shares Austerlitz's name, the gare d'Austerlitz, which when he saw it gave Austerlitz a felt "premonition that he was coming closer to his father [a Holocaust victim who disappeared in Paris] . . . an idea came to him of his father's leaving Paris from this station"—one of the nodes in the Nazi prisoner transport system—on the way to his death in a concentration camp.[112]

The story's main narrative, which moves with a critical slowness, is on the duration involved in the protagonist's recovery of his name, Austerlitz. It's a story of a gradual becoming that he undergoes as he investigates the details of his origins. The story's slowness is articulated through yet another artistic genre that participates in Sebald's drama. Just as Sebald's text performs a slowness that allows for a critical look at the Holocaust as it painstakingly amplifies a single, historically affected/afflicted life, at a critical moment in the story, Austerlitz himself performs a slowness; he slows down a Nazi propaganda film while seeking to find images of his mother. In a crucial part of the bio/historical narrative, Austerlitz has obtained a cassette copy of a film the Nazis made in the Czech concentration camp, Theresienstadt, entitled *Der Führer schenkt den Juden eine Stadt* (The Führer gifts the Jews a city).[113] On his initial viewing of the fourteen-minute video, he strains to catch a glimpse of his mother as he observes a rapid concatenation of images of "various tasks being carried out. . . . an unbroken succession of strangers' faces," and a variety of leisure scenes: concert-going, gardening, playing, and reading, all of which merely "flickered" before his eyes.[114] After trying unsuccessfully to find his mother's face "among those fleeting faces," he got "the idea of having a slow motion copy of the fourteen-minute fragment from Theresienstadt made, one which would last a whole hour."[115]

The effect of the reproduced film is very much like the effects achieved by film directors who practice what have come to be called "slow movies"[116]—for example, Andrei Tarkovsky, who said that his "long-take style,"[117] . . . developed in opposition to the rapid montage style of his fellow countryman, Sergei Eisenstein, gives the viewer "an opportunity to live through what is on screen as if it were his own life, to take over the experience imprinted in time on the screen."[118] Accordingly, once Austerlitz has slowed down the Nazi propaganda film, making it four times its original length, he is able to enter the demoralized world of the Theresienstadt inmates and find an image of his mother. Slowed down, the film reveals "previously hidden objects and people. . . . The men and women employed in the workshops now looked as if they were toiling in their sleep . . . [and those moving about] seemed to be hovering rather than walking, as if their feet no longer touched the ground, . . . [and] strangest of all, said Austerlitz, was the transformation of sounds in this slow-motion version [for example] . . . the merry polka of some Austrian operetta composer . . . had become a funeral march dragging along at a grotesquely . . . sluggish pace."[119] Thus, in the role of a film editor, as in his role as an architectural historian, Austerlitz reproduces the Holocaust the way the text as a whole enacts it: slowly, painstakingly, and obliquely.

Crucially, for purposes of my analysis, Sebald involves Austerlitz in one other film commentary, one in which he ponders the question I raise at the outset of this chapter, that of the adequacy of words to capture events. Austerlitz describes a moment in Paris's *Bibliothéque Nationale* where he is "watching a short black and white film [about the library] . . . *Toute la Memoire du monde* . . . made by Alain Resnais," which, he says, "assumed ever more monstrous and fantastic dimensions in my imagination." He reports, "it struck me that the scholars, together with the whole apparatus of the library, formed an immensely complex and constantly evolving creature which had to be fed with myriads of words, in order to bring forth myriads of words in its own turn."[120] Certainly, as Austerlitz is suggesting, as words about the Holocaust-as-event keep accumulating, they don't add up to an ultimate closure of its meaning; they only thicken the flow of words, which (as I suggested at the outset) "hover in the vicinity of that historical catastrophe without definitively capturing it." Nevertheless, to borrow from an observation of David Albahari attributed to a similar historical ambiguity, the ancestry of immigrant refugees to which the word *background* has been applied: "Background is the wrong word, but better that word than none at all."[121]

Conclusion: The Holocaust After Handke, Kertész, and Sebald

That statement in Albahari's novel, which is peopled with (among others) refugee artists and writers settled in Banff, Canada, accords with the primary problem of the three writers whose works I analyze in this chapter. It is about lending temporal depth to biographies, about giving dislocated people historical presence while at the same time rethinking the political and ethical approach to their events of displacement. Albahari's character-mediated insistence on the need for *a* word, wrong or not, to lend temporal depth to diverse individuals in the novel, however, references only one side of a text's durational effects. As I've put it elsewhere, "After [Henri] Bergson, we must recognize that *subjects* are durations that encounter external durations. The apprehension of events is entangled with recollection"[122] because "the body *is* something other than a mathematical point. . . . it is the recollections of memory that link . . . instants to each other and interpolate the past in the present. . . . It is therefore memory that makes the body something other than instantaneous and gives it a duration in time."[123] Hence, a novel's or a story's aesthetic (durational) subjects are encountered by readers who are also durations. Just as Tarkovsky's viewers are durations given "an opportunity to live through what is on screen as if it were his own life, to take over the experience imprinted in time on the screen,"[124] Handke's, Kertész's, and Sebald's compositional styles, deployed with durational subjects, punctuate their texts in ways that impose on their readers the need to reflect on their own temporal trajectories, to "live through" what is in the pages. Moreover, because their readers, like Bakhtin's authors, are "axiological yet to be," their approaches to the Holocaust articulate in each of the texts an "ethics of the event."[125] As a result, the experiences of their protagonists impose on readers a task of sense-making that encourages not only a rethinking of the Holocaust—seen through lenses that articulate biography with history—but also parallel phenomenological reflections in which they confront the ethical comportment toward events of their own durational selves.

Ultimately, what is fundamentally shared in Handke's, Kertész's, and Sebald's texts are the observations and acts through which Holocaust-affected individuals seek to reclaim "unclaimed experience."[126] All three testify obliquely to the Holocaust's "fracturing of time and civilization" (as I put it above) by creating durational subjects involved in coming to terms with the ways that the past inflects the management of their presents. What I want to stress with respect to what their texts can do for readers (and for the event)—beyond the suggestion that readers are encouraged to reflect on their own durational trajectories (the mingling of biographical time with historical time)—is to encourage an ethico-political attunement derived through an incessant temporalization of encounters with persons and things in one's every day experience.

As the writers accomplish such effects, what should draw our analytic attention are their aesthetic strategies, especially the textual vehicles to which they turn to formulate what must be thought anew. Thus, to emphasize the primary pedagogy, I want to retrieve from my readings of the three exemplary contributions to a reformulation of what Kertész calls "Holocaust culture"—*how* the texts think the political. I want to end by picking up key encounters that testify to the ways the three writers enact "time," which (to quote Rancière again) "means the form of coexistence of facts that defines a situation and the mode of connection between events that defines a story" because the ways they tell the stories serve to counteractualize the Holocaust by amplifying it from a passing and now abstract historical moment to a series of concrete, experiential, and enduring effects that must be continually engaged.

Handke's aesthetic strategy in his *Slow Homecoming* is to temporalize space to help his protagonist Valentine Sorger recognize that the violent history with which he is associated as an Austrian is not one he must passively accept. To quote from my earlier analysis, Sorger realizes that "history is not a mere sequence of evils which someone like me can do nothing but despise." Recognizing that the northern landscape he investigates at the beginning of his spatial and identity migrations is "episodic," he is ultimately able to see that he, as a becoming subject, participates in temporalizing space and is thus (allegorically) able to challenge the way history is sedimented as an impenetrable, seemingly fixed facticity. Among the most significant thought vehicles involved in his revelations about time and history are the landscape paintings of Paul Cézanne. Through Sorger's engagement with them, Handke transforms them from mere pictures hanging on museum walls into lessons about the dynamics of subjective apprehension, that is, about the process through which consciousness develops an awareness of its immediate surroundings and by extension its relationship with historical time. Because Cézanne captures "the world in the process of becoming perceptible," Handke's Sorger is able to transcend passivity and recognize *his* participation in the process of his self-making as he renders his experiential and historical worlds perceptible.

In contrast with Handke's turn to art, Kertész is able to make sense of *his* experiences and the event within which they transpire by turning to philosophical and literary texts. His philosophical apprenticeship begins with Schopenhauer, who he says "had the abiding merit of leading me to Kant,"[127] whose critical philosophy shapes his subjected-centered ethical posture, while the writers who influence his account of his camp experiences, especially Kafka and Camus, and a familiarity with detective fiction, shape the distancing ironic style that emerges in his protagonist, Köves, who recounts the patient management of his time in the camps.

To repeat part of the passage in which Köves encounters the man who follows him from the train, seeking an explanation for his dispassionate reflection on his camp experience (which prompts him to explain the strategy through which he managed his day-to-day life in the camp): "I came up with 'Time,'" he says, adding, "By the time one has passed a given step, put it behind one, the next one is already there. By the time one knows everything one has already understood it all. And while one is coming to understand everything, a person does not remain idle: he is already attending to his new business, living, acting, moving, carrying out each new demand at each new stage. Were it not for that sequencing in time, and were the entire knowledge to crash in upon a person on the spot in one fell swoop, it might well be that neither one's brain nor one's heart would cope with it."[128] That passage, along with many others, articulates not only a biohistory of a victim but also the philosophical orientation within which that biohistory is recovered and framed, specifically the Kantian philosophical revolution that locates time within the subjects' structure of apprehension rather than in the object world.

Sebald reverses that emphasis. He maps the biohistory of his subject by having that subject recover time in the material world. As Sebald's text assembles a variety of artistic genres to mediate Austerlitz's experience—photography, film, music, art history, and architecture—he uses them to temporalize the material world in ways that recover a microhistory of the Holocaust as it is available in the biography of an individual. Thus, fascism's emergence within the German-Italian axis is treated not in macro-geopolitical terms but in material details, for example, the "boom" in Austerlitz's maternal grandfather's "fez- and slipper-making factory," when "Mussolini's men had taken to wearing that semi-Oriental item of headgear the fez."[129]

As I have suggested, however, the primary materialization of time throughout Sebald's story is articulated through the architectural observations that arise continually in the encounters between Austerlitz and Sebald's narrator. Buildings, especially railway stations, are the most notable parts of the built world that Sebald's story temporalizes. Beginning with Antwerp's Centraal Station and proceeding through a wide variety of buildings, his architectural narrative allows the Theresienstadt concentration camp's architecture of death to emerge both during and after its time. Sebald's text, like that of Handke and Kertész, re-punctuates the Holocaust to locate its endurance in the world, where it remains pervasively accessible when one knows where and how to look.

Introduction: Deferrals, Punctuations, Media Textualities

1. Michael J. Shapiro, *For Moral Ambiguity: National Culture and the Politics of the Family* (Minneapolis: University of Minnesota Press, 2001), 18–19.

2. Shapiro, *For Moral Ambiguity*, 22.

3. The quotations are from the "Afterword," in Michael J. Shapiro, *The Political Sublime* (Durham, NC: Duke University Press, 2018), 169.

4. See Paul Ricoeur, *Time and Narrative*, vol. 1, trans. Kathleen McLaughlin and David Pellauer (Chicago: University of Chicago Press, 1983), 38.

5. Daniel Just, "Aesthetics of Blankness: Political Imagination in Marguerite Duras's Hybrid Narratives," *The Romantic Review* 101, no. 3 (May 2010): 360–61. For Duras's explication of that aesthetic, see "La Destruction La Parole: Entretien avec Marguerite Duras par Jean Narboni et Jacques Rivette," *Cahiers de cinéma* 217 (Novmeber 1969): 45–69, at http://derives.tv/la-destruction-la-parole/.

6. Beth Hinderliter et al., eds. "Introduction," in *Communities of Sense: Rethinking Aesthetics and Politics* (Durham, NC: Duke University Press, 2009), 19.

7. I am borrowing a phrase applied to Jacques Derrida's text, *Glas*. See David Wills, "Derrida and Aesthetics: Lemming (reframing) the Abyss," in *Jacques Derrida and the Humanities*, ed. Tom Cohen, 117 (New York: Cambridge University Press, 2008).

8. See Jacques Rancière, *The Emancipated Spectator*, trans. Gregory Elliott (New York: Verso, 2009), 75.

9. See Wills, "Derrida and Aesthetics," 113.

10. Wills, "Derrida and Aesthetics."

11. Jennifer DeVere Brody, *Punctuation: Art, Politics, and Play* (Durham, NC: Duke University Press, 2008), 12. Although her study is a thorough and very creative treatment of punctuation, it sticks closely to punctuation as "marks," while my approach takes punctuation as a concept/metaphor that ranges beyond marks to a wide variety of pauses and deferrals in diverse artistic media genres.

12. Theodor W. Adorno, "Punctuation Marks," *The Antioch Review* 48, no. 3 (summer 1990): 300–301.

13. Godelieve Mercken-Spaas, "An Interview with Alain Robbe-Grillet and Lillian Dumont," *The French Review* 50, no. 4 (March 1977): 653.

14. Roy Armes, *The Films of Alain Robbe-Grillet* (Amsterdam: John Benjamin B. V., 1981), 141.

15. J.-F. Lyotard, *Discourse, Figure*, trans. Antony Hudek and Mary Lyndon (Minneapolis: University of Minnesota Press, 2011), 212.

16. The quotations are from a reading of the film by Mike Kitchell,

"Slow Slidings of Pleasure," http://eostiakefilm.com/reviews/slowslidingsofpleasure.hmtl.

17. Roland Barthes, *Camera Lucida: Reflections on Photography*, trans. Richard Howard (New York: Hill and Wang, 1982), 26–27.

18. André Bazin, "The Ontology of the Photographic Image," *Film Quarterly* 13, no. 4 (summer 1960): 8, 163.

19. Gilles Deleuze and Félix Guattari, *What Is Philosophy?*, trans. Hugh Tomlinson and Graham Burchell (New York: Columbia University Press, 1994), 51.

20. Deleuze and Guattari, *What Is Philosophy?*, 145; the latter quotations are from Gilles Deleuze, *Difference and Repetition*, trans. Paul Patton (New York: Columbia University Press, 1994), 136.

21. Deleuze and Guattari, *What Is Philosophy?*, 49.

22. See Jean-Paul Sartre, *The Family Idiot: Gustave Flaubert 1821–1857*, trans. Carol Cosman (Chicago: University of Chicago Press, 1987), 25.

23. Quoted in George Craig et al., eds., *The Letters of Samuel Beckett, Volume 2, 1941–1956* (Cambridge: Cambridge University Press, 2011).

24. See Gilles Deleuze and Félix Guattari, *Kafka: Toward a Minor Literature*, trans. Dana Polan (Minneapolis: University of Minnesota Press, 1986), 26. Deleuze and Guattari note, "'The Great Swimmer' is undoubtedly one of the most Beckett-like of Kafka's texts" (94, n25).

25. I'm quoting here from a reference to the conversation in the *New York Times Book Review*, Sunday, November 13, 2011, 6.

26. Leo Bersani, *The Death of Stéphane Mallarmé* (New York: Cambridge University Press, 1982), 4.

27. The concept of an event space belongs to the architectural theorist Bernard Tschumi. See his *Architecture and Disjunction* (Cambridge, MA: MIT Press, 1994).

28. Daniel Libeskind, "Between the Lines," in *Daniel Libeskind: The Space of Encounter* (London: Thames and Hudson, 2001), 28.

29. Daniel Libeskind, quoted in James E. Young, *At Memory's Edge: Afterimages of the Holocaust in Contemporary Art and Architecture* (New Haven, CT: Yale University Press, 2002), 175.

30. Roland Barthes, "From Work to Text," in *Image Music Text*, trans. Stephen Heath (New York: Hill and Wang, 1977), 158.

31. Young, *At Memory's Edge*, 163.

32. Young, *At Memory's Edge*.

33. Libeskind, "Between the Lines," 23.

34. The quotation is from Young, *At Memory's Edge*, 165.

35. Johann Gottlieb Fichte, *Addresses to the German Nation*, trans. R. F. Jones and G. H. Turnbull (Chicago: The Open Court, 1922), 68.

36. Fichte, *Addresses to the German Nation*, 69.

37. Analyzed in Michael J. Shapiro, *Methods and Nations: Cultural Governance and the Indigenous Subject* (London: Routledge, 2004), 37.

38. Shapiro, *Methods and Nations*. The inner quotation is from Roth's story, "Rare and Ever Rarer in This World of Empirical Facts," in *The Collected Stories of Joseph Roth*, trans. Michael Hoffman (New York: W. W. Norton, 2002), 66.

39. For a review of such aspects of cultural governance, see Shapiro, *Methods and Nations*.

40. Fredric Jameson, *The Ancients and the Postmoderns: On the Historicity of Forms* (New York: Verso, 2017), 3.

41. For an account of the religious ferment among those alternatives to Luther's rebellion, see Michael Massing, *Fatal Discord: Erasmus, Luther and the Fight for the Western Mind* (New York: HarperCollins, 2018).

42. Jameson, *The Ancients and the Postmoderns*, 4.

43. Emile Durkheim, *The Elementary Forms of Religious Life*, trans. Joseph Ward Swain (New York: George Allen and Unwin Ltd., 1915), 51.

44. Durkheim, *The Elementary Forms of Religious Life*, 59.

45. The quotation is from Tanael Joachimjan, "What Makes a Country Great? Meet Haiti's People," *New York Times*, January 12, 2018, https://www.nytimes.com/2018/01/12/opinion/what-makes-a-country-great-meet-haitis-people.html? action=click&pgtype=Homepage&clickSource=story-heading&module=opinion-c-col-left-region&region=opinion-c-col-left-region&WT.nav=opinion-c-col-left-region.

46. See Fernand Braudel, *Afterthoughts on Material Civilization and Capitalism*, trans. Patricia Ranum (Baltimore: Johns Hopkins University Press, 1977).

47. See William E. Connolly, "The Evangelical-Capitalist Resonance Machine," *Political Theory* 33, no. 6 (December 2005): 869–86.

48. Connolly, "The Evangelical-Capitalist Resonance Machine," 872.

49. Connolly, "The Evangelical-Capitalist Resonance Machine," 874.

50. See their pamphlet, "Ten Good Reasons to Eliminate Funding for the National Endowment for the Arts," https://www.heritage.org/report/ten-good-reasons-eliminate-funding-the-national-endowment-orthe-arts.

51. The expression belongs to Jacques Rancière, *The Politics of Aesthetics*, trans. Gabriel Rockhill (London: Continuum, 2004), 20.

52. Rancière, *The Politics of Aesthetics*, 23.

53. Philip Dick, "Who Is a SF Writer?," in *The Shifting Realities of Philip K. Dick*, ed. Lawrence Sutin (New York: Pantheon, 1995), 73.

54. Steven Shaviro, *Discognition* (London: Repeater Books, 2015), 8–9.

55. The quotation is from Bernard Stiegler, *Technics and Time 3: Cinematic Time and the Question of Malaise* (Stanford, CA: Stanford University Press, 2011), 91.

56. Stiegler, *Technics and Time 3*, 16.

57. The quotation is from a commentary on Stiegler's *Technics and*

Time 3, by Patrick Grogan, "Experience of the Industrial Temporal Object," in *Stiegler and Technics*, ed. Christina Howells and Gerald Moore (Edinburgh: Edinburgh University Press, 2013), 103.

58. See obituary, "Dan Talbot, Impresario of Art Films, Is Dead at 91," by Anita Gates, *New York Times*, December 31, 2017, https://www.nytimes.com/2017/12/31/obituaries/dan-talbot-dead.html? _r=0.

59. Durkheim, *The Elementary Forms of Religious Life*, 39.

60. The quotation is from Shaviro, *Discognition*, 9.

61. See Galations 5:17: "For the flesh desires what is contrary to the Spirit, and the Spirit what is contrary to the flesh. They are in conflict with each other, so that you are not to do whatever you want."

62. Philip Dick, *The Three Stigmata of Palmer Eldritch* (London: Orion, 1964), 41.

63. Dick, *The Three Stigmata of Palmer Eldritch*, 145.

64. Dick, *The Three Stigmata of Palmer Eldritch*, 193.

65. Barry Lopez, *Arctic Dreams* (New York: Scribners, 1986), 201.

66. See Michael J. Shapiro, *Studies in Trans-Disciplinary Method: After the Aesthetic Turn* (London: Routledge, 2012), 9–10.

67. Shapiro, *Studies in Trans-Disciplinary Method*, 10.

68. Shapiro, *Studies in Trans-Disciplinary Method.*

69. Shapiro, *Studies in Trans-Disciplinary Method.* The internal quotation is from a study by two members of the Oakridge Laboratory social science staff: David B. Bobrow and Alan R. Wilcox, "Dimensions of Defense Opinion: The American Public," *Papers of the Peace Research Society (International)*, vol. 6 (1966), 140.

70. Jacques Rancière, "Fictions of Time," in *Rancière and Literature*, ed. Grace Hellyer and Julian Murphet (Edinburgh: Edinburgh University Press, 2017).

71. Rancière, "Fictions of Time."

72. See Michel Foucault, *The Archaeology of Knowledge*, trans. A. M. Sheridan Smith (New York: Pantheon, 1972), 120.

73. The expression belongs to Gertrud Koch, "The Aesthetic Transformation of the Image of the Unimaginable: Notes on Claude Lanzmann's *Shoah*," *October* 48 (spring 1989): 15–24.

74. Koch, "The Aesthetic Transformation of the Image of the Unimaginable," 20.

75. For an analysis of Lanzmann's approach to a "fiction of the real," see Richard Brody, "Witness: Claude Lanzmann and the Making of 'Shoah,'" *The New Yorker*, March 12, 2012, https://www.newyorker.com/magazine/2012/03/19/witness-5.

76. The quotations are from Jacob Mikanowski, "Lessons on the Holocaust, From Warsaw's No. 35 Tram," *New York Times*, February 17, 2018, http://comment-news.com/source/www.nytimes.com/2018/02/17/opinion/sunday/poland-holocaust.html/.

77. See Saishigo's treatment of Bazin, "The 'Image-fact' in Bazin and

Bresson," *Luminous Era: On Cinema, Philosophy and the Aesthetics of Existence*, May 25, 2012, https://lesiecledelumiere.wordpress.com/2012/05/25/the-image-fact-in-bazin-and-bresson/.

78. Saishigo, "The 'Image-fact' in Bazin and Bresson," 21–22.

79. André Bazin, "An Aesthetic of Reality: Cinematic Realism and the Italian School of Liberation," in *What Is Cinema, Volume 2*, trans. Hugh Gray (Berkeley: University of California Press, 1971).

80. Saishigo, "The 'Image-Fact' in Bazin and Bresson."

81. Sandro Bernardi, "Rossellini's Landscapes: Nature, Myth, History," in *Roberto Rossellini: Magician of the Real*, ed. David Forgacs, Sarah Lutton, and Geoffrey Nowell-Smith (London: BFI, 2001), 51.

82. Antoine-Nicolas de Condorcet, *Sketch for a Historical Picture of the Progress of the Human Mind* [1795], trans. June Barraclough (London: Noonday, 1955), 100.

83. Rune Saugmann Andersen, *Remediating Security* (Copenhagen: Department of Political Science, University of Copenhagen, 2014), 37.

84. See Mattathias Schwartz, "Who Killed the Kiev Protesters?" *New York Times*, May 30, 2018, https://www.nytimes.com/2018/05/30/magazine/ukraine-protest-video.html.

85. Eyal Weizman, *Forensic Architecture: Violence at the Threshold of Detectability* (New York: Zone Books, 2017), 97.

86. Weizman, *Forensic Architecture*, 98–99.

87. Saugmann Andersen, *Remediating Security*, 42.

88. The quotation is from Robert Gooding-Williams, "Du Bois's Counter-Sublime," *The Massachusetts Review* 35, no. 2 (summer 1994): 207; see W. E. B. Du Bois, *Black Reconstruction: An Essay toward a History of the Part Which Black Folk Played in the Attempt to Reconstruct Democracy in America: 1860–1880* (New York: Free Press, 1935), 350.

89. Pascal Gielen, "Performing the Common City," in *Interrupting the City: Artistic Constitutions of the Public Sphere*, ed. Sander Bax, Pascal Gielen, and Bram Leven (Amsterdam: Antennae Valiz, 2016), 283.

90. See Quentin Stevens, *The Ludic City: Exploring the Potential of Public Spaces* (London: Routledge, 2007).

91. The quotation is from Susan Laxton, "The Guarantor of Chance: Surrealism's Ludic Practices," *Papers of Surrealism* #1 (winter 2003), www.surrealismcentre.ac.uk/papers of surrealismjournal/1/acrobat_files/laxton.pdf.

92. Laxton, "The Guarantor of Chance."

93. See Mark Godfrey and Zoe Whitney, eds., *Soul of a Nation: Art in the Age of Black Power* (London: D.A.P., 2017), 210.

94. Yara Sharif, *Architecture of Resistance: Cultivating Moments of Possibility within the Palestinian/Israeli Conflict* (London: Routledge, 2017), 194.

95. Gilles Deleuze, *Cinema 1*, trans. Hugh Tomlinson and Barbara Habberjam (Minneapolis: University of Minnesota Press, 1986), 64.

96. Teju Cole, "Victory in the Shadows," *New York Times*, August

10, 2017, https://www.nytimes.com/2017/08/10/magazine/victory-in-the-shadows.html.

97. Rancière, "Fictions of Time."

98. Michael Foucault, *Lectures on the Will to Know*, trans. Graham Burchell (London: Palgrave/Macmillan, 2013), 2.

Chapter One: How "Popular" Music Thinks the Political

1. Adorno, "Punctuation," *Antioch Review* 48, no. 3 (summer 1990): 300–301.

2. Jacques Rancière, "Contemporary Art and the Politics of Aesthetics," in Beth Hinderliter et al., eds., *Communities of Sense* (Durham, NC: Duke University Press, 2009), 31.

3. See M. M. Bakhtin, *Problems of Dostoevsky's Poetics*, trans. Caryl Emerson (Minneapolis: University of Minnesota Press, 1984), 97.

4. See David Michael Hertz, *The Tuning of the Word: The Musico-Literary Poetics of the Symbolist Movement* (Carbondale: Southern Illinois University Press, 1987), and for a similar comparison, see Elizabeth McCombie, *Mallarmé and Debussy: Unheard Music, Unseen Text* (Oxford: Clarendon Press, 2003).

5. Hertz, *The Tuning of the Word*, 18.

6. Hertz, *The Tuning of the Word*, 19.

7. Hertz, *The Tuning of the Word*, 17–18.

8. Hertz, *The Tuning of the Word*, 57.

9. Hertz, *The Tuning of the Word*, 30–31.

10. John Ashbery, "Introduction: In Raymond Roussel," in Michael Foucault, *Death and the Labyrinth: The World of Raymond Roussel,* trans. Charles Ruas (Garden State, NY: Doubleday, 1986), xv.

11. Foucault, *Death and the Labyrinth*, 7.

12. See Raymond Roussel, *How I Wrote Certain of My Books,* trans. Trevor Winkfield (New York: Exact Change, 2005).

13. I discuss and elaborate that comparison in Michael J. Shapiro, *Methods and Nations: Cultural Governance and the Indigenous Subject* (London: Routledge, 2004), 93.

14. Foucault, *Death and the Labyrinth*, 177.

15. Leon Botstein, "Beyond the Illusions of Realism: Painting and Debussy's Break with Tradition," in *Debussy and His World*, ed. Jane Fulcher, 150 (Princeton, NJ: Princeton University Press, 2001).

16. I am here paraphrasing and quoting a passage from Jann Pasler, *Writing through Music: Essays on Music, Culture, and Politics* (New York: Oxford University Press, 2008), 38.

17. I am borrowing the word from David Wills, who attributes that figural effect to both Jacques Derrida and Mallarmé: "Derrida and Aesthetics: Lemming (reframing the abyss)," in *Jacques Derrida and the Humani-*

ties: A Critical Reader*, ed. Tom Cohen, 114 (New York: Cambridge University Press, 2002).

18. Foucault, *Death and the Labyrinth*, 23.

19. Foucault, *Death and the Labyrinth*, 2.

20. I am quoting my remarks on the music-nationhood relationship in an earlier investigation: Shapiro, *Methods and Nations*, 89–90. The inner quotations are from Houston A. Baker Jr., *Modernism and the Harlem Renaissance* (Chicago: University of Chicago Press, 1987), 71.

21. Baker, *Modernism and the Harlem Renaissance*, 50–51.

22. Baker, *Modernism and the Harlem Renaissance*, 101.

23. Hertz, *The Tuning of the Word*, 20.

24. Michael Sokolove, *New York Times Magazine*, February 13, 2005, http://www.nytimes.com/2005/02/13/magazine/clang.html.

25. See Roman Jakobson and Morris Halle, *Fundamentals of Language* (The Hague: Mouton, 1971).

26. Greg Hainge, "Is Pop Music?," in *Deleuze and Music*, ed. Ian Buchanan and Marcel Swiboda, 36 (Edinburgh: Edinburgh University Press, 2004).

27. Nathaniel Mackey, "Other: From Noun to Verb," *Representations* 39 (summer 1992): 59.

28. Gabriel Solis, *Monk's Music: Thelonious Monk and Jazz History in the Making* (Berkeley: University of California Press, 2008), 37.

29. The hyphenated expression is borrowed from Wills, "Derrida and Aesthetics," 114.

30. See Coltrane's remarks on his *Alabama* reported in Sasha Feinstein, "From *Alabama* to *A Love Supreme*: The Evolution of a John Coltrane Poem," *The Southern Review* 23, no. 2 (April 1996): 315–27.

31. Scott Deveaux, "'Nice Work If You Can Get It': Thelonious Monk and Popular Song," *Black Music Research Journal* 19, no. 2 (autumn 1999): 169.

32. George Lipsitz, *Dangerous Crossroads: Popular Music, Postmodernism, and the Poetics of Place* (New York: Verso, 1994), 63.

33. The analysis of black talk is in Ben Sidran, *Black Talk* (New York: Da Capo, 1971). The quotation is my summary of his argument in Shapiro, *Methods and Nations*, 89.

34. Solis, *Monk's Music*, 30.

35. From Ross Russell, "Bebop," in *The Art of Jazz*, ed. Martin Williams (New York: Oxford University Press, 1959), 172.

36. Chris Bachelder, "Way Down Yonder," a review of *King Zeno* by Nathaniel Rich, *New York Times Book Review*, January 21, 2018, 9.

37. Christopher Small, *Music of the Common Tongue: Survival and Celebration in African American Music* (New York: River Run Press, 1987), 382.

38. The quotation is my paraphrase of Small's argument: Shapiro, *Methods and Nations*, 91.

39. Deveaux, "Nice Work If You Can Get It," 174.

40. The quotation is from Michael C. Finke's analysis of metapoesis in Russian literature, where the term applies to the way "authorial words engage a very specific addressee or set of addressees," *Metapoesis* (Durham, NC: Duke University Press, 1995), 5.

41. Mackey, "Other: From Noun to Verb," 52.

42. Mackey, "Other: From Noun to Verb," 53.

43. Mackey, "Other: From Noun to Verb," 61.

44. Mackey, "Other: From Noun to Verb," 68.

45. Hainge, "Is Pop Music?," 43.

46. *Master of My Domain*, September 27, 2008, http://masterofmy-publicdomain.blogspot.com/2008/09/rock-roll-killed-your-hit-parade.html.

47. *Master of My Domain*, 49.

48. *Master of My Domain*.

49. Allen J. Scott, "The Cultural Economy: Geography and the Creative Field," *Media, Culture and Society* 21, no. 6 (1999): 814.

50. Scott, "The Cultural Economy," 813.

51. Jennifer Lynn Stoever, *The Sonic Color Line: Race and the Cultural Politics of Listening* (New York: NYU Press, 2016), 3.

52. Mark Anthony Neal, *What the Music Said* (New York: Routledge, 1999), 21.

53. Arthur Kempton, *Boogaloo: The Quintessence of American Popular Music* (New York: Pantheon, 2003), 17.

54. Kempton, *Boogaloo*, 244.

55. Kempton, *Boogaloo*.

56. Kempton, *Boogaloo*, 248.

57. See M. M. Bakhtin, "Discourse and the Novel," trans. Caryl Emerson, in *The Dialogic Imagination*, ed. Michael Holquist, 259–422 (Austin: University of Texas Press, 1981).

58. Roland Barthes, *The Rustle of Language*, trans. Richard Howard (New York: Hill and Wang, 1986), 123.

59. James Ellroy, "High Darktown," in *Hollywood Nocturnes* (New York: Dell, 1994), 170.

60. Ellroy, *Hollywood Nocturnes*, 174.

61. Richard Middleton, "Through a Mask Darkly: Voices of Black Folk," in *Voicing the Popular* (New York: Routledge, 2006), 37–89.

62. Gillian Lane-Mercier, "Translating the Untranslatable: The Translator's Aesthetic, Ideological and Political Responsibility," *Target* 9, no. 1 (January 1997): 47.

63. For the former, see Martin Lefebvre, "Introduction," in *Landscape and Film*, ed. Martin Lefebvre (London: Routledge, 2006), xii; for the latter, see Lefebvre, "Between Setting and Landscape in Cinema," in *Landscape and Film*.

64. Lefebvre, "Between Setting and Landscape in Cinema," 28.

65. Lefebvre, "Between Setting and Landscape in Cinema," 22.

66. Lefebvre, "Between Setting and Landscape in Cinema," 23.

67. See Stephen Hunter, "At the Altar of the Game," *Washington Post*, May 1, 1998, http://www.washingtonpost.com/wp-srv/style/longterm/movies/videos/hegotgamehunter.htm.

68. Jacques Rancière, *The Politics of Aesthetics*, trans. Gabriel Rockhill (New York: Continuum, 2004), 24.

69. Here I am quoting Jacques Rancière's analysis of Erich Auerbach's insights about Western literary fiction. See his "Fictions of Time," in *Rancière and Literature*, ed. Grace Hellyer and Julian Murphet, 27 (Edinburgh: Edinburgh University Press, 2016).

70. William Brooks, "Simple Gifts and Complex Accretions," in *Copland Connotations: Studies and Interviews*, ed. Peter Dickinson, 104 (Woodbridge, UK: Boydell Press, 2002).

71. Aaron Copland, *Music and Imagination* (Cambridge, MA: Harvard University Press, 1952), 101.

72. Thomas Mann, *The Theme of the Joseph Novels* (Washington, DC: Library of Congress, 1942), 14–15.

73. Alan Howard Levy, *Musical Nationalism: American Composers' Search for Identity* (Westport, CT: Greenwood Press, 1983), 110.

74. The term *ethnogenesis* belongs to William Boelhower, *Through a Glass Darkly: Ethnic Semiosis and American Literature* (New York: Oxford University Press, 1986).

75. See Jessica Burr, "Copland, the West and American Identity," in *Copland Connotations*, ed. Dickinson, 27.

76. Elizabeth B. Crist, *Music for the Common Man: Aaron Copland during the Depression and War* (New York: Oxford University Press, 2005), 51.

77. See Sally Brick, "'Of Mice and Men': Copland, Hollywood, and American Musical Modernism," *American Music* 23, no. 4 (winter 2005): 433.

78. Brick, "Of Mice and Men," 71.

79. Brick, "Of Mice and Men," 27.

80. Brick, "Of Mice and Men," 111.

81. The concept of a melodic landscape is treated in John Snydal and Marti Hearst, "ImproViz: Visual Explorations of Jazz Improvisato," http://www.offhanddesigns.com/jon/docs/snydal_improViz.pdf.

82. Michel Chion, *Audio-Vision: Sound on Screen*, trans. Claudia Gorbman (New York: Columbia University Press, 1994), 8.

83. George Lipsitz, *Dangerous Crossroads: Popular Music, Postmodernism and the Poetics of Place* (New York: Verso, 1994), 36–37.

84. The quoted lines are from the lyrics of "He Got Game."

85. Carter Mathes, *Imagine the Sound* (Minneapolis: University of Minnesota Press, 2015), 4.

86. Mathes, *Imagine the Sound*, 8.

87. Tricia Rose, "Orality and Technology: Rap Music and Afro-

American Cultural Resistance," *Popular Music and Society* 13, no. 4 (winter 1999): 39.

88. Mark Anthony Neal, *What the Music Said* (New York: Routledge, 1999), 161.

89. Reginald Thomas, "The Rhythm of Rhyme: A Look at Rap Music as an Art Form from a Jazz Perspective," in *African American Jazz and Rap*, ed. James L. Conyers, 165 (Jefferson, NC: McFarland, 2001).

90. Thomas, "The Rhythm of Rhyme," 167.

91. The expression belongs to Henry Louis Gates Jr., *The Signifying Monkey: A Theory of Afro-American Literary Criticism* (New York: Oxford University Press, 1988), 52.

92. Rose, "Orality and Technology," 40.

93. Krin Gabbard, "Race and Reappropriation: Spike Lee Meets Aaron Copland," *American Music* 18, no. 4 (winter 2000): 371.

94. Rancière, *The Politics of Aesthetics*, 12.

95. Rancière, *The Politics of Aesthetics*, 65.

96. Stephanie Zacharek's review of *Inside Man*, in *Salon*, March 24, 2006, http://www.salon.com/2006/03/24/inside_man/.

97. David Sterritt, *Spike Lee's America* (Malden, MA: Polity, 2013), 5.

98. The expression was introduced by Fernando Solanas and Octavi Getino, "Towards a Third Cinema," https://ufsinfronteradotcom.files.wordpress.com/2011/05/tercer-cine-getino-solonas-19691.pdf.

99. Sohail Daulatzai, *Fifty Years of The Battle of Algiers: Past as Prologue* (Minneapolis: University of Minnesota Press, 2016), 3.

100. Peter Matthews, "*The Battle of Algiers*: Bombs and Boomerangs" (Criterion: 2004), 11.

101. Eric Breitbart, "The Invisible Prison: Representing Algiers on Film," in *Walls of Algiers: Narratives of the City through Text and Image*, ed. Zeynep Çelik, Julia Clancy-Smith, and Frances Terpak, 163 (Seattle: University of Washington Press, 2009).

102. Michael J. Shapiro, "Slow Looking: The Ethics and Politics of Aesthetics," *Millennium* 37, no. 1 (2008): 193.

103. I am taking the description of Braithwaite's observation from Walter Mignolo's use of it in his treatise on "the colonial difference": *Local Histories/Global Designs* (Princeton, NJ: Princeton University Press, 2000), 4.

104. Ben Highmore, "Colonial Spacing—Control and Conflict in the Colonial and Neocolonial City," in *Cityscapes*, 72 (New York: Palgrave, 2005).

105. Shapiro, "Slow Looking," 192.

106. Pontecorvo's remarks are in the second DVD of the Criterion Collection version of the film (2004), in which there are interviews.

107. Peter Matthews, "*The Battle of Algiers*: Bombs and Boomerangs" (Criterion, 2004), 8.

108. Michael Chanan, "Outsiders: The Battle of Algiers and Political Cinema," *Sight and Sound* 17, no. 6 (June 2007): 38.

109. See Highmore, "Colonial Spacing," 70–91.

110. The only professional actor in the film is Jean Martin, who plays Colonel Mathieu, the leader sent to crush the rebellion. Yacef Saadi, who was a leader in the actual rebellion, plays himself (with the name Djafar).

111. Highmore, *Cityscapes*, 80 (in the inner quotes, he is quoting Solinas).

112. Bensmaia is here quoted in Anne Donaday, "The Multilingual Strategies of Postcolonial Literature: Assia Djebar's Algerian Palimpsest," *World Literature Today* 74, no. 1 (winter 2000): 28.

113. Russell A. Potter, *Spectacular Vernaculars* (Albany: State University of New York, 1995), 131.

114. Mildred Mortimer, "Language and Space in the Fiction of Assia Djebar and Leila Sebbar," *Research in African Literatures* 19, no. 3 (autumn 1988): 305.

115. Shapiro, *Methods and Nations*, 30. The inner quotations belong to Assia Djebar, quoted in Donaday, "The Multilingual Strategies of Postcolonial Literature," 122.

116. Michael J. Shapiro, "Bowling Blind: Post Liberal Civil Society and the Worlds of Neo-Tocquevillean Social Theory," *Theory and Event* 1, no. 1 (1997). The inner quotation is from Tzvetan Todorov's reading of Tocqueville's report on Algeria. See his "Tocqueville's Nationalism," *History and Anthropology* 4, no. 2 (April 1990): 360.

117. Shapiro, "Bowling Blind." The quotation is from Alexis de Tocqueville, "Notes du Voyage en Algeries de 1841," *Oeuvre Complète,* ed. J. P. Mayer and André Jardin (Paris: Gallimard, 1958), vol. 5, part 2, 192.

118. Shapiro, "Bowling Blind." The inner quotations are from Timothy Mitchell, *Colonizing Egypt* (New York: Cambridge University Press, 1988), 58–59.

119. Donald Pease, "José Martí, Alexis de Tocqueville, and the Politics of Displacement," in *José Martí's "Our America,"* ed. Jeffrey Belnap and Raúl Fernandez, 29–30 (Durham, NC: Duke University Press, 1998).

120. Maurice Peress, *Dvorak to Duke Ellington* (New York: Oxford University Press, 2004), 25.

121. Peress, *Dvorak to Duke Ellington*, 23.

122. Salman Rushdie, *Imaginary Homelands* (New York: Penguin, 1992), 15.

123. Salman Rushdie, *The Ground Beneath Her Feet* (New York: Henry Holt, 1999), 93.

124. Gregory Clark, *Civic Jazz* (Chicago: University of Chicago Press, 2015), 3–4.

125. Clark, *Civic Jazz*, 7.

126. Giovanni Russonello, "Wayne Shorter, Jazz's Abstruse Elder, Isn't Done Innovating Yet," *New York Times*, September 12, 2018, https://www.nytimes.com/2018/09/12/arts/music/wayne-shorter-emanon.html.

127. Russonello, "Wayne Shorter, Jazz's Abstruse Elder, Isn't Done Innovating Yet," 101.

128. The CD of the Adderley quintet's *Somethin' Else* with Miles Davis is available on YouTube, https://www.youtube.com/results? search_query=somethin+else+cannonball+adderley+full+album+.

129. *Somethin' Else*, 31.

130. *Somethin' Else.*

131. Clark, *Civic Jazz*, 150.

132. The CD of the Roberts-Fleck musical encounter, entitled "Across the Imaginary Divide," is available on YouTube, https://www.youtube.com/watch?v=TeOXF5WhfsU.

133. Robert Gooding-Williams, "Du Bois's Counter-Sublime," *Massachusetts Review* 35, no. 2 (summer 1994): 207.

134. See W. E. B. Du Bois, *Black Reconstruction: An Essay Toward a History of the Part Which Black Folk Played in the Attempt to Reconstruct Democracy in America: 1860–1880* (New York: Free Press, 1935), 350.

Chapter Two: Urban Punctuations

1. See Alan Smart and Josephine Smart's use of punctuation as a metaphor to treat the way the "world is punctuated by barriers": "Time-space Punctuation: Hong Kong's Border Regime and Limits on Mobility," *Pacific Affairs* 81, no. 2 (summer 2008): 175.

2. Lewis Mumford, *The City in History: Its Origins, Its Transformations, and Its Prospects* (New York: Harcourt, 1961), 569.

3. From Thomas Daniell's introduction, "Articles of Faith," to Sanford Kwinter, *Requiem: For the City at the End of the Millennium* (Houston, TX: Actar, 2010), 10.

4. Pascal Gielen, "Performing the Common City: On the Crossroads of Art, Politics and Public Lives," in *Interrupting the City: Artistic Constitutions of The Public Sphere*, ed. Sander Bax, Pascal Gielen, and Bram Leven, 283 (Amsterdam: Valiz Antennae, 2016).

5. See Derek Hillard, "Walther Ruttmann's Janus-Faced View of Modernity: The Ambivalence of Description in 'Berlin, Die Sinfonie de Grofstadt,'" *Monatshefte* 96, no. 1 (spring 2004): 78–79.

6. Richard Will, "Time, Morality, and Humanity in Beethoven's 'Pastoral' Symphony," *Journal of the American Musicological Society* 50, no. 2–3 (summer–autumn, 1997): 320.

7. As Adorno points out, "To understand Beethoven means to understand *tonality*"; Theodor W. Adorno, *Beethoven: The Philosophy of Music*, trans. Edmund Jephcott (Stanford, CA: Stanford University Press, 1998), 112.

8. See Christopher Hatch, "The Wondrous Trumpet Call in Beethoven's *Fidelio*," *The Opera Quarterly* 15, no. 1 (1999): 5.

9. Hatch, "The Wondrous Trumpet Call in Beethoven's *Fidelio*," 6, 7.

10. Will, "Time, Morality, and Humanity in Beethoven's 'Pastoral' Symphony," 278–79.

11. Will, "Time, Morality, and Humanity in Beethoven's 'Pastoral' Symphony," 284.

12. Will, "Time, Morality, and Humanity in Beethoven's 'Pastoral' Symphony," 312.

13. Will, "Time, Morality, and Humanity in Beethoven's 'Pastoral' Symphony," 317.

14. Will, "Time, Morality, and Humanity in Beethoven's 'Pastoral' Symphony," 319.

15. Will, "Time, Morality, and Humanity in Beethoven's 'Pastoral' Symphony," 320–21.

16. Anton Kaes, "Leaving Home: Migration and the Urban Experience," *New German Critique* 74 (summer 1998): 190.

17. Hillard, "Walter Ruttmann's Janus-Faced View of Modernity," 90.

18. Kaes, "Leaving Home," 181.

19. Hillard, "Walter Ruttmann's Janus-Faced View of Modernity," 90.

20. See Georg Simmel, "The Metropolis and Mental Life," in *The Sociology of Georg Simmel*, ed. and trans. Kurt H. Wolf (New York: Free Press, 1964).

21. Frank Martin Lehman, "Reading Tonality through Film: Transformational Hermeneutics and the Music of Hollywood" (PhD dissertation, Harvard University, 2012); http://www.academia.edu/4309608/Reading_Tonality_Through_Film_Transformation_Theory_and_the_Music_of_Hollywood_Dissertation_.

22. From David Bordwell, "The Musical Analogy," *Yale French Studies*, no. 60 (1980): 144.

23. Anton Kaes, "The Phantom of the Apocalypse: Metropolis and Weimar Modernity," in *Noir Urbanisms: Dystopic Images of the Modern City*, ed. Gyan Prakash, 28 (Princeton, NJ: Princeton University Press, 2010).

24. Andrew Webber, "Symphony of a City: Motion Pictures and Still Lives in Weimar Berlin," in *Cities in Transition*, ed. Andrew Webber and Emma Wilson, 68 (New York: Wallflower Press, 2008).

25. In Thomas Shadt's 2002 remake of Ruttmann's film, the symphonic metaphor is retained, but the tonal disjuncture is less prominent. The emphasis is on the ways in which industrial technology suborns human movement so that machines seem to control human agency.

26. Ash Amin and Nigel Thrift, *Reimagining the Urban* (Malden, MA: Polity, 2002), 84.

27. Linda Poon, "What a City's 'Soundscape' Reveals about Its Character," CITYLAB, September 17, 2015, http://www.citylab.com/tech/2015/09/what-a-citys-soundscape-reveals-about-its-character/405733/.

28. Henri Lefebvre, *The Production of Space*, trans. Donald Nicholson-Smith (New York: Wiley-Blackwell, 1992), 227.

29. Quentin Stevens, *The Ludic City* (New York: Routledge, 2007), 1.

30. Randy Martin speaking on his concept of "the social kinesthetic" at the Movement Research Studies Project, "Performing the Changing City: Public Space, Transformative Events and Creative Action in New York," published subsequently in *Elsewhere*, February 13, 2015, https://movementresearch.org/publications/critical-correspondence/elsewhere-randy-martin-on-performing-the-changing-city.

31. Randy Martin, "A Precarious Dance, A Derivative Sociality," *TDR* 56, no. 4 (winter 2012): 77.

32. David Garrioch, "Sounds of the City: The Soundscape of Early Modern European Towns," *Urban History* 30, no. 1 (2003): 5.

33. Garrioch, "Sounds of the City."

34. Garrioch, "Sounds of the City," 18.

35. Garrioch, "Sounds of the City," 22.

36. Garrioch, "Sounds of the City," 15.

37. I am quoting a close reading of the documentary; Amanda Holmes, "Backstage Pass to the City: The Soundscape of *Suite Habana*," *Studies in Spanish and Latin American Cinemas* 12, no. 2 (June 2015): 126.

38. Holmes, "Backstage Pass to the City."

39. See Jacques Attali, *Noise: The Political Economy of Music*, trans. Brian Massumi (Minneapolis: University of Minnesota Press, 1985).

40. Jean-Paul Thibaud, "The Sonic Composition of the City," in *The Auditory Culture Reader*, ed. Michael Bull and Les Back, 329 (Amsterdam: Berg, 2003).

41. Thibaud, "The Sonic Composition of the City," 332.

42. Thibaud, "The Sonic Composition of the City," 329.

43. Gregory Clark, *Civic Jazz* (Chicago: University of Chicago Press, 2015), 150.

44. See Attali, *Noise*.

45. This illustration from the HBO *Treme* series is treated at greater length in an earlier investigation: Michael J. Shapiro, *Politics and Time: Documenting the Event* (Cambridge: Polity, 2016), 76–84.

46. Ralph Ellison, "Remembering Jimmie," in *Living with Music: Ralph Ellison's Jazz Writings*, ed. Robert G. O. Meally, 47 (New York: Morrow, 1999).

47. Kirchner describes what he tries to capture in his painting in his *Tagebuch* (diary), quoted in Charles W. Haxthausen, "A New Beauty: Ernst Ludwig Kirchner's Images of Berlin," in *Berlin: Culture and Metropolis*, ed. Charles W. Haxthausen and Heidrum Surh, 67 (Minneapolis: University of Minnesota Press, 1990). I am quoting from my reading of Kirchner's painting elsewhere: Michael J. Shapiro, *The Time of the City: Politics, Philosophy and Genre* (New York: Routledge, 2010), 166.

48. Patricia Phillips, "Creating Democracy: A Dialogue with Krzysztof Wodiczko," *Art Journal* 62, no. 4 (winter 2003): 33.

49. Krzysztof Wodiczko, *Critical Vehicles: Writing, Projects, Inter-*

views (Cambridge, MA: MIT Press, 1999), 104. The original account of the bâton d'étranger is in Krzysztof Wodiczko, *Art public, art critique: Textes, propos, et documents* (Paris: École Normale Supérieure des Beaux-Arts, 1995).

50. The outer quotation is from my earlier account of Wodiczko's inventions: Michael J. Shapiro, *Cinematic Political Thought: Narrating Race, Nation and Gender* (Edinburgh: Edinburgh University Press, 1999), 70. The inner quotation is from Wodiczko, *Art public, art critique*, 212.

51. Wodiczko, *Art public, art critique.*

52. Phillips, "Creating Democracy," 35–36.

53. Phillips, "Creating Democracy," 38.

54. Gerrit Wiesmann, "An Invisible Artwork Reminds Austria of Its Nazi Past," *New York Times*, March 16, 2018, https://www.nytimes.com/2018/03/16/arts/the-voices-susan-philipsz-heldenplatz.html.

55. Wiesmann, "An Invisible Artwork Reminds Austria of Its Nazi Past."

56. See Sander Bax, Pascal Gielen, Bram Ieven, "Introduction," in Bax et al., *Interrupting the City*, 11.

57. Bax et al., *Interrupting the City*, 14.

58. Krzysztof Ziarek, *The Force of Art* (Stanford, CA: Stanford University Press, 2004), 12.

59. Gielen, "Performing the Common City," 282.

60. Paul Routledge, "Sensuous Solidarities: Emotion, Politics and Performance in the Clandestine Insurgent Rebel Clown Army," *Antipode* 44, no. 2 (2012): 432.

61. M. M. Bakhtin, "Forms of Time and Chronotope in the Novel," in *The Dialogic Imagination*, trans. Caryl Emerson and Michael Holquist, ed. Michael Holquist, 159 (Austin: University of Texas Press, 1982).

62. From a review of Fellini's documentary *I Clown*, by Philip French, *The Guardian*, October 26, 2014, https://www.theguardian.com/film/2014/oct/26/i-clowns-review-philip-french-fellini-1970.

63. Federico Fellini, *A Journey into the Shadow*, documentary *I Clown* DVD (RaroVideo, 2011), booklet, 11, 13.

64. Fellini, *A Journey into the Shadow*, 16.

65. Peta Tait, "Circus Oz Larrikinism [Mischievousness]: Good Gender Sport," *Contemporary Theater Review* 14, no. 3 (2004): 79.

66. Tait, "Circus Oz Larrikinism," 81.

67. M. M. Bakhtin, *Rabelais and His World*, trans. Helene Iswolsky (Bloomington: Indiana University Press, 1984), 101.

68. Bakhtin, *Rabelais and His World*, 199.

69. Routledge, "Sensuous Solidarities," 433.

70. Laszlo Krasznahorkai, *The Melancholy of Resistance*, trans. George Szirtes (New York: New Directions, 1998), 92.

71. Elias Canetti, *Crowds and Power*, trans. Carol Stewart (New York: Farrar, Straus and Giroux, 1984), 31.

72. Gielen, "Performing the Common City," 283.

73. Tessa Overbeek, "Embodying the Possibilities of Public Space—Circus Amok: An Interview with Jennifer Miller," in Bax et al., *Interrupting the City*, 207.

74. Overbeek, "Embodying the Possibilities of Public Space," 205.

75. Circus Amok website, http://www/cicusamok.org/circus/.

76. Overbeek, "Embodying the Possibilities of Public Space," 206.

77. Overbeek, "Embodying the Possibilities of the Public Space," 211.

78. See Stevens, *The Ludic City*.

79. Peter Dickinson, "John Cage and His Musicircus," *The Guardian*, June 20, 2014, https://www.theguardian.com/music/2014/jun/20/john-cage-and-his-musicircus.

80. Dickinson, "John Cage and His Musicircus."

81. Richard Fleming, "Listening to Cage: Nonintentional Philosophy and Music," *Cogent Arts and Humanities* 3, no. 1 (2016): 31, https://www.cogentoa.com/article/10.1080/23311983.2015.1088733.

82. Fleming, "Listening to Cage," 37.

83. Fleming, "Listening to Cage," 47.

84. John Cage quoted in Jann Pasler, *Writing through Music* (New York: Oxford University Press, 2008), 10.

85. Pasler, *Writing through Music*, 42.

86. Pasler, *Writing through Music*, 175.

87. Pasler, *Writing through Music*, 176.

88. Pasler, *Writing through Music*, 166.

89. Susan Laxton, "The Guarantor of Chance: Surrealism's Ludic Practices," *Papers of Surrealism* #1 (winter 2003), www.surrealismcentre.ac.uk/papers of surrealismjournal/1/acrobat_files/laxton.pdf.

90. Laxton, "The Guarantor of Chance."

91. Michel Tournier, *Friday, or the Other Island*, trans. Norman Denny (Harmondworth, UK: Penguin, 1974).

92. Ian Watt, "Robinson Crusoe as Myth," in *Robinson Crusoe: An Authoritative Text, Backgrounds, and Sources of Criticism*, ed. Michael Shinagel, 322 (New York: W. W. Norton, 1975).

93. The quotation is from my reading of the novel in an earlier investigation: Michael J. Shapiro, "Weighing Anchor: Postmodern Journeys from the Life-World," in *Reading the Postmodern Polity* (Minneapolis: University of Minnesota Press, 1992), 52.

94. Tournier, *Friday, or the Other Island*, 46.

95. Shapiro, "Weighing Anchor," 53.

96. Lefebvre, *Practices of Space*, 227. I am also drawing on the discussion of it in Stevens, *The Ludic City*, 33.

97. Stevens, *The Ludic City*, 1.

98. Stevens, *The Ludic City*.

99. The quoted expression is from Peter Pal Pelbart's explication of the sense of Maurice Blanchot's conception of community: *Cartography of Exhaustion* (Minneapolis: Univocal, 2015), 108.

100. Blanchot, *Cartography of Exhaustion*. See also Maurice Blanchot, *The Unavowable Community*, trans. Pierre Joris (New York: Station Hill Press, 1988).

Chapter Three: Architectural Punctuations

1. See Mark Godfrey and Zoe Whitney, eds., *Soul of a Nation: Art in the Age of Black Power* (London: D.A.P., 2017), 210.

2. Bernard Tschumi, "Violence and Architecture," in *Architecture and Disjunction* (Cambridge, MA: MIT Press, 1994), 121.

3. Tschumi, "Violence and Architecture," 122.

4. Tschumi, "Violence and Architecture," 123.

5. Richard Ross, *Architecture of Authority* (New York: Aperture, 2007), 140.

6. Michael Hays, "Crack," *Assemblage* 20 (April 1993): 42.

7. Tschumi, "Violence and Architecture," 124.

8. See Ted Gregory, "The Black Panther Raid and the Death of Fred Hampton," *Chicago Tribune*, September 3, 2008, http://www.chicago tribune.com/news/nationworld/politics/chi-chicagodays-pantherraid-story -story.html.

9. See the interview, "Eyal Weizman on Global Politics and Forensic Architecture," *Theory Talks #69*, December 21, 2015, http://www .theory-talks.org/2015/03/theory-talk-69. html.

10. Eyal Weizman, *Forensic Architecture: Violence at the Threshold of Detectability* (New York: Zone Books, 2017), 51.

11. Even the "FBI firearms examiner who showed real integrity . . . proved the Panthers fired, at most, one shot at the police—compared to the police, who raided Hampton's apartment and shot at the Panthers ninety-nine times." Reported by Jeffrey Hass, "The Assassination of Fred Hampton by the FBI and Chicago Police, Forty Years Later," *Monthly Review*, December 1, 2009, https://monthlyreview.org/2009/12/01/the-assassination -of-fred-hampton-by-the-fbi-and-chicago-police-forty-years-later/.

12. Hass, "The Assassination of Fred Hampton by the FBI and Chicago Police, Forty Years Later."

13. Albena Yaneva, *Five Ways to Make Architecture Political* (London: Bloomsbury, 2017), 32.

14. See Bernard Tschumi, *Questions of Space: Lectures on Architecture* (London: E. G. Bond Ltd, 1990).

15. Tschumi, *Questions of Space*, 35.

16. See Andreas Huyssen, *Presents Past: Urban Palimpsests and the Politics of Memory* (Stanford, CA: Stanford University Press, 2003), 51.

17. Jacques Rancière, "Fictions of Time," in *Rancière and Literature*, ed. Grace Hellyer and Julian Murphet (Edinburgh: Edinburgh University Press, 2016), 25.

18. Sorapoj Techakraisri, "MahaNakhon: A Pixelated Punctuation Mark on the Bangkok Skyline," CTBUH *Research Paper*, 2015, ctbuh.org/papers.

19. Stephen Graham, *Vertical: The City from Satellites to Bunkers* (London: Verso, 2016), 134.

20. James Abbott, "Louis Sullivan: Architectural Modernism and the creation of Democratic Space," *The American Sociologist* 31, no. 1 (spring 2000): 63.

21. Abbott, "Louis Sullivan," 77.

22. Yaneva, *Five Ways to Make Architecture Political*, 7.

23. Yaneva, *Five Ways to Make Architecture Political*, 39.

24. Yaneva, *Five Ways to Make Architecture Political*, 37.

25. Colin Harrison, *Bodies Electric* (New York: St. Martins), 19–20.

26. Abbott, "Louis Sullivan," 78.

27. The quotation is from my reading of the novel in an earlier investigation: Michael J. Shapiro, *For Moral Ambiguity: National Culture and the Politics of the Family* (Minneapolis: University of Minnesota Press, 2001), 76.

28. Joe Gores, *32 Cadillacs* (New York: Mysterious Press, 1992), 34.

29. Shapiro, *For Moral Ambiguity*, 76.

30. Geoff Manaugh, *A Burglar's Guide to the City* (New York: Farrar, Straus and Giroux, 2016), 9.

31. Manaugh, *A Burglar's Guide to the City*, 10.

32. Manaugh, *A Burglar's Guide to the City*, 90.

33. Sally Bushell, "The Slipperiness of Literary Maps: Critical Cartography and Literary Cartography," *Cartographica* 47, no. 3 (2012): 154.

34. Qiu Xiaolong, *When Red Is Black* (New York: Soho, 2004).

35. See Sigfried Giedion, *Building in France, Building in Iron, Building in Concrete* (Los Angeles: Getty Center for the History of Art, 1995).

36. Detlief Mertins, "The Enticing and Threatening Face of Prehistory: Walter Benjamin and the Utopia of Glass," *Assemblage* 29 (April 1996): 8.

37. Xiaolong, *When Red Is Black*, 125.

38. Xiaolong, *When Red Is Black*, 23.

39. Xialong, *When Red Is Black*, 154, 23.

40. Xialong, *When Red Is Black*, 37.

41. See, for example, Julia Leyda, "Home on the Range: Space, Nation, and Mobility in John Ford's *The Searchers*," *The Japanese Journal of American Studies*, no. 13 (2002): 83–106.

42. The quotation is from Umberto Eco's reading of the film *Casablanca*: "'Casablanca': Cult Movies and Intertextual Collage," *SubStance* 14, no. 2 (1985): 5.

43. The first is the opening shot from inside the Edwards home, where

Martha looks out at the prairie; the second is shot from inside the small hut where Martha lies after having been raped and killed by Comanches, and the third is from inside a cave where Ethan Edwards and his nephew are seeking refuge from a Comanche war party.

44. I am borrowing the expression from Beatriz Colomina's figuring of the optics of domestic architecture, "The Split Wall: Domestic Voyeurism," in *Sexuality and Space*, ed. Beatriz Colomina, 113 (New York: Princeton Architecture Press, 1992).

45. Alessandro Baricco, *City*, trans. Ann Goldstein (London: Penguin, 2002), 158–59.

46. I am using quotations because the remark is a reference to Martin Heidegger's title *Was Heisst Denken?* See Martin Heidegger, *What Is Called Thinking?*, trans. J. Glen Gray (New York: Harper and Row, 1968), a translation of *Was Heisst Denken?*, which could be translated as *What Calls for Thinking?*

47. The quoted expression belongs to John Whiteman, "On Hegel's Definition of Architecture," *Assemblage* 2 (February 1987): 7.

48. The outer quotations are from my analysis of Brown's argument in Michael J. Shapiro, *Cinematic Political Thought: Narrative Race, Nation and Gender* (New York: NYU Press, 1999), 104. The inner quotations are from Peter Brown, *Authority and the Sacred* (New York: Cambridge University Press, 1995), 69.

49. Erwin Panofsky, *Gothic Architecture and Scholasticism* (New York: Meridian, 1958), 43.

50. Panofsky, *Gothic Architecture and Scholasticism*, 16–17.

51. Panofsky, *Gothic Architecture and Scholasticism*, 68.

52. See, for example, Maurice de Wulf, *An Introduction to Scholastic Philosophy* (Eugene, OR: Wipf and Stock, 2003).

53. Jacques Attali, *Noise: The Political Economy of Music*, trans. Brian Massumi (Minneapolis: University of Minnesota Press, 1985), 6.

54. See my response to Attali's position: Michael J. Shapiro, *Methods and Nations: Cultural Governance and the Indigenous Subject* (London: Routledge, 2004), 73.

55. Shundana Yusaf, "Salt Lake City Tabernacle," in SAH *Archipedia*, ed. Gabrielle Esperdy and Karen Kingsley (Charlottesville: University of Virginia Press, 2012), http://sah-archipedia.org/buildings/UT-01-035-0039.

56. For a summary of Tschumi's event-oriented perspective on architecture, see Y-Jean Mun-Delsalle, "Bernard Tschumi's Architecture Is Not Just about Space and Form but Also the Events Happening Inside, *Forbes*, September 7, 2005, https://www.forbes.com/sites/yjeanmundelsalle/2015/09/07/bernard-tschumis-architecture-is-not-just-about-space-and-form-but-also-the-events-happening-inside/#ff2f75576051.

57. Bernard Tschumi, *Tschumi on Architecture: Conversations with Enrique Walker* (New York: Monachelli Press, 2006), 24.

58. The expression belongs to the sociologist George Ritzer, whose

expression is quoted in Steven Kurutz, "An Ode to Shopping Malls," *New York Times*, July 26, 2017, https://www.nytimes.com/2017/07/26/fashion/an-ode-to-shopping-malls.html? _r=0.

59. See Walter Benjamin, *The Arcades Project*, trans. Howard Eiland and Kevin McLaughlin (Cambridge, MA: Harvard University Press, 2002). For an analysis of the commercial and perceptual implications of the historical trajectory of shopping from the arcades to the mall, see Anne Friedberg, *Window Shopping: Cinema and the Postmodern* (Berkeley: University of California Press, 1993).

60. See, for example, Quentin Tarantino's *Jackie Brown* (1997), in which the architecture of the mall is an important element in the plot.

61. Martin Lefebvre, "Between Setting and Landscape," in *Landscape and Film*, ed. Martin Lefebvre, 28 (London: Routledge, 2006).

62. For a good reading of how the mall in the film exercises its effects, see Anne Friedberg, *Window Shopping* (Berkeley: University of California Press, 1993), 122–24.

63. William Leach, *Land of Desire* (New York: Pantheon, 1993), 62–63.

64. Jonathan Sterne, "Sounds Like the Mall of America: Programmed Music and the Architectonics of Commercial Space," *Ethnomusicology* 41, no. 1 (winter 1997): 23.

65. Sterne, "Sounds Like the Mall of America," 25.

66. Sterne, "Sounds Like the Mall of America," 31.

67. Sterne, "Sounds Like the Mall of America."

68. Paul Virilio, *Speed and Politics*, trans. Mark Polizotti (New York: Semiotext(e), 1986), 30.

69. Yve-Alain Bois, "Introduction" to Sergei M. Eisenstein, "Montage and Architecture," trans. M. Glenny, *Assemblage* 10 (1989): 117.

70. Bois, "Introduction."

71. Eisenstein, "Montage and Architecture," 6.

72. David Denby, "Which Is the Best le Carré Novel," *The New Yorker*, August 6, 2014, http://www.newyorker.com/culture/cultural-comment/best-le-carre-novel.

73. See, for example, "The Effect of Film on Bernard Tschumi," in *Architects and Artisans*, November 2012, http://architectsandartisans.com/2012/11/the-effect-of-film-on-bernard-tschumi/.

74. Noël Burch, *Theory of Film Practice* (Princeton, NJ: Princeton University Press, 1981), 18.

75. Burch, *Theory of Film Practice*.

76. See Randy Martin, "A Precarious Dance, a Derivative Sociality," *TDR/The Drama Review* 56, no. 4 (winter 2012): 76.

77. The quotation is from Randy Martin's *Knowledge LTD*, quoted in John Andrew, "Nonknowledge as Capacity: Randy Martin's *Knowledge LTD* and the Limits of Rationality in the Age of the Derivative," *Social Text*,

March 20, 2017, https://socialtextjournal.org/nonknowledge-as-capacity-randy-martins-knowledge-ltd-and-the-limits-of-rationality-in-the-age-of-the-derivative/.

78. Conrad Hilton, quoted in Annabel Jane Wharton, *Building the Cold War: Hilton International Hotels and Modern Architecture* (Chicago: University of Chicago Press, 2001), 8.

79. See Sara Fregonese and Adam Ramadan, "Hotel Geopolitics: A Research Agenda," *Geopolitics* 20, no. 4 (August 2015): 794.

80. Fregonese and Ramadan, "Hotel Geopolitics," 802.

81. Fregonese and Ramadan, "Hotel Geopolitics," 794.

82. The quotation is from Linda McDowell, Adina Batnitzky, and Sarah Dyer, "Division, Segmentation, and Interpellation: The Embodied Labors of Migrant Workers in a Greater London Hotel," *Economic Geography* 83, no. 1 (January 2007): 3.

83. Siegfried Kracauer, *The Mass Ornament: Weimar Essays* (Cambridge, MA: Harvard University Press, 1995), 181.

84. Michael J. Shapiro, "The Sublime Today: Re-Partitioning the Global Sensible," *Millennium* 34, no. 3 (August 2006): 678.

85. Janet R. Jakobsen, "Queer Is? Queer Does? Normativity and the Problem of Resistance," GLQ 4, no. 4 (1998): 526.

86. Marissa R. Campos, "Queering Architecture: Appropriating Space and Process" (thesis, University of Cincinnati, 2014), https://etd.ohiolink.edu/pg_10?0::NO:10:P10_ACCESSION_NUM:ucin1397466885.

87. Elizabeth Bronfen, "Femme Fatale—Negotiations of Tragic Desire," *New Literary History* 35, no. 1(winter 2004): 104.

88. Michael J. Shapiro, "*Neo-Noir* and Urban Domesticity: The Wachowski Brother's *Bound*," in Michael J. Shapiro, *The Time of the City* (New York: Routledge, 2010), 76.

89. Henri Lefebvre, *The Production of Space*, trans. Donald Nicholson Smith (Cambridge, MA: Basil Blackwell, 1991), 92–93.

90. Daniel Bertrand Monk, *An Aesthetic Occupation: The Immediacy of Architecture and the Palestine Conflict* (Durham, NC: Duke University Press, 2002), 5.

91. See Eyal Weizman, *Hollow Land: Israel's Architecture of Occupation* (New York: Verso, 2007), 7.

92. Weizman, *Hollow Land*, 185.

93. Weizman, *Hollow Land*, 256.

94. Yara Sharif, *Architecture of Resistance: Cultivating Moments of Possibility within the Palestinian/Israeli Conflict* (London: Routledge, 2017), 194.

95. Sharif, *Architecture of Resistance*, 13.

96. Sharif, *Architecture of Resistance*, 41.

97. Sharif, *Architecture of Resistance*, 48.

98. Sharif, *Architecture of Resistance*, 30.

99. Sharif, *Architecture of Resistance*, 59.

100. See Michel de Certeau, *The Practice of Everyday Life* (Berkeley: University of California Press, 1984).

101. Sharif, *Architecture of Resistance*, 67.

102. See Ana Cristina Mendes, "Walled in/Walled Out in the West Bank: Performing Separation Walls in Hany Abu-Assad's *Omar*," *Transnational Cinema* 6, no. 2 (August 2015): 129.

103. Helga Tawil-Souri, "Cinema as the Space to Transgress: Palestine's Territorial Trap," *Middle East Journal of Culture and Communication* 7, no. 2 (2014): 172.

104. Eyal Weizman, *The Least of All Possible Evils* (London: Verso, 2011), 108.

105. Weizman, *The Least of All Possible Evils*, 111.

106. See the report on a forensic architecture exhibit, reported by Michael Kimmelman, "Forensics Helps Widen Architecture's Mission," *New York Times*, April 6, 2018, https://www.nytimes.com/2018/04/06/arts/design/forensic-architecture-human-rights.html.

Chapter Four: Image Punctuations

1. André Bazin, "The Ontology of the Photographic Image," *Film Quarterly* 13, no. 4 (summer 1960): 8.

2. Bazin, "The Ontology of the Photographic Image," 4–5.

3. Bazin, "The Ontology of the Photographic Image," 8.

4. Bazin, "The Ontology of the Photographic Image," 9.

5. Bazin, "The Ontology of the Photographic Image."

6. Teju Cole, "Victory in the Shadows," *New York Times Magazine*, August 10, 2017, https://www.nytimes.com/2017/08/10/magazine/victory-in-the-shadows.html.

7. Cole, "Victory in the Shadows."

8. Cole, "Victory in the Shadows."

9. Cole, "Victory in the Shadows."

10. Drew Thompson, May 2015, "Ruminations? Or, Ruinations? In the Work of Santu Mofokeng," http://africasacountry.com/2015/05/ruminations-or-ruinations-in-the-work-of-santu-mofokeng/.

11. Patricia Hayes, "Santu Mofokeng, photographs: 'the violence is in the knowing,'" *History and Theory* 48, no. 4 (December 2009): 34–35.

12. Hayes, "Santu Mofokeng, photographs: 'the violence is in the knowing,'" 36.

13. See Kaja Silverman, *The Threshold of the Visible World* (New York: Routledge, 1986), 184.

14. Silverman, *The Threshold of the Visible World*, 186.

15. The quoted expressions belong to Gilles Deleuze, who attributes a deforming of the canvass to Francis Bacon, whose images were aimed at

avoidance of "figurative givens and psychic clichés." See his *Francis Bacon: The Logic of Sensation*, trans. Daniel W. Smith (Minneapolis: University of Minnesota Press, 2005), 71–72.

16. Santu Mofokeng, "Trajectory of a Street Photographer," quoted in Annabelle Wienand, "Santu Mofokeng: Alternative Ways of Seeing (1996–2013)," *Safundi: The Journal of South African and American Studies* 15, no. 2–3 (December 2014): 309.

17. Wienand, "Santu Mofokeng."

18. Hayes, "Santu Mofokeng, photographs: 'the violence is in the knowing,'" 42.

19. Georges Didi-Huberman, "The Art of Not Describing: Vermeer—the Detail and the Patch," *History of the Human Sciences* 2, no. 2 (June 1989): 164, 165.

20. Roland Barthes, *Camera Lucida: Reflections on Photography*, trans. Richard Howard (New York: Hill and Wang, 1982), 26–27.

21. Didi-Huberman, "The Art of Not Describing," 149, 163.

22. Michael Fried's reading of Barthes's *Camera Lucida*: "Barthes's Punctum," *Critical Inquiry* 31, no. 3 (spring 2005): 560.

23. Walter Benjamin, "A Short History of Photography," https://monoskop.org/images/7/79/Benjamin_Walter_1931_1972_A_Short_History_of_Photography.pdf, 7.

24. Barthes, *Camera Lucida*, 84.

25. Barthes, *Camera Lucida*, 97.

26. For Barthes, the *punctum* is traumatic; it is derived from the Latin for *trauma*.

27. See, for example, James Attlee, "Towards Anarchitecture: Gordon Matta-Clark and Le Corbusier," *Tate Research Publications*, July 1, 2007, http://www.tate.org.uk/research/publications/tate-papers/07/towards-anarchitecture-gordon-matta-clark-and-le-corbusier.

28. Matta-Clark quoted in Attlee, "Towards Anarchitecture."

29. The quotation is from the sculptor, Ned Smyth, who often accompanied Matta-Clark on his forays into abandoned buildings: "Gordon Matta-Clark," April 2004, http://www.artnet.com/Magazine/Features/smyth6-4-04.asp.

30. Nicolai Ouroussoff, "Timely Lessons from a Rebel, Who Often Created by Destroying," *New York Times*, March 3, 2007, http://www.nytimes.com/2007/03/03/arts/design/03matt.html.

31. Jennifer Shields, *Collage and Architecture* (New York: Routledge, 2014), 153.

32. Shields, *Collage and Architecture*.

33. Matta-Clark quoted by Juan Manuel Simon-Barallorbre, in *City Slivers and Fresh Kills: The Films of Gordon Matta-Clark*, ed. Steven Jenkins (San Francisco: Cinematheque, 2004).

34. Matta-Clark quoted in Pamela M. Lee, *Object to be Destroyed* (Cambridge, MA: MIT Press, 2000), 67.

35. Matta-Clark quoted by Jane Martin, "Views of the Impossible," in *City Slivers and Fresh Kills*, ed. Steven Jenkins.

36. The quotations in the sentence belong to Nicolai Ouroussoff, "Timely Lessons from a Rebel, Who Often Created by Destroying," *New York Times*, March 2, 2007, http://www.nytimes.com/2007/03/03/arts/design/03matt.html? mcubz=0.

37. Didi-Huberman, "The Art of Not Describing," 138.

38. Didi-Huberman, "The Art of Not Describing," 146.

39. Didi-Huberman, "The Art of Not Describing," 147.

40. Didi-Huberman, "The Art of Not Describing," 147–48.

41. Didi-Huberman, "The Art of Not Describing," 149.

42. Didi-Huberman, "The Art of Not Describing," 155.

43. Didi-Huberman, "The Art of Not Describing," 156.

44. Didi-Huberman, "The Art of Not Describing."

45. Didi-Huberman, "The Art of Not Describing," 152.

46. Didi-Huberman, "The Act of Not Describing." 155.

47. Michel Foucault accords the primary responsibility for creating the modern viewer to Edouard Manet. See his *Manet and the Object of Painting*, trans. M. Barr (London: Tate, 2009), 16.

48. Meyer Schapiro, *Paul Cézanne* (New York: H. N. Abrams, 1988), 10.

49. Schapiro, *Paul Cézanne*, 11.

50. Maurice Merleau-Ponty, *Sense and Nonsense*, trans. Hubert Dreyfus and Patricia Allen Dreyfus (Evanston, IL: Northwestern University Press, 1964), 12.

51. Norman Turner, "Cézanne, Wagner, Modulation," *Journal of Aesthetics and Art Criticism* 56, no. 4 (fall 1998): 10.

52. Turner, "Cézanne, Wagner, Modulation," 2.

53. Turner, "Cézanne, Wagner, Modulation," 2–3, 10, 14.

54. Turner, "Cézanne, Wagner, Modulation," 10.

55. Wim Wenders, *The Pixels of Paul Cézanne: And Reflections on Other Artists*, trans. Jen Alleja (London: Faber and Faber, 2018), 182–83.

56. See Jonah Lehrer, *Proust Was a Neuroscientist* (New York: Houghton Mifflin, 2008), 102.

57. Lehrer, *Proust Was a Neuroscientist*, 115.

58. Lehrer, *Proust Was a Neuroscientist*, 98.

59. Lehrer, *Proust Was a Neuroscientist*, 107.

60. Lehrer's term, *Proust Was a Neuroscientist*, 102.

61. Merleau-Ponty, *Sense and Nonsense*, 13.

62. I am quoting from Howard Caygill's rendering of Walter Benjamin's notions about the role of chromatics in his writings on the philosophy of experience: *Walter Benjamin: The Colour of Experience* (London: Routledge, 1998), 83.

63. See Simon O' Sullivan, *Art Encounters: Deleuze and Guattari* (London: Palgrave Macmillan, 2006), 42.

64. George Heard Hamilton, "Cézanne, Bergson and the Image of Time," *College Art Journal* 16, no. 1 (autumn 1956): 11–12.

65. Gilles Deleuze, *Cinema 1*, trans. Hugh Tomlinson and Barbara Habberjam (Minneapolis: University of Minnesota Press, 1986), 64.

66. Jonathan Crary, *Suspensions of Perception: Attention, Spectacle, and Modern Culture* (Cambridge, MA: MIT Press, 2001), 297.

67. Rilke quoted in Crary, *Suspensions of Perception.*

68. Connie Byrne and William O. Lopez, "*Nashville*," in *Robert Altman: Interviews*, ed. Robert Sterritt, 20 (Jackson: University of Mississippi Press, 2000).

69. An earlier version of my reading of *Red Desert* is in Michael J. Shapiro, *The Political Sublime* (Durham, NC: Duke University Press, 2018), 116–23; Peter Handke, "The Lesson of *Mont Sainte-Victoire*, in *Slow Homecoming*, trans. Ralph Mannheim (New York: Macmillan, 1985), 155.

70. Handke, "The Lesson of Mont Sainte-Victoire," 145.

71. Handke, "The Lesson of Mont Sainte-Victoire."

72. Antonioni quoted in Matthew Gandy, "Landscapes of Deliquescence," *Transactions of the Institute of British Geographers* 28, no. 2 (June 2003): 225.

73. Peter Brunette, "Deserto Rosso Red Desert," in *The Cinema of Italy*, ed. Giorgio Bertinellini and Gian Piero Brunetta (London: Wallflower, 2004), 159.

74. As Merleau-Ponty puts it, for Cézanne, a personality is "no more than a combination of colors," *Sense and Nonsense*, 16.

75. Merleau-Ponty, *Sense and Nonsense*, 15.

76. Richard Misek, *Chromatic Cinema: A History of Screen Color* (Chichester, UK: Wiley-Blackwell, 2007), 65.

77. Brunette, "Deserto Rosso Red Desert," 158.

78. Brunette, "Deserto Rosso Red Desert."

79. Brunette, "Deserto Rosso Red Desert," 184.

80. Brunette, "Deserto Rosso Red Desert," 186. The lesson Handke drew from Cézanne's rendering of a landscape is responsive to a different project from Antonioni's, one in which he desired to overcome the violent history associated with his Austrian heritage (of "death cult masters") and celebrate "the people of the present," as he pursues his character's (and thus his) "peace-fostering *form* that can be perpetuated by anyone (even me)."

81. Handke, "The Long Way Around," in *Slow Homecoming*, 114.

82. Didi-Huberman, "The Art of Not Describing," 164.

83. Joe McElhaney, *The Death of Classical Cinema: Hitchcock, Lang, Minelli* (Albany: State University of New York Press, 2006), 239.

84. The expression belongs to Matthew Gandy, "Landscapes of Deliquescence in Michelangelo Antonioni's 'Red Desert,'" *Transactions of the Institute of British Geographers* 28, no. 2 (June 2003): 221.

85. The quotations are from Mark Le Fanu, "In This World," published with the Criterion Collection DVD version of *Red Desert* (2010), 9.

86. The quoted reference to Chirico is from Gandy, "Landscapes of Deliquescence in Michelangelo Antonioni's 'Red Desert,'" 227.

87. Cole, "Victory in the Shadows."

88. The quotation is from David Forgacs, "Antonioni: Space, Place, Sexuality," in *Spaces in European Cinema*, ed. Myrto Konstantarakos, 103 (Exeter, UK: Intellect, 2000).

89. See Forgacs, "Antonioni," 102, for the quotation on anchorage and beyond for the space versus place distinction applied to Antonioni's films.

90. Pascal Bonitzer, *Decadrage: Peinture et Cinéma* (Paris: Editions de l'Etoile, 1987), 97 (my translation).

91. The quoted segment is from Peter Brunette, "Deserto Rosso Red Desert," in *The Cinema of Italy*, ed. Giorgio Bertellini and Gian Piero, 158 (London: Wallflower, 2004).

92. William Arrowsmith, *Antonioni: The Poet of Images* (New York: Oxford University Press, 1995), 97.

93. Louis-Georges Schwartz, "Typewriter: Free Indirect Discourse in Deleuze's *Cinema*," *SubStance* 34, no. 3, issue 108 (2005): 107.

94. Schwartz, "Typewriter," 111.

95. See Jean Mitry, *The Aesthetics and Psychology of the Cinema*, trans. Christopher King (Bloomington: Indiana University Press, 2000), 216.

96. See Gilles Deleuze, *Cinema 2: The Time Image*, trans. Hugh Tomlinson and Robert Galeta (Minneapolis: University of Minnesota Press, 1989), 272.

97. Jacques Lacan, "The Eye and the Gaze," chapter 6 in *The Four Fundamental Concepts of Psycho-Analysis*, trans. Alan Sheridan (London: Penguin, 1979), 73.

98. Michelangelo Antonioni quoted in Juhani Pallasma, *The Architecture of Vision: Existential Space in Cinema* (Helsinki: Rakennustieto Oy, 2001), 123.

99. Deleuze, *Cinema 1*, 64.

100. Patricia Pisters, *The Matrix of Visual Culture* (Stanford, CA: Stanford University Press, 2003), 22.

101. Quotations from Ouroussoff, "Timely Lessons from a Rebel."

102. The outer quotation is from Deleuze, *Cinema 2*, 9, quoting Claude Ollier.

103. I chose that sentence to juxtapose it with a commentator's statement about Martin Scorcese's film *Silence* (2017): "*Silence* gives enormously satisfying evidence of a filmmaker *thinking* his way through the film: making visual and dramatic choices": Andrew Tracy, "Silence," *Cinema Scope*, http://cinema-scope.com/currency/silence-martin-scorsese-ustaiwanmexico/.

104. The quotation is from Martin Walsh's commentary on the film: "Antonini's Narrative Design," *Jump Cut*, no. 8 (1975), https://www.ejumpcut.org/archive/onlinessays/JC08folder/PassengerWalsh.html.

105. Noël Burch, *Theory of Film Practice* (Princeton, NJ: Princeton University Press, 1981), 18.

106. I am quoting Michael Tawa's observation here. See his *Agencies of the Frame: Tectonic Strategies in Cinema and Architecture* (Newcastle, UK: Cambridge Scholars, 2010), 151.

107. Ira Jaffe, *Slow Movies* (New York: Wallflower, 2014), 3.

108. Jack Turner, "Antonioni's *The Passenger* as Lacanian Text," *Other Voices* 1, no. 3 (January 1999), http://othervoices.org/1.3/turner/passenger.php.

109. The quotation is Walter Benjamin's view of Hamlet's desire for death in his *Trauerspiel* investigation: *The Origin of German Tragic Drama,* trans. John Osborne (New York: Verso, 1998), 137.

110. Jacques Lacan, "Desire and the Interpretation of Desire in *Hamlet*," *Yale French Studies*, no. 55/56 (1977): 11, 12.

111. Lacan, "Desire and the Interpretation of Desire in *Hamlet*," 29.

112. Lacan, "Desire and the Interpretation of Desire in *Hamlet*," 17.

113. Tawa, *Agencies of the Frame*, 151.

114. I am basing that shot designation on the shot-by-shot account of the screenplay in "Analysis of Michelangelo Antonioni's *The Passenger*," dyllopuspress.com/idyllopus/film/p_one.htm.

115. Lacan, "Desire and the Interpretation of Desire in *Hamlet*," 25.

116. See Deleuze on affection images in *Cinema 1*, 65.

117. Leo Bersani and Ulysse Dutoit, *Forms of Being: Cinema, Aesthetics, Subjectivity* (London: BFI, 2004), 21.

118. Sven Lindqvist, *"Exterminate All the Brutes": One Man's Odyssey into the Heart of Darkness and the Origins of European Genocide*, trans. Joan Tate (New York: New Press, 1996), 3.

119. The quotation is from Arrowsmith, *Antonioni: The Poet of Images*, 153.

120. Lindqvist, *"Exterminate All the Brutes,"* 104.

121. Lindqvist, *"Exterminate All the Brutes,"* 46.

122. See Lillian Dumont, "An Interview with Alain Robbe-Grillet," *The French Review* 50, no. 4 (March 1977): 653.

123. The quotation is from Seymour Chatman, *Antonioni, or, The Surface of the World* (Berkeley: University of California Press, 1985), 192.

124. Didi-Huberman, "The Art of Not Describing," 156.

125. Michel Foucault, *The Birth of Biopolitics*, trans. Graham Burchell (New York: Palgrave, 2008), 3.

126. Hayes, "Santu Mofokeng, photographs: 'The violence is in the knowing,'" 42.

127. See Antonio Gramsci, *Prison Notebooks*, trans. Joseph A. Buttigieg (New York: Columbia University Press, 1975), where he distinguishes organic intellectuals from disinterested, "traditional intellectuals."

128. Cole, "Victory in the Shadows."

129. See Gilles Deleuze and Félix Guattari, *A Thousand Plateaus*, trans.

Brian Massumi (Minneapolis: University of Minnesota Press, 1987), 109, and John Protevi, *Political Affect* (Minneapolis: University of Minnesota Press, 2009), 49, for a similar explication of trans-assemblage encounters.

130. Cole, "Victory in the Shadows."

131. Cole, "Victory in the Shadows."

132. The quotation is from Ronald Bogue's analysis of Cézanne in "Gilles Deleuze: The Aesthetics of Force," *The Journal for the British Society for Phenomenology* 24, no. 1 (January 1993): 57.

133. Handke, "The Lesson of *Mont Sainte-Victoire*," 141.

134. Handke, "The Lesson of *Mont Sainte-Victoire*," 180.

135. Handke, "The Lesson of *Mont Sainte-Victoire*," 179.

136. Handke, "The Lesson of *Mont Sainte-Victoire*," 190.

137. I do an extended analysis of Handle's subject-in-process in Michael J. Shapiro, "Toward a Politicized Subject: Peter Handke and Language," *Boundary* 2, no. 8 (winter/spring 1985): 393–418.

138. See Gilles Deleuze, *Cinema 2: The Time Image*, trans. H. Tomlinson and R. Galeta (Minneapolis: University of Minnesota Press, 1989), 272.

139. Deleuze, *Cinema 1*, 64.

140. Peter Handke, *The Inner World of the Outer World of the Inner World* (New York: Seabury Press, 1974), 105.

141. I am quoting from Alphonso Lingis, "Concepts and Colours," in *Deleuze/Guattari and the Arts: Intensities and Lines of Flight*, ed. Antonio Calcagno, Jim Vernon, and Steve G. Lofts, 83 (New York: Rowman and Littlefield, 2014).

142. For an analysis of what he calls "affective tonality," see Matthew Hawkin, "The Concept of Affective Tonality and Its Manifestation as Narrative Experience in the Short Film, *Bullseye*," http://core.ac.uk/download/pdf/30620172.pdf.

143. Karl Ove Knausgaard, *Autumn*, trans. Invild Burkey (New York: Penguin, 2017), 144.

144. Antonioni quoted in Chatman, *Antonioni, or, The Surface of the World*, 185.

145. That formulation belongs to Chatman, *Antonioni, or, The Surface of the World*, 192.

146. Knausgaard, *Autumn*, 133.

147. I am quoting here from a convenient summary supplied by Filippo Del Lucchese, "Monstrous Individuations: Deleuze, Simondon and Relational Ontology," *Differences: A Journal of Feminist Cultural Studies* 20, no. 2–3 (2009): 181.

148. See Jacques Rancière, "Aesthetic Separation, Aesthetic Community: Scenes from the Aesthetic Regime of Art," *Art and Research* 2, no. 1 (summer 2008): 1–14.

149. Rancière, "Aesthetic Separation, Aesthetic Community," 4.

Chapter Five: Holocaust Punctuations

1. Michael J. Shapiro, *War Crimes, Atrocity, and Justice* (Cambridge: Polity, 2015), 159.

2. Laszlo Krasznahorkai, *War and War*, trans. George Szirtes (New York: New Directions, 2006), 196.

3. Shapiro, *War Crimes, Atrocity, and Justice*, 160.

4. Jacques Rancière, "Fictions of Time," in *Rancière and Literature*, ed. Grace Hellyer and Julian Murphet, 25–41 (Edinburgh: Edinburgh University Press, 2016), 25–41.

5. Rancière, "Fictions of Time," 26.

6. Imre Kertész, *The Holocaust as Culture*, trans. Thomas Cooper (Calcutta, India: Seagull Books, 2011), 43.

7. "Imre Kertész: Memoirs of a Survivor" (interview with Tibor Fischer, *Independent*, January 11, 2008, http://www.independent.co.uk/arts-entertainment/books/features/imre-kert-sz-memoirs-of-a-survivor-769521.

8. Rancière, "Fictions of Time," 27.

9. Ann Smock, "Translator's Introduction," in Maurice Blanchot, *The Space of Literature: A Translation of "L'Espace littéraire,"* trans. Ann Smock, 3 (Lincoln: University of Nebraska, 1989).

10. Michel Foucault, "The Thought from Outside," in *Foucault/Blanchot*, trans. Jeffrey Mehlman and Brian Massumi (New York: Zone, 1990), 21–22.

11. The quotations are from Alain Badiou's chapter "The Ethic of Truths," in his *Ethics: An Essay on the Understanding of Evil*, trans. Peter Hallward (New York: Verso, 2001), 43.

12. From Imre Kertész, Nobel Prize acceptance speech quoted in Bettina von Jagow, "Representing the Holocaust, Kertész's *Fatelessness* and Benigni's *La vita e bella*," trans. Sabine Prechtar, in *Imre Kertész and Holocaust Literature*, ed. Louise O. Vasvari and Steven Totosy de Zepetnek, 79 (West Lafayette, IN: Purdue University Press, 2005).

13. The quotation belongs to Roberto Calasso, who, better than any contemporary writer, captures the force of Kafka's prose. See his *K*, trans. Geoffrey Brock (New York: Alfred A. Knopf, 2005), 24.

14. Michael J. Shapiro, "Affirming the Political: Tragic Affirmations versus Gothic Displacements," in *The Politics of Moralizing*, ed. Jane Bennett and Michael J. Shapiro, 233 (New York: Routledge, 2002).

15. Aeschylus, *Seven against Thebes*, trans. A. W. Verrall, in A. W. Verrall, *The Seven against Thebes of Aeschylus* (London: Macmillan, 1887), 147.

16. Michael J. Shapiro, *For Moral Ambiguity: National Culture and the Politics of the Family* (Minneapolis: University of Minnesota Press, 2001), 21.

17. Specifically, Adorno stated that "to write a poem after Auschwitz is barbaric," but since acknowledged, "Perennial suffering has as much right to expression as a tortured man has to scream; hence, it may have been

wrong to say that after Auschwitz you could no longer write poems." Theodor W. Adorno, *Negative Dialectics*, trans. E. B. Ashton (New York: Continuum, 1973), 362.

18. Vivian Liska, *When Kafka Says We* (Bloomington: Indiana University Press, 2009), 151.

19. Liska, *When Kafka Says We*, 152.

20. Jacques Rancière, *Figures of History*, trans. Julie Rose (Cambridge: Polity, 2014), 49–50.

21. Lanzmann's approach to a "fiction of the real" is described and quoted in Richard Brody, "Witness: Claude Lanzmann and the making of 'Shoah,'" *The New Yorker*, March 12, 2012, https://www.newyorker.com/magazine/2012/03/19/witness-5.

22. For descriptions and analyses of Forgács's films, see Bill Nichols and Michael Renov, eds., *The Films of Peter Forgács* (Minneapolis: University of Minnesota Press, 2011).

23. See Kertész, *The Holocaust as Culture*, 61.

24. The future anterior, the will-have-been of events, is the main focus of my recent investigation of political temporalities: Michael J. Shapiro, *Politics and Time: Documenting the Event* (Cambridge: Polity, 2016).

25. The expression is from Claude Romano's analysis of the temporal phenomenology of events: *Event and Time*, trans. Stephen E. Lewis (New York: Fordham University Press, 2014).

26. The expression belongs to Liska, *When Kafka Says We*, 151.

27. See M. M. Bakhtin, *Art and Answerability*, trans. Vadim Liapunov (Austin: University of Texas Press, 1990), 13.

28. See M. M. Bakhtin, "Forms of Time and of the Chronotope in the Novel: Toward a Historical Poetics," in M. M. Bakhtin, *The Dialogic Imagination*, trans. Caryl Emerson and Michael Holquist (Austin: University of Texas Press, 1981), 84–258.

29. M. M. Bakhtin, "The Bildungsroman and Its Significance in the History of Realism," in *Speech Genres and Other Late Essays*, trans. Vern W. McGee (Austin: University of Texas Press, 2002), 25.

30. The expression is Bernard Tschumi's concept for the functioning of the built environment. See, for example, Bernard Tschumi, "Violence and Architecture," in *Architecture and Disjunction* (Cambridge, MA: MIT Press, 1994).

31. Peter Handke, "The Long Way Around," in *Slow Homecoming*, trans. Ralph Manheim (New York: Macmillan, 1988), 3.

32. Handke, "The Long Way Around," 65, 66.

33. Handke, "The Long Way Around," 60.

34. Handke, "The Long Way Around," 9.

35. Handke, "The Long Way Around," 33.

36. Handke, "The Long Way Around," 48.

37. The quotation is from Hugo Caviola's reading of the novella:

"*Ding-Bild-Schift:* Peter Handke's Slow Homecoming to a 'Chinese' Austria," *Modern Fiction Studies* 36, no. 3 (fall 1990): 383.

38. The concept of Philopoesis belongs to Cesare Casarino: "Philopoesis: A Theoretico-Methodological Manifesto," *boundary 2* 29, no. 1 (2002): 65–96.

39. Peter Handke, "The Lesson of Mont Sainte-Victoire," in *Slow Homecoming*, 141.

40. Handke, "The Lesson of Mont Sainte-Victoire," 145.

41. See J.-F. Lyotard, *Discourse, Figure*, trans. Antony Hudek and Mary Lyundon (Minneapolis: University of Minnesota Press, 2011), 24.

42. Handke, "The Long Way Around," 38.

43. Handke, "The Lesson of Mont Sainte-Victoire," 159.

44. Handke, "The Long Way Around," 3.

45. Handke, "The Long Way Around," 136.

46. Handke, "The Long Way Around," 21–22.

47. Handke, "The Long Way Around," 114.

48. Gilles Deleuze, "Nomad Thought," in *The New Nietzsche*, ed. David B. Allison, 149 (New York: Delta, 1977).

49. Deleuze, "Nomad Thought."

50. Rosi Braidotti, "Nomadic Ethics," *Deleuze Studies* 7, no. 3 (2013): 343.

51. John K. Noyes, "Nomadism, Nomadology, Postcolonialism," *Interventions* 6, no. 2 (2004): 161.

52. The concept belongs to Paul Virilio, quoted in Noyes, "Nomadism, Nomadology, Postcolonialism," 163.

53. Rosi Braidotti, quoted in Noyes, "Nomadism, Nomadology, Postcolonialism," 164.

54. Peter Handke, *Short Letter, Long Farewell*, trans. Ralph Manheim (New York: Avon, 1974), 11–12.

55. Michael J. Shapiro, "Toward a Politicized Subject: Peter Handke and Language," *Boundary 2* 13, no. 2/3 (winter–spring 1985): 414.

56. Handke, *Slow Homecoming*, 3.

57. The concept of conceptual personae is developed in Gilles Deleuze and Félix Guattari's *What Is Philosophy?*, trans. Hugh Tomlinson and Graham Burchell (New York: Columbia University Press, 1994), 61–83.

58. M. M. Bakhtin, *Problems of Dostoevsky's Poetics*, trans. Caryl Emerson (Minneapolis: University of Minnesota Press, 1984), 18.

59. Peter Handke, *The Innerworld of the Outerworld of the Innerworld* (New York: Seabury, 1974), 106–7.

60. M. M. Bakhtin, "Discourse in the Novel," in *The Dialogic Imagination*, trans. Michael Holquist and Caryl Emerson (Austin: University of Texas Press, 1981), 297.

61. That construction comes up in Imre Kertész, *The Union Jack*, trans. Tim Wilkinson (New York: Melville House, 2009), 16.

62. Kertész, *The Holocaust as Culture*, 41.

63. Imre Kertész, *Dossier K.*, trans. Tim Wilkinson (Brooklyn, NY: Melville House, 2006), 58–59.

64. "Imre Kertész, "The Art of Fiction No. 220," and interview with Luisa Zielinski, *Paris Review* 205 (summer 2013), https://www.theparisreview.org/interviews/6235/imre-Kertész-the-art-of-fiction-no-220-imre-Kertész.

65. Kertész, "The Art of Fiction No. 220."

66. Gilles Deleuze, *Francis Bacon: The Logic of Sensation*, trans. Daniel W. Smith (Minneapolis: University of Minnesota Press, 2002), 71.

67. Deleuze, *Francis Bacon*, 71–72.

68. Kertész, *The Holocaust as Culture*, 31.

69. Frantz Fanon, *Black Skin, White Masks*, trans. Richard Philcox (New York: Grove Press, 2008).

70. Imre Kertész, *Fatelessness*, trans. Tim Wilkinson (New York: Vintage, 2004), 12.

71. Kertész, *Dossier K*, 130–31.

72. The expression is Kertész's in *The Holocaust as Culture*, 30.

73. Kertész, *The Holocaust as Culture*, 13.

74. Kertész, *The Holocaust as Culture*, 21–22.

75. James R. Martel, *The Misinterpellated Subject* (Durham, NC: Duke University Press, 2017), 6–7.

76. Martel, *The Misinterpellated Subject*, 201.

77. Kertész, *Fatelessness*, 57.

78. Kertész, *Fatelessness*, 80.

79. Kertész, *Fatelessness*, 171–72.

80. Kertész, *Fatelessness*, 247.

81. Kertész, *Fatelessness*, 249.

82. Kertész, *Dossier K*, 9.

83. Imre Kertész's *Fiasco*, trans. Tim Wilkinson (New York: Melville House, 2011), 74.

84. Kertész, *Fiasco*, 247, 72.

85. Kertész, *Dossier K*, 167.

86. Kertész, *Kaddish for an Unborn Child*, 43.

87. See, for example, the philosophical references in his novella, *The Union Jack*, trans. Tim Wilkinson (New York: Melville House, 209).

88. Kertész, *Dossier K*, 79.

89. Kertész, *The Holocaust as Culture*, 65–66.

90. The quotation is from James Wood's "Introduction" to W. G. Sebald, *Austerlitz* (New York: Modern Library, 2001), xviii.

91. Gilles Deleuze and Félix Guattari, *Kafka: Toward a Minor Literature*, trans. Dana Polan (Minneapolis: University of Minnesota Press, 1986), 17.

92. That commentary on Kafka's paradoxical temporal structure is in Dorrit Cohen, *Transparent Minds* (Princeton, NJ: Princeton University Press, 1978), 195. See also J. M. Coetzee's commentary (and critique of Co-

hen), which discerns a similar temporal structure: "Time, Tense and Aspect in Kafka's 'The Burrow,'" *MLN* 96, no. 3 (April 1981): 565.

93. Franz Kafka, *The Trial*, trans. Breon Mitchell (New York: Schocken, 1999), 200.

94. See W. G. Sebald, "To the Brothel by Way of Switzerland: On Kafka's Travel Diaries," in *Campo Santo*, trans. Anthea Bell (New York: Random House, 2005), 135–40.

95. W. G. Sebald, "Strangeness, Integration, and Crisis: On Peter Handke's Play *Kaspar*," in *Campo Santo*, 56.

96. Sebald, *Austerlitz*, 68.

97. Sebald, *Campo Santo*, 56.

98. Sebald, *Austerlitz*, 91.

99. Sebald, *Austerlitz*, 92–93.

100. See the interview with Sigrid Loffler, "Wildes Denken," quoted in Amir Eshel, "Against the Power of Time: The Poetics of Suspension in W. G. Sebald's 'Austerlitz,'" *New German Critique*, no. 88 (winter 2003): 75.

101. Sebald, *Austerlitz*, 100.

102. Sebald, *Austerlitz*, 101.

103. Eshel, "Against the Power of Time," 74.

104. James Wood, "Introduction," in Sebald, *Austerlitz*, xii.

105. Patricia Drechsel Tobin, *Time and the Novel: The Genealogical Imperative* (Princeton, NJ: Princeton University Press, 2015), 6.

106. Sebald, *Austerlitz*, 5.

107. Sebald, *Austerlitz*, 7.

108. Eshel, "Against the Power of Time," 71.

109. His quotation is from Gilles Deleuze's gloss on Bergsonian temporality; see his *Bergsonism*, trans. Hugh Tomlinson and Barbara Habberjam (New York: Zone, 1988), 58.

110. Deleuze, *Bergsonism*, 53.

111. Sebald, *Austerlitz*, 104.

112. Sebald, *Austerlitz*, 291.

113. Sebald, *Austerlitz*, 246.

114. Sebald, *Austerlitz*, 245–46.

115. Sebald, *Austerlitz*, 246–47.

116. For details of the practice, see Ira Jaffe, *Slow Movies: Countering the Cinema of Action* (New York: Wallflower, 2014).

117. I am quoting from Elizabeth Zelensky, "Tarkovsky, Science and Faith," *Religions: A Scholarly Journal* (2014): 17, http://www.qscience.com/doi/abs/10.5339/rels.2014. science.17.

118. Andrei Tarkovsky, *Sculpting in Time*, trans. Kitty Hunter Blair (Austin: University of Texas Press, 2012), 183.

119. Sebald, *Austerlitz*, 147.

120. Sebald, *Austerlitz*, 261.

121. David Albahari, *Globetrotter*, trans. Ellen Elias Bursac (New Haven, CT: Yale University Press, 2014), 50.

122. See Michael J. Shapiro, "Afterword: It's All about Duration," in *The Political Sublime* (Durham, NC: Duke University Press, 2018).

123. I am quoting from Deleuze, *Bergsonism*, 25–26.

124. Andrei Tarkovsky, *Sculpting in Time*, trans. Kitty Hunter Blair (Austin: University of Texas Press, 2012), 183.

125. I am using the expression from the title of Levi Bryant's analysis of Deleuze and ethics: "The Ethics of the Event: Deleuze and Ethics without Αρχή," in *Deleuze and Ethics*, ed. Nathan Jun and Daniel W. Smith, 21–43 (Edinburgh: Edinburgh University Press, 2011).

126. I'm borrowing that expression from Cathy Caruth's analysis of the temporality of trauma. See her *Unclaimed Experience: Trauma, Narrative and History* (Baltimore: Johns Hopkins University Press, 1996).

127. Kertész, *Dossier K*, 167.

128. Kertész, *Dossier K*, 249.

129. Sebald, *Austerlitz*, 166.